INVITATION TO MVS

Logic and Debugging

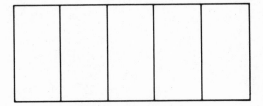

Harry Katzan Jr.
Davis Tharayil

PBI
a petrocelli
book
new york / princeton

Typesetting by Backes Graphics
Designed by Diane L. Backes

Printed in the United States of America
    4 5 6 7 8 9 10

Library of Congress Cataloging in Publication Data

Invitation to MVS.

    Includes index.
    1. MVS (Computer system) I. Katzan, Harry. II. Tharayil, Davis. III. Title.
QA76.6.I6   1984   001.64'2   84-6996
ISBN 0-89433-081-0

To
Anthony
&
Theresa
Tharayil

To
MFK
&
KAK

Contents

Preface

MVS is an acronym for "multiple virtual storage," a concept descriptive of IBM's most complex operating system for the System/370 family of computers. This system is appropriately named "Operating System/MVS" or simply "MVS" for short. MVS represents the state of the art in operating-system technology. MVS serves also as a point of reference in the area of operating systems because of its widespread utilization and as an effective model for future systems-development.

MVS is a comprehensive system that exists as a mysterious black box to most users. This is primarily the case because introductory material is not readily available in a convenient form. The objective of this book is to describe the structure and function of MVS in a straightforward and readable manner. Once a basic understanding of MVS is obtained, the reader can utilize the information for debugging of application programs and for obtaining improved service from the MVS system.

This book is intended for any person desiring in-depth knowledge of MVS without wading through the lengthy and tedious reference documents. Anyone involved with MVS, from managers to programmers, could benefit from the book. Special emphasis is given in the book to debugging so that the subject matter is of particular interest to systems programmers.

Chapter 14, entitled "MVS Summary", gives a synopsis of the entire book. It is here that the interested reader can obtain an overview of MVS before delving into its detailed intervals. The glossary serves as a handy reference to the important acronyms used in the MVS world.

Harry Katzan, Jr.
Davis Tharayil

1 Introduction to MVS

1.1 EVOLUTION OF THE MVS ENVIRONMENT

Early information-processing systems were limited in scope and flexibility. The most significant characteristic was that data-processing operations were performed serially with a limited set of system resources. Thus, for example, the amount of main storage usable by an application program might have been limited to 20,000 bytes, such that a program would have to be divided into small segments and executed serially in the processing unit. The operating environment was a single job, running in the batch mode. Even though all the resources of the computing system were available to the single user, they could not be utilized in their entirety. The obvious result was valuable resources being literally wasted. The operating environment was characterized also by manual intervention between jobs; and this, together with job setup time, was a major contributor to inefficient use of total system resources. Significant increases in computer power and the intervention of autonomous input/output facilities, overlapping CPU, and input/output activity reinforced the need for more efficient utilization of system resources.

Twenty five years ago, central processing units were capable of executing instructions in thousandths of a second; today's CPUs execute instructions in billionths of a second. For example, IBM's currently announced 3084 processing units have a cycle time of 26 nanoseconds. In an older system like the IBM 1401, main storage ranged from 1,400 to 16,000 bytes. The IBM 3084 model Q64 has a main storage size of 67,108,864 bytes (64 meg) with a storage access cycle time of 312 nanoseconds. The number and speed of the data channels attached to the CPUs have been tripled in the last decade. Currently, IBM supports up to 24 channels on their latest processors. All block multiplexer channels are capable of transfering data at a maximum rate of 3 million bytes/second using the data-streaming feature across a 1-byte interface. Storage capacity on the new IBM 3380 disk drive is over 200 times larger than the early models of the IBM 1311 disk drives. Dramatic improvements have been made in the area of printing (17,000 lines per minute on an IBM 3800 printer), remote job entry systems, and interactive system devices such as CRTs, etc. This overview does not even consider teleprocessing applications and equipment that did not exist 20 years ago.

Software has been developed to utilize the hardware advances. Resulting operating systems can execute several programs concurrently and can to some extent more fully utilize the resources of the computer system.

1

During the pre-operating system days (early 1950s) operators had to set up each job step and manually allocate devices for that step. With the aid of written instructions, operators had to collect the object deck for the program, along with any necessary subroutine decks, and feed them into the system card reader. At the end of the job step the operator had to deallocate the devices for the step and prepare for the next step. The operation's environment was totally manual. During the early 1960s two rudimentary operating systems, PCP (*P*rimary *C*ontrol *P*rogram) and DOS (*D*isk *O*perating *S*ystem), came into existence. These operating systems tried to automate operations by mechanizing interjob transitions. Device allocation for the jobs was done manually, but these operating systems had the ability to search the subroutine libraries on tape or disk and automatically retrieve the necessary programs. Systems in this class only execute one job at a time.

In 1967 the operating system MFT (*M*ultiprogramming with *F*ixed number of *T*asks) was announced for the third generation operating system OS/360. A fixed number of job(s) could run concurrently on the system. JCL (*J*ob *C*ontrol *L*anguage) enhancements attempted to separate the applications programs from operational considerations such as device types, device allocations, address, and timing of execution. Better control of the output was achieved through spooling systems such as HASP. The possibility of multiprogramming opened up interactive program development facilities such as TSO (*T*ime *S*haring *O*ption) and RJE (*R*emote *J*ob *E*ntry) systems.

The next step in the evolution of operating systems was MVT (*M*ultiprogramming with *V*ariable number of *T*asks). Additional multiprogramming capabilities of these systems placed a greater importance on workload management, resource management, and data management. More high-level languages, such as PL/I, ALGOL, APL, and Basic, came into existence in support of programming development efforts. During 1972 three new operating systems were announced: SVS (*S*ingle *V*irtual *S*torage system), VS1, and VM/370 (*V*irtual *M*achine *F*acility). Virtual storage gave greater flexibility to programmers. The need for complex overlay techniques became obsolete. Device independence for data access opened the gateway for data base technology. The need for bigger programs and support for a large number of users gave birth to the operating system MVS (*M*ultiple *V*irtual *S*torage system) in 1974.

As we can see through the evolution of the operating systems, the purpose of the operating system is to increase the productivity of a computer installation by dynamically allocating its resources, such as hardware (CPU time, main storage, I/O devices, etc.) and information (data and programs). An operating system also increases the productivity of the human resources (operators, programmers, and system analysts) by automating an installation's computer operations, and work load management, data management, and resource management functions.

The various capabilities of the operating system can be classified into three sorts, namely: supervisor management, data management, and job management. *Supervisor Management*, initially known as the resource manager, has the primary function of allocating main storage and I/O devices for a job. New methods were developed to share resources between jobs dynamically rather than statically as in early operating systems. The effective use of direct-access storage devices was the next evolutionary step in operating-systems technology. Direct-access storage capacity and the speed of the devices have tripled in the last decade. This necessitated sharing the same device among different users and distinguishing between data files and devices. The component of the operating system that does the above function is appropriately named *data management*. *Job management* provides the logical interface between supervisory management routines and an application program.

1.2 CHARACTERISTICS OF THE MVS ENVIRONMENT

The MVS operational environment consists of a combination of the following characteristics:

- Large computer systems

    IBM 370/30XX/43XX class computers.

    Up to 64 million bytes of real storage.

    Block multiplexer channels capable of transferring 3 MEG bytes of data/sec.

    Fast I/O devices.

- Large number of concurrent users

    The number of concurrent users in an MVS environment is theoretically unlimited. (However, there are practical limitations due to the main storage and external page storage capacity. MVS can currently support 1,635 concurrent address spaces.)

- Teleprocessing

    Modern on-line applications such as data entry, data inquiry, and data collection. (These applications became very common due to the increased power and the faster execution time of the central processing unit.)

- Data base

    Larger storage devices made it easy to store large volumes of data. The refinement of data storage methods for efficient storage and retrieval became data bases.

- Time sharing

  More users started to use the system interactively. Using a technique called time slicing, CPU could distribute its computing power between time-sharing users and batch jobs.

- Batch processing

  In an MVS environment, we see more batch jobs running concurrently; this is achieved through the efficient use of the system resources by the operating system.

The hardware environment for MVS is conceptualized in figure 1.1.

MVS is a multipurpose operating system designed to enhance the functional capabilities of the underlying computer system. In the context of the book, it is feasible to introduce the MVS environment from two complementary points of view:

- The software structure of the operating system.
- The hardware structure of the operating system.

It is important to recognize that even though we have selected this approach, MVS can also be considered an operational concept, relatively independent of the underlying hardware. Thus, MVS can be viewed as a total approach to effective computer utilization.

1.3 SOFTWARE STRUCTURE OF MVS

The software structure of MVS is divided into three major functional areas: job management, supervisor management, and data management.

1.3.1 Job Management

Job management activities can be subdivided into two categories: command processing and job processing.

Command Processing

This function consists of sending a command from a program or console and scheduling it for processing. Subsequently, the command is executed by invoking the master scheduler, which initiates the command processing as a unit of work for the system.

Job Processing

The job processing function consists of

1. Reading Jobstream JCL into the system and spooling it into auxiliary storage (DASD). The system component that does this is called "JES" (*Job Entry Subsystem*).
2. Next, another component called "CONVERTER" is given control to convert the JCL into INTERNAL TEXT for the machine recognition.

SYSTEM

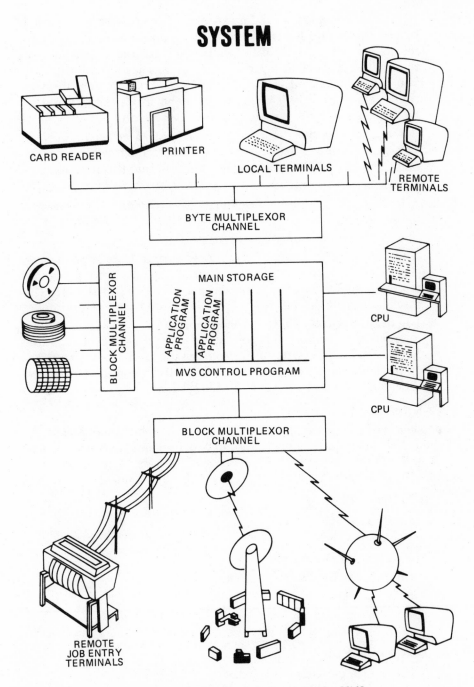

Figure 1.1 The hardware environment for MVS.

3. INITIATOR requests a job for execution. This request is forwarded to JES, since JES is controlling initial job selection. JES in turn selects a job according to its priority and returns a JOBNAME to the INITIATOR. (This priority is the initial selection priority that you specified in your JCL as /*PRIORITY; or it is your installation's default priority if you specified none. This priority is not to be confused with the dispatching priority of a job.)

4. Before a job can execute, certain control blocks have to be created. The system knows the presence of a job through control blocks only. The INTERPRETER is given control to do this function.

5. Next function to be performed is the ALLOCATION of data sets.

6. After completing all the above functions successfully, a job is ready for execution.

7. The INITIATOR attaches a JOB STEP TASK.

8. While the job is executing, it produces output. Output processing (SYSOUTS) is done by JES. It collects all the output for a job and spools it into DASD for later printing at the end of the job. (In special cases the output can be printed at step termination time.)

9. The next function of a job processing is the TASK TERMINATION. In order to accomplish this, job management uses a special routine called "TERMINATOR." JES also helps the job management clean up the mess made by a job. At this stage all of the system resources allocated to a job are returned to the system.

1.3.2 Supervisor Management

Supervisor management activities can be subdivided into nine categories. These activities are involved with resource management and are summarized in the following sections. Each function is covered in later chapters, and the total software structure is conceptualized in figure 1.2.

- Supervisory Control
  - Interruption handlers
  - Dispatcher
  - Memory switch routines
  - Inter-processor communication
  - Schedule processing
  - Locking manager
  - Exit processing
- Task Management
  - Creation & deletion of subtasks
  - WAIT/POST services— ENQ/DEQ services
  - SPI processing

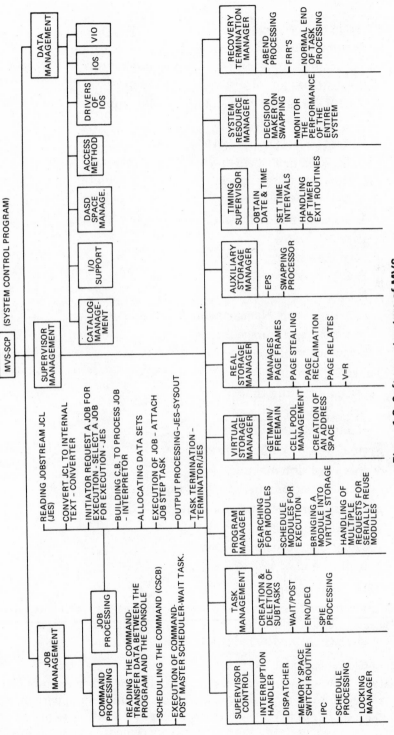

Figure 1.2 Software structure of MVS.

- Program Management
    - Searching for LOAD MODULES
    - Schedule LOAD MODULES for execution
    - Load MODULES into VIRTUAL STORAGE
    - HANDLE multiple requests for serially reusable modules
- Virtual Storage Management
    - GETMAIN/FREEMAIN services
    - CELL POOL management
    - Creates an address space
- Real Storage Management
    - Manage page FRAMES
    - Page STEALING
    - Page reclamation
    - Page release
    - Manages V=R space
- Auxiliary Storage Management
    - External page storage management
    - Swapping processor
- Timer Supervisor
    - Obtain date and time
    - Set time intervals
    - Handle timer exit routines
- System Resource Management
    - Swap decision making
    - Monitor performance of the entire system
- Recovery Termination-Management
    - Abend processing
    - Functional recovery routines
    - Normal end of task processing

1.3.3 Data Management

Data management activities can be subdivided into seven categories. These activities are concerned with file and input/output operations and are summarized in the following sections.

Catalog Management

Catalog management routines are used by the other components of the system and the application programs to locate and update information in a catalog. In MVS the master catalog is a VSAM data set. In order to request services from the catalog management, the requestor first creates a catalog paramenter list (CTGPL) to describe the request, along with a catalog field parameter list (CTGFL) to describe the specific fields of information, and then issues CATLG macro instruction. This macro instruction results in a supervisory call (SVC 26), and the supervisory routine(s) does the requested function.

MVS catalog management also provides support for old OS catalogs through CVOL processor.

I/O Support

OPEN, CLOSE, and EOV routines are classified under I/O Support. OPEN routine prepares the data set for processing after verification of volume and the data set password (if one exists). For standard label tape output, OPEN routine writes the data-set label. The last thing OPEN does is pass control to access method executors.

CLOSE routine determines device-dependent processing, as in the case of a tape data set where it writes tape marks, processes labels, and re-positions the tape. In the case of a direct access data set, CLOSE writes file mark and updates the F1 DSCB in the VTOC. CLOSE routine also restores to pre-open status the data control block/access method control block. Then it returns to the caller.

EOV routine makes it possible for the applications programs to process multivolume data sets without knowing when the end of one volume was reached and the next volume's processing began. It also makes it possible to process concatenated data sets with like or unlike character-istics. For tape output, EOV writes the trailor labels, rewinds the tape, and requests the operator for a new tape mount. For direct access out-put, EOV gets more space on the same volume or on a new volume and updates the corresponding VTOC.

DASD Storage Management (DASDM)

DASD storage management routines control the allocation of space on direct-access storage volumes. Control is effected by manipulating different types of DSCBs on the VTOCs of each DASD volume. DSCBs are the data set labels that contain the characteristics of the data set or data space as well as the physical tracks at which the data set resides. DADSM consists of an ALLOCATE routine, an EXTEND routine, a SCRATCH routine, and a PARTIAL RELEASE routine. In addition to these, DADSM also contains VTOC-related service routines, such as RENAME (SVC 30), OBTAIN (SVC 27), LSPACE (SVC 78), and PRO-TECT (SVC 98).

Access Methods

Access method routines move data between the main storage and an I/O device. Depending on the organization of data, these routines are divided into the following groups:

- Sequential

  BSAM (basic sequential access method)

  QSAM (queued sequential access method)

- Indexed sequential

  ISAM (indexed sequential access method)

Access to an ISAM file can be through

  QISAM (sequential access)

  BISAM (direct access)

- Direct

  BDAM (basic direct access method)

- Partitioned

  BPAM (basic partitioned access method)

MVS provides an access method that is specifically designed to take advantage of virtual storage and is called "VSAM" (virtual storage access method). It supports entry-sequenced, key-sequenced, and relative record data sets.

Telecommunications access methods, such as BTAM (basic telecommunication access method), TCAM (telecommunication access method), and VTAM (virtual telecommunication access method), move data as messages. These access methods are also called *subsystems* and have their own address spaces.

Access method routines take away much of the device-dependent coding, channel programming, and buffer management from application programming and have greatly enhanced data management in application programs.

I/O Supervisor

IOS (Input/output supervisor) is responsible for starting I/O operations devices and for monitoring the events taking place in devices, control units, and channels. Before starting an I/O operation, IOS makes sure of the availability of a datapath to the device and that a channel program is provided by the DRIVER(S). IOS then stores the address of the channel program in a location in memory called *channel address word*. It then issues a start I/O instruction. At the completion of an I/O operation, IOS performs termination processing.

Other functions provided by the IOS are

1. responding to I/O events;
2. restoring the availability of I/O resources (channels, control units, devices);
3. purging or restoring an I/O operation.

I/O Supervisor Drivers

Programs and access methods that directly interface with the IOS are called "DRIVERS." Most of the access methods use EXCP driver as their interface to IOS. There are other drivers such as ASM, VSAM, VTAM, and OLTEP. The program manager uses a driver called "FETCH," and JES3 has its own DRIVER.

Standard access method issues an EXCP or EXCPVR macro instruction to request an I/O operation. This in turn invokes the EXCP driver. The DRIVER fixes control blocks in real storage and converts the virtual storage address of the channel command words into a real storage address. Finally, it requests IOS to start the I/O operation by issuing a STARTIO macro instruction. IOS gets control at this time; and if the device path is available, it starts the I/O operation by issuing a STARTIO instruction. If the request cannot be started immediately, IOS queues the request for later execution.

Virtual I/O

Virtual I/O or VIO is a facility in MVS to handle temporary data sets by using only virtual storage or paging space. The application program using the VIO data set is not aware that it is not using a real DASD file. VIO simulates virtual track for a device (the type of the VIO device is specified during system generation), and it is written to auxiliary storage when the virtual track or buffer is full. VIO offers the following performance advantages:

- Elimination of device allocation and data management overhead (no VTOC search/update).
- More efficient use of DASD space if block size is less than 4,096.
- I/O is done by the auxiliary storage manager which has a better I/O load-balancing capability.

1.4 HARDWARE STRUCTURE OF MVS

There are five major hardware resources in an MVS system: devices, control units, channels, main storage, and the central processing unit(s). A sample configuration is given in figure 1.3 and is referenced in subsequent sections.

1.4.1 Devices

These are the actual machines that transcribe or store data. Figure 1.3 indicates how any of the devices can be addressed individually.

An I/O address consists of a channel specification, a control unit specification, and a device address specification. The I/O address is 16 bits. The first 8 bits represent the channel address, and the next 8 bits collectively represent a control unit and an I/O device. But, for all practical

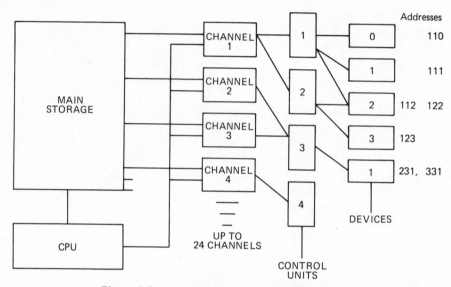

Figure 1.3 Sample MVS hardware configuration.

purposes, the control unit address is the next 4 bits, and the device address is the last 4 bits. Thus the first device address (note the address starts from 0), which is connected to control unit 1 and channel 1, would be 0110. Device 3 has two addresses, since this device is attached through two control units. Addresses for device 3 are 112 and 122. Now consider the device on control unit 3. Control unit 3 is connected to two different channels. Thus the same device can be accessed through two different channels and has two different addresses: 231 and 331.

As mentioned earlier, the internal computing speed of a fourth generation computer has increased tremendously and is measured in nanoseconds, while the operation speed of I/O devices still has mechanical limitations. If the devices were to connect directly to CPU, the CPU would be waiting most of the time for the completion of an I/O operation. The electronic computing speed is limited by the mechanical speed of a device. Another problem is the manner in which data is received from a device. The CPU can only fetch or store data to main storage according to the ACCESS WIDTH of a particular machine. (In the case of system 370 models 168 and 3084, access width is double word, containing 8 bytes.)

The various devices handle data differently, for example, bits in the case of DASD and bytes in the case of magnetic tape units.

1.4.2 Control units

These units provide a data path from a device to a channel and from a channel back to a device, as summarized in figure 1.4.

A controller can handle up to 16 devices of similar characteristics. Rather than duplicating the same circuit in each device to collect and assemble data bytes and to validate them, all the necessary circuits are incorporated in the control units. This makes devices more efficient, faster, and above all cheaper. Controllers are often integrated within a single unit.

1.4.3 Channels

The main function of a channel is to relieve the CPU from data transfer operations: it permits data processing to proceed concurrently with I/O operations. Channel assembles data for memory cells by replacing cyclic check characters and inserting parity bits in each data byte. The action is reversed when channel receives data from main storage. Channel disassembles data by removing parity bit from each byte and by generating cyclic check characters after each block of data.

During I/O processing, the CPU asks the channel to do an I/O operation and continues processing. Only when the channel finishes an I/O operation does the CPU need to take care of the data. This type of concurrent processing of CPU and channel is called *I/O overlap*. Throughput of the system can be increased by increasing the I/O overlap.

1.4.4 Main Storage

In order for the CPU to execute an instruction, the instruction and the related data must be in main storage at the time of execution. An MVS installation can have up to 64 million bytes of main (or real) storage. The amount of real storage in MVS has an indirect relationship to the performance of the system.

Let us briefly look at the components of main storage. Main storage is divided into 2K blocks (1K=1,024 bytes). Associated with each block of storage is a 7-bit area where the operating system keeps track of storage key for that particular block. The first 4 bits represent the access key. Whenever there is a FETCH or STORE of data, this storage key is matched against the requestor's access key before allowing access to the block of

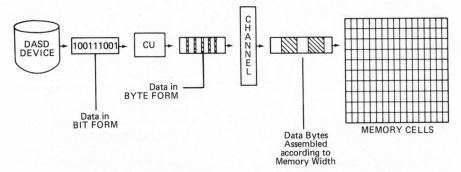

Figure 1.4 Data representation along the datapath from a DASD device to main storage.

data. The key-matching process is controlled by the setting of the next bit, called the "FETCH protection bit." If this FETCH protection bit is off, then no key checking is done for FETCH operations; but STORE type operations still require a Key-match condition. If FETCH protection bit is on, then both FETCH and STORE operations require a Key-match condition.

The next (sixth bit) bit is called a *reference bit*. Each time a reference to the 2k block of storage is made, either through FETCH or STORE operation, this bit is turned on.

The change bit (seventh bit) is set when a STORE type operation is done at a location in the corresponding storage block. Later it will become apparent that most of the storage manipulation is done in 4K blocks. Then why is the storage blocked by 2K bytes? The answer is that the same hardware is used for other operating systems such as DOS where the addressing scheme is for 2K blocks; so, it is a matter of compatibility. Also, the protection architecture was developed before IBM's virtual storage concept.

The blocks are further subdivided into CELLS. Each CELL corresponds to the access width of a particular model.

A main storage configuration is depicted in figure 1.5, which summarizes the various components as follows:

- Memory (storage) cells contain data.
- The memory address register contains the address of a reference location in memory.

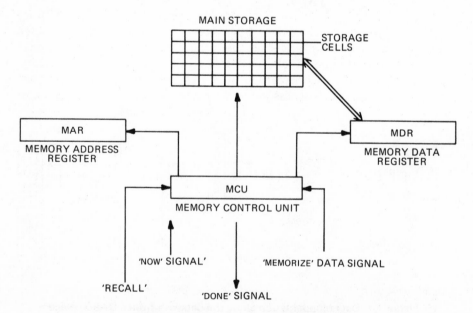

Figure 1.5 Main storage environment.

- The memory data register contains the data from or to memory cell.
- The memory control unit contains the logic to perform access to main storage or memory cells.

Two types of access to main storage are requested by CPU and channel to MCU.

Store Access

Store access stores data in memory cells. This can be requested by channel or CPU. The request alerts the memory control unit by a MEMORIZE signal. The requester places the data-to-be-stored in the data register and the address of the memory cell to which it is going. The requester then issues a NOW signal to the control unit. Assuming it is free to accept the request, the control unit fetches the data from the data register and places it in the memory cell referenced by the address register. When it is done, the control unit signals DONE to the requester and the store access is completed.

Fetch Access

The requester, namely a channel or CPU, issues a RECALL signal to the memory control unit. After placing the memory address of the data-to-be-fetched in the address register, the requester issues a NOW signal. The control unit fetches the data from main storage according to the MAR address and places the data in the data register.

After the control unit places the data in the data register, it issues a DONE signal to the requester. The requester now can access the data from the data register.

1.4.5 Central Processing Unit

The central processing unit, which is summarized in figure 1.6, is composed of two units, an I-UNIT (instruction unit) and an E-UNIT (execution unit). I-UNIT fetches the instruction, decodes it, fetches the operands, and issues instructions to E-UNIT for execution. The E-UNIT, under control of micro program, executes the instruction. It is capable of executing a new instruction during every machine cycle.

Fetching an Instruction

The instruction control unit signals the memory control unit to RECALL (see figure 1.7). When the memory control unit is ready to accept the signal, the instruction control unit transfers the content of the instruction address register to the memory address register. After the transfer is complete, the instruction control unit signals NOW to the memory control unit, whose function at this time is to pick up the address in the memory address register, go to that location in main storage, and fetch the content (usually 8 bytes). This content, which is the next instruction to be executed by the CPU, is transferred to the memory data register. When the transfer is complete, the memory control unit signals a DONE condition to the instruction control unit, which in turn transfers the instruction in the memory data register to the Instruction register. This instruction is decoded by the ID and signals the E-Unit for execution. The ICU increments the instruction address register by the length of the fetched instruction in order to address the next instruction during the next machine cycle. The length of the fetched instruction can be determined by the first two bits of the OP-CODE. If these bits are 00, the instruction length is 2 bytes. A binary 11 indicates the instruction is 3 halfwords or 6 bytes long. Any other combination is for a 2-halfword or 4-byte long instruction. The same process is repeated with the new value in the instruction address register.

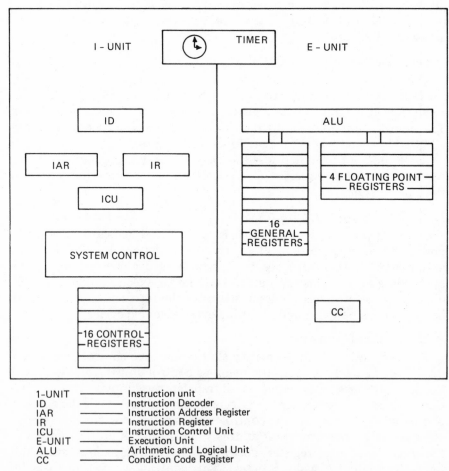

1-UNIT	——	Instruction unit
ID	——	Instruction Decoder
IAR	——	Instruction Address Register
IR	——	Instruction Register
ICU	——	Instruction Control Unit
E-UNIT	——	Execution Unit
ALU	——	Arithmetic and Logical Unit
CC	——	Condition Code Register

Figure 1.6 CPU logical components.

In high-performance machines, instructions are prefetched and stored in auxiliary instruction buffers for future execution. In any case the address in the instruction address register points to the next instruction to be executed.

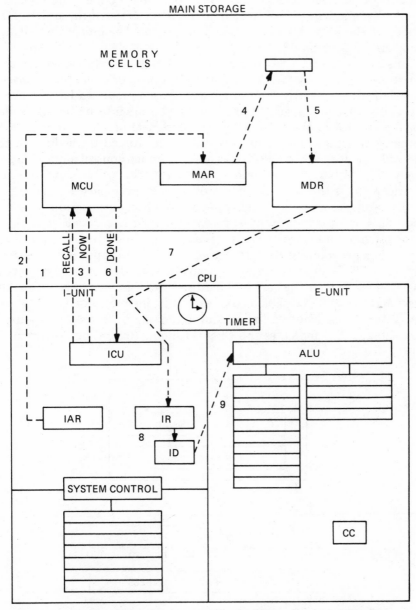

Figure 1.7 Basic functions performed by the CPU to fetch an instruction.

1.4.6 Program Status Word

The program status word (see figure 1.8) is located in CPU. It governs the status of the system at any given point in time. PSW is a combination of some of the CPU components that we already looked at, namely the instruction address register and condition code register. The PSW also consists of flags and masks which indicate the status of the system. The length of the PSW is a double word or 8 bytes. The bits in the PSW are numbered 0 through 63.

Bits 12 through 15 deserve special attention and are called *flag bits.* These are denoted by "EMWP." If the E bit is on or equal to 1 (binary), this indicates this PSW is in extended control mode. In later systems, especially virtual storage systems, more and more information is needed for the control of the CPU. When the designers of the system decided to carry this information in PSW, they were forced to distinguish the old and new formats of the PSW as basic extended control modes, respectively. The M bit is for machine-check mask. This will be covered later.

The W bit is the wait bit. When this flag is on (binary 1), the system is in a hardware wait state. CPU does not fetch any instruction when this wait bit is on. It is important to distinguish a hardware wait from a software program wait. Software wait is accomplished by issuing a WAIT macro in a program. In the latter case, the program is put in a wait state, but the CPU is enabled to execute instructions for other programs in the system. But, in the case of a hardware wait, the wait bit in the PSW is set and the CPU is disabled from executing instructions. Thus the wait bit distinguishes whether the system is running or in a WAIT status. If the W bit is 0, it indicates the CPU is running (executing instructions).

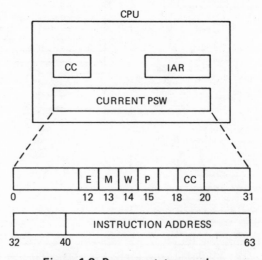

Figure 1.8 Program status word.

Now in order to distinguish between the supervisor state and problem program state, there is an indicator in the PSW called the P bit. If the P bit is a binary 1, then the system is executing in problem program status, or else it is executing in supervisor state. In supervisor state CPU is allowed to execute any instructions, including "privileged" instructions. But in the problem program state only a subset of instructions (excluding privileged instructions) are allowed to be executed by the CPU.

The instruction address portion of the PSW contains the address of the next instruction to be executed. We saw how the instruction address register is incremented according to the length of the previous instruction. One exception to this rule is the EXECUTE (EX) instruction. When the CPU encounters the subject instruction of execute, the instruction address register or the address portion of the PSW is not updated.

1.4.7 Registers

The CPU contains 16 general purpose registers and 4 floating point registers for application programmers' use. There are also 16 control registers for system control functions. Dynamic address translation hardware for virtual storage machines and timer hardware are also part of the CPU.

1.5 MULTIPROCESSING SYSTEMS

A *Multiprocessing System* (MP) allows more than one CPU to share the computing workload. Through this method of sharing tasks between each other, the availability of the system increases. Even if one CPU is down, the other CPU (or CPUs in the future) can take over the functions of the failing unit. At present there are only 4 CPUs (IBM 3084 MP) sharing the tasks, but there are facilities for 16 CPUs to share in the future. There are two types of MP system combinations.

1.5.1 Tightly Coupled Multiprocessing

In a tightly coupled multiprocessing system (figure 1.9), CPUs share all available main storage, and only one copy of the operating system (control program) resides in storage. In addition, processor-to-processor communication is accomplished via storing of data in shared storage and via direct processor-to-processor signals (both program and hardware initiated).

The multiprocessor communication unit connects both CPUs and, through a configuration console, provides the operator with a facility to divide an multiprocessing system into two unit processor (UP) systems. Main storage and channels can also be partitioned between the system according to the needs. This facility allows engineers to isolate and repair any failing hardware component without bringing down the entire system.

Channels and control units can be shared between CPUs. A device that can be accessed from all CPUs is called *symmetric*. If a device cannot be addressed through all CPUs, it is called *asymmetric*.

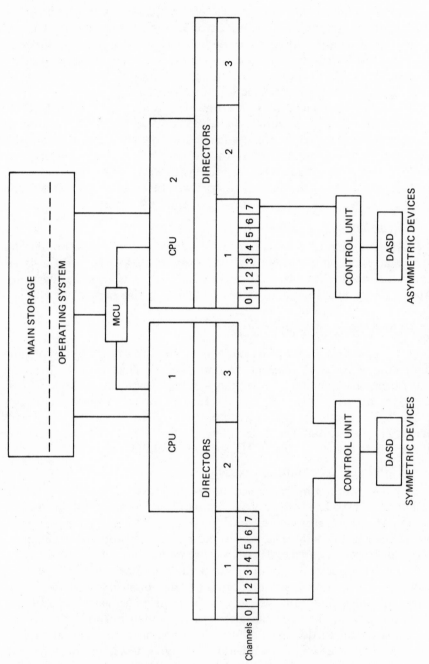

Figure 1.9 Tightly coupled multiprocessing system.

A CPU in a multiprocessing system without channels connecting to it, is called an *Attached Processor*. No I/O operation can be initiated through an attached processor. This can be thought of as adding power to the existing CPU. But if I/O bound jobs are running on this attached processor, every time an I/O operation is called for, the attached processor has to evoke the other CPU to access the data from the channel. This situation can create a bottleneck in the performance of the system.

Since there are two or more CPUs executing tasks concurrently and sharing the same main storage, there is a problem in data integrity and validity. This problem is solved by adding hardware features such as prefixing and software features such as locking. These features are covered later.

1.5.2 Loosely Coupled Multiprocessing

In a loosely coupled multiprocessing system (figure 1.10), each CPU has its own main storage. The only connection between the two CPUs is through a hardware component called a *channel-to-channel adaptor*. In this configuration there is always a GLOBAL CPU which reads in all the jobs to the system and then puts them in a job queue. This queue will exist on a direct access storage device accessible from both systems. Asymmetric multiprocessing system software (ASP) supports from 2 to 33 systems connected via channel-to-channel adapters.

The JES2 multi-access spool facility supports loosely coupled systems without the channel-to-channel adapters. Through shared DASD (shared spool volume) JES2 supports up to seven systems. Multiple copies of the operating system (MVS) exist for this configuration, one in each of the CPU's main storage. Once selected from the job queue by one CPU, a job is executed in that CPU alone. No switching of CPUs is done for a task as in a tightly coupled MP system.

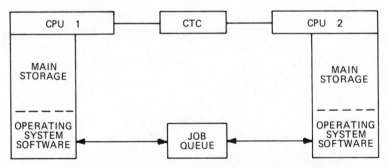

Figure 1.10 Loosely coupled multiprocessing system.

1.6 CHANNEL PROGRAMMING

In the same manner in which the CPU executes instructions, the channel executes commands. In fact, both of them can execute at the same time. All the CPU has to do is initiate the I/O operation by executing a start I/O (SIO) instruction. Since this instruction is a privileged one, the CPU can only execute it in the supervisor state.

As covered in the data management section, the IOS does all the I/O functions for the system. Before issuing an SIO, it has to do some housekeeping routines. This includes setting up of channel command words. It also includes putting the address of the first command word in a fixed location in memory or main storage (at location 72) called *Channel Address Word*. After setting all these, the I/O supervisor issues a SIO instruction. The operand of this instruction is the channel and device address to which the I/O operation is directed. If the requested channel and device can accept the command, the channel fetches the first channel command word from the main storage pointed by the channel address word. Once channel processing is initiated, the CPU can do its processing independently of the channel operation. If the channel rejects the SIO, a condition code is set, and it is up to the IO supervisor to determine the final disposition of the command.

1.6.1 Channel Command Word

The channel command word is depicted in figure 1.11, and its components are summarized as follows:

Command Code

This directs the channel for a specific I/O operation. The command codes we are interested in are READ and WRITE; their command codes are 02 and 01 respectively.

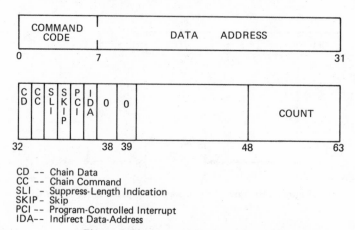

CD -- Chain Data
CC -- Chain Command
SLI - Suppress-Length Indication
SKIP- Skip
PCI -- Program-Controlled Interrupt
IDA-- Indirect Data-Address

Figure 1.11 Channel command word.

Data Address

This is the address of data in main storage from which channel picks up data for a WRITE operation. But for a READ, this address contains the area in main storage to which the channel will assign data.

Flags

There are seven flag bits in CCW. Seven of them will be covered in detail. When the channel completes the operation specified by a channel command word, it can terminate the I/O operation or continue, depending on the CD (chain data) or CC (command chain) flags chain data. When CD bit is on (1), the channel fetches the next sequential command word. The address portion of this channel command word defines a new storage address and a new byte count for the original I/O operation. Both command words pertain to the same I/O record that the channel is working on. When the chain data (CD) flag is on, the channel will not examine the command code portion of the next channel command word, but uses the same command code from the previous one. This flag is very useful in scatter reading of a record into different locations in main storage. In a WRITE operation this can be used to collect data from different locations to write as a single record.

Chain Command

If this flag is 1, the next sequential channel command word is fetched. This new word specifies a new I/O operation on the same I/O device. The new operation is only initiated at normal completion of the current operation.

Skip Flag

This flag allows the channel to receive data from a device but not transmit it to main storage. Consider a WRITE CHECK operation. It consists of a WRITE operation followed by a READ to check the validity of the data just written. In order to implement this, we need a command chain flag set in the WRITE CCW and a skip flag set in the READ CCW.

SLI Flag

This flag bit is called *suppress length indicator*. It is used to indicate that the number of bytes specified on the byte count of channel command word may not be the same as the number of bytes from a block of data.

Every time the channel receives a byte of data, it decrements the data count field by 1. And when the count field becomes 0, it indicates the end of a command operation. But suppose there are still data remaining in a block even after the data count field in the channel command word reaches 0. Then the operation will terminate with an I/O error. The above condition is possible in variable length records and in other cases, but we don't want the I/O operation terminated with an error. This is accomplished by setting this SLI flag in the corresponding channel command word that operates on a variable length record.

1.6.2 Transfer In Channel

Another channel command necessary for a general understanding of I/O operations is TIC (transfer in channel). This enables us to jump and execute CCWs other than in a normal sequential fashion. TIC does for a channel program what the BRANCH instruction does for the CPU program.

The format of this channel command word is the same as all other commands. The channel ignores the flag bytes and the byte count. The form of a TIC command is given in figure 1.12. The data address in a TIC CCW points to the next channel command word to be executed. Some of the general rules to code a TIC CCW are the following:

- The data address in a TIC must be on a doubleword boundary.
- The next channel command word pointed to by the address in a TIC should not be another TIC command.
- Command and data chaining (CC and CD) are transmitted through TIC.
- If a channel command word does not indicate chaining and is not a TIC, then it is the last CCW of the channel program.

1.6.3 Initial Program Loading

Initiate INITIAL PROGRAM LOAD (IPL) by selecting or typing the load unit address on the system control panel or on the console IPL screen (depending on the CPU model) and by hitting the LOAD button or by activating the IPL screen. When the operator hits or activates the LOAD, a machine action takes place. From the device address dialed, the system reads 24 bytes and places this data at storage location 0 through 23. After this, the channel is given control. Looking at fixed storage location 0 through 23 in the System/370 reference summary, we see that location 0 through 7 contains initial program loading PSW; location 8 through 15, initial program loading CCW1; and from 16 through 23, initial program loading CCW2. When the channel gets control, it picks up the first channel

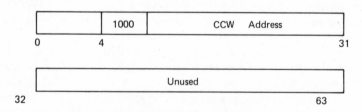

Figure 1.12 Transfer channel command.

command word (CCW1) from location 8 through 15. This channel command word is used to read in additional ones at a different location in storage. The next channel command word at location 16 will TIC to this newly built channel program to bring in the copy of the operating system. When the channel finishes, another automatic action takes place: the CPU picks up the IPL PSW from location 0 through 7 and makes *this* PSW the current one. According to the status of the system, indicated by the current PSW, the system either will be in a hardware wait state or will start executing instructions according to the address portion of the PSW.

1.7 INTERRUPTS

There are three ways to load the current PSW and thus gain control of the system. The first is through the automatic action at IPL. The second is to issue the LPSW (LOAD PSW) instruction. The third and final way to introduce a current PSW to the system is through interrupts. There are six types of interrupts in the System/370 architecture. They are identified as external interrupt, supervisor call, program interrupt, machine check interrupt, I/O interrupt, and restart interrupt.

1.7.1 Interrupt Processing

When an interrupt occurs, through a hardware mechanism, a PSW swap occurs. The PSW in the CPU (current PSW) is stored in a pre-assigned area in memory as the old PSW. There are six slots for each of the different types of interrupts. Also there are six corresponding PSWs (new PSWs) for each of the six different types of interrupts. Hardware loads the corresponding new PSW into the CPU. This PSW now becomes the current PSW.

Fixed storage locations (see figure 1.13) for old PSWs are from 24 through 63. Each PSW is 8-bytes long. The order of PSWs is ESPMI. The old PSW for RESTART is stored in location 8 through 15. New PSWs are stored from location 88 through 127. The RESTART new PSW is stored at location 0 through 7.

The address portion of the new PSWs points to interrupt-handling routines for the corresponding interrupts. These routines are part of the supervisor. In effect, we can say that when an interrupt happens, the control of the CPU is given to the supervisor.

1.7.2 Interrupt Handling

Supervisor routines examine the cause of the interrupt and take appropriate actions. After it has finished processing the interrupt, the supervisor issues a LPSW instruction to give control to an application program which has the highest dispatching priority and is in ready status. That program executes until another interrupt occurs. This form of interrupt

MAIN STORAGE FIXED LOCATIONS

0	RESTART NEW PSW
8	RESTART OLD PSW
24	
	EXTERNAL OLD PSW
32	SUPERVISOR CALL OLD PSW
40	PROGRAM OLD PSW
48	MACHINE–CHECK OLD PSW
56	INPUT/OUTPUT OLD PSW
88	EXTERNAL NEW PSW
96	SUPERVISOR CALL NEW PSW
104	PROGRAM NEW PSW
112	MACHINE–CHECK NEW PSW
120	INPUT/OUTPUT NEW PSW

Figure 1.13 Interrupt storage areas.

processing continues. This is how, in MVS, the CPU is effectively given control of different programs or tasks by the supervisor to permit fast response to conditions of high priority.

Some examples of interrupts are

- Time interval has expired (external interrupt).
- Instruction executed causes an abnormal condition (program check interrupt).
- An I/O operation has completed (I/O interrupt).
- An even parity byte is found (machine check interrupt).*
- Somebody hit the restart button on the system console panel (restart interrupt).

(*NOTE: Integrity of a byte is accomplished through odd parity.)

Just because we have one of these interrupt-causing events does not mean that we have an interrupt. It all depends on whether the CPU is enabled or disabled for that particular interrupt. (*Enabled* means interrupt is allowed, and *disabled* means interrupt of CPU is not allowed.)

1.7.3 Masking

If the CPU is disabled for I/O interrupts, these interrupts remain pending. But, on the other hand, external and machine check interrupts may get lost, and others will stay pending. There are more than 20 types of program check interrupts. Some of them can be disabled through PSW masks. If the CPU is disabled for these types of program check interrupts and they do occur they will be lost.

1.7.4 Input/Output Interrupts

Bit 6 in current PSW indicates where I/O interrupts are enabled or disabled. If bit 6 is a 0, this means I/O interrupts are disabled. If this bit is a 1, then we have to check control register 2 for further identification of channels to which I/O interrupts are enabled. Bits 0 through 31 in control register 2 correspond to channels 0 through 31. If any of these bits are 1s, the corresponding channels are allowed for I/O interrupts, or they are disabled for I/O interrupts.

An I/O interrupt causes the current PSW to be stored at a location for input/output old PSW (at location 56), and the channel status word (CSW) is stored at location 64. A new PSW from location 120 is loaded into the CPU and becomes the current PSW.

1.7.5 External Interrupts

Bit 7 of current PSW is the external mask. If this bit is a 1, check control register 0 for the particular types of external interrupts allowed. If this bit is 0, external interrupts are disabled.

1.7.6 Program Check Interrupts

The only types of program checks that can be disabled are fixed-point overflow, decimal overflow, exponent underflow, and significance check. These masks are in the current PSW from bit position 20 through 23.

1.7.7 Machine Check Interrupts

If bit 13 in the current PSW is a 1, then check control register 14 for different classes of machine checks that are enabled.

1.7.8 SVC Interrupt

The only type of interrupt that *cannot* be disabled is the supervisory call interrupt.

When a supervisory control is encountered in the user program, an SVC interrupt occurs. Due to the interrupt, the PSW in the CPU is stored in SVC old PSW location (location 32) in main storage. Note the address portion of this PSW points to the next sequential instruction within the user program. The SVC new PSW is brought to the CPU by the automatic action of the hardware. This new PSW now becomes the current PSW. The address portion of this current PSW points to the SVC first level interrupt handler (FLIH) routine. Thus the routine gets control. If this routine wants another supervisory routine and issues a supervisory call, another SVC interrupt happens. Then the current PSW would be stored in the old SVC PSW location overlaying the user program's PSW. Thus, it would never be possible to return to the user program. Moreover, this will create an endless loop of SVC interrupts.

All of these problems are due to the fact that SVC interrupts cannot be disabled. Later, how the system takes care of the situation will be covered.

2 Virtual Storage

The primary concept contributing to the effectiveness and efficiency of an MVS system is *virtual storage*. Storage management is an important aspect of operating system design, and virtual storage is the most recent step in its evolutionary chain.

2.1 EVOLUTION OF STORAGE MANAGEMENT TECHNOLOGY

In IBM's major operating system line, storage management has evolved through five systems: OS/PCP, OS/MFT, OS/MVT, SVS, and finally MVS.

2.1.1 OS/PCP Primary Control Program

In a PCP system (figure 2.1a) only one job can run at a time. The job is loaded to a fixed location in main storage. The only other program that shares main storage is the PCP system control program. The primary objective of the system is to automate many of the operator interactions with the system during the execution of a job. Even though the PCP system achieved these objectives, there are some disadvantages to it:

1. Programming was restricted to the size of the main storage.

2. Because the program was larger than the main storage, it was the responsibility of the programmer to break the program into overlay structure. This took a considerable amount of time and talent.

3. On the other hand, small programs could not utilize the full potential of the resources; thus, a substantial portion of the system resources were idle during execution of each job.

4. Set-up time for a job was greater than its execution time. Thus, due to idle time, system resources were wasted considerably.

5. Jobs could run only serially, one a time. Thus the system as a whole was underutilized.

In fact, input/output spooling was only available in later versions, on an unsupported basis. OS/PCP is not used today.

2.1.2 OS/MFT–Multiprogramming with a Fixed Number of Tasks

The OS/MFT system (figure 2.1b) tries to take advantage of the system resources by multiprogramming. Main storage is divided into partitions. Each job can run in one of the specified partitions. Even though this operating system produces more throughput than the PCP system, it still has its disadvantages:

29

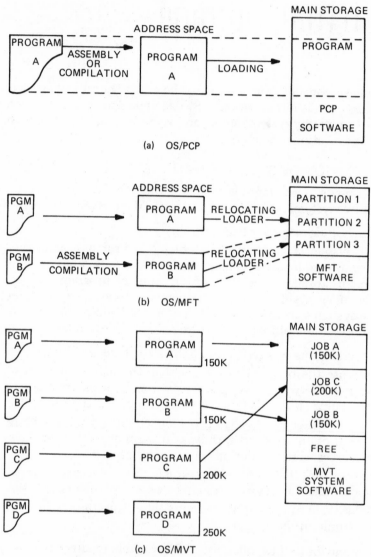

Figure 2.1 Evolution of storage management.

a. The number of partitions specified at system generation time limits the number of active jobs in the system.
b. Jobs are pre-assigned to a particular partition according to the size of the program.
c. Since partition sizes are pre-set at system generation time, small jobs will not utilize partition space efficiently. In an environment where the main storage requirements of all jobs are known before-

hand, OS/MFT is a reasonable operating system to achieve the objectives of an installation.

d. MFT uses each partition serially. Allocation for a device, if not satisfied, puts a job in a wait state. This waiting job will hold its main storage partition during that idle period. (The solution of this problem leads to the next stage of the operating system development.)

Surprisingly, OS/MFT is still used today in installations with a rigidly controlled work load.

2.1.3 OS/MVT-Multiprogramming with a Variable Number of Tasks

OS/MVT (figure 2.1c) tries to solve the drawbacks of the MFT system by allowing the main storage to be dynamically shared between active jobs. Jobs are loaded into main storage one after another until there is no more room in main storage. Thus jobs need not be loaded into a pre-assigned partition, as was the case in OS/MFT.

Let us assume there are four jobs ready to be executed by the system: Job A, Job B, Job C, and Job D. According to the priority, Job A is allocated main storage (150K) before execution. The next highest priority job, Job C and Job B, get 200K and 150K of storage respectively. Since our conceptual system has only 100K of storage left, even though Job D is ready to execute, Job D has to wait.

Now let us assume that Job C has finished. Even though now there are 300K of storage available, Job D cannot start because Job D needs 250K of contiguous storage. This type of problem is called *fragmentation* of main storage. This problem occurred due to the restriction that Job D be loaded in contiguous main storage. The above restriction is called *static relocation*.

2.1.4 Static Relocation and Assembly

When a program is assembled or compiled, the compiler generates an address space for the program. The address space consists of machine instructions, data descriptions, and I/O descriptions for the program. In generating the machine instructions for a program, a compiler uses relative displacement from the beginning of the program, which is usually 0. And all other addresses are contiguous from that beginning location. The linkage editor can expand and resolve the compiler-generated address space by including other address space of other programs. In any case, the net effect is an address space whose starting address is 0. The base register also contains 0. When this program is loaded into main storage for execution, the loader loads this address space into a contiguous area in main storage. In order for this program to execute correctly, all the loader has to do is change the base register that contains 0 (origin of the address space) to the beginning address of the main storage at which the address space is loaded. This type of relocation of a program into main storage is called *static relocation* (figure 2.2).

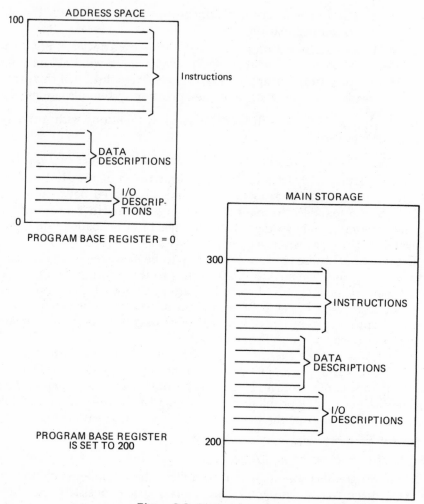

Figure 2.2 Static relocation.

Thus one of the major disadvantages of the MVT system is the main-storage fragmentation. Another disadvantage or limitation is the dynamic allocation of storage required by the executing program. In order to avoid this situation, the MVT system allocates the maximum-sized region the user requested through his job card. Even a small step in a job, during a wait for an event, wastes the main-storage resource allocated to that whole job.

2.1.5 Roll-in/Roll-out

The problem of storage allocation is addressed by the roll-in–roll-out feature of MVT. If this feature is in effect, a high-priority job can cause a rollout of a low-priority waiting job. The exact image of the waiting job and its main-storage addresses are copied onto an external device by rollout. During the roll-in operation, the job has to read into the original main-storage locations it occupied before a roll-out. This restriction limits the effectiveness of the roll-in–roll-out feature in achieving dynamic allocation of main storage. But it is a milestone in the development of virtual storage systems, which utilize the main storage on a dynamic basis.

2.1.6 Dynamic Relocation

If the address space is segmented into smaller units, each starting with a relative address 0, we will be able to load our program into different segments of main storage. The only restriction is that each segment of main storage be contiguous to the size of our address space unit.

Another problem to be solved is the address translation of each unit in relation both to others and to main storage segments. This type of translation is called dynamic relocation. This is done through a hardware feature called *dynamic address translation*. This hardware component translates our relative segment address into real storage addresses during program execution. Since this dynamic address translation is taking place during execution, our program address space is no longer bounded by its real storage locations, even during execution. Thus, there is an opportunity to manage or re-allocate main storage during program execution in contrast to static relocation (figure 2.3).

This idea gave birth to the concept of virtual storage systems. Virtual storage allows a large addressing capability that exceeds the size of physi-

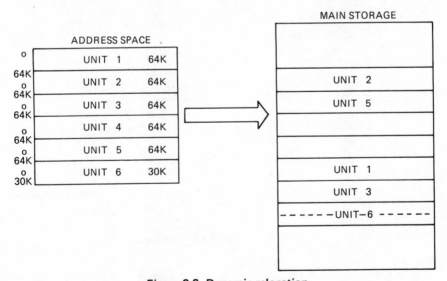

Figure 2.3 Dynamic relocation.

cal main storage. In virtual storage systems, addresses are created and referenced relative to virtual storage rather than the main storage seen in the previous systems.

2.1.7 OS/VS1 and OS/VS2 Release 1-Single Virtual Storage System

OS/VS1 and OS/VS2 are each virtual storage system with only a single virtual storage. *Virtual storage* is one large address space. The size of the virtual storage is 16 million bytes. This 16-meg limitation of virtual storage is due to the IBM 360/370 addressing scheme. A 24-bit address can represent a value from 0 through 16,777,215. Thus virtual storage is the biggest address space that the hardware addressing-scheme permits.*

Virtual storage is mapped into a combination of main (real) storage and external storage (DASD) (see figure 2.4). Any virtual storage not allocated to a program need not exist anywhere. Programs and data occupy contiguous locations in virtual storage but need not be in main storage.

In a single virtual storage system (SVS), one big address space (16 meg) exists for the system. This is just an address range for the system and not to be confused with a physical medium for storage. When programs are loaded for execution, each individual address space is given a contiguous virtual storage address as in static relocation. The maximum number of jobs that can be loaded for execution depends on the virtual storage

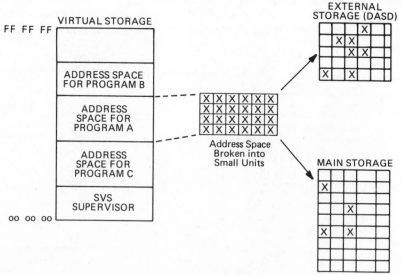

Figure 2.4 Single virtual storage.

---

*In later versions of MVS software permit 31-bit addressing. This gives an address space of 2 billion bytes.

address range, which is 0 through 16,777,215. The address space of a program which is loaded into virtual storage or mapped into the virtual storage address is considered broken down into smaller units. The size of each unit is 2K (2,048 bytes) in VS1 and 4K (4,096 bytes) in VS2. Each unit in both versions of the system is called a *page*. As we have seen before, a hardware mechanism called dynamic address translation performs the mapping between the virtual storage address and its current physical location either in main storage or in external page storage.

The following list summarizes the concept of virtual storage as presented thus far:

- Virtual storage is an addressing scheme. The system is given an address range of 0 through 16,777,215 location. When a program is said to be *loaded into virtual storage*, it means the program is given addresses within the virtual address range for its data, instruction, and I/O descriptions. This address range for a program has to be contiguous on virtual storage but not in main storage.
- Virtual storage is an address space that exceeds the size of main storage.
- A hardware mechanism (DAT) performs a mapping between virtual storage addresses and its current physical location.
- When a requested address is not in main storage, the data requested is brought into main storage from an external storage device.

2.1.8 Multiple Virtual Storage (MVS) System

In this system each user gets an address space (range) that is 16 million bytes long. In other words, each user gets the maximum virtual address for his own use. So there are multiple virtual address spaces in this system —thus the name "MVS" (see figure 2.5).

Some system components, such as master scheduler, job entry subsystem, and telecommunication access method, have their own virtual address spaces. Each the batch job and each TSO user also gets one virtual address space. Even though the number of virtual address spaces is theoretically unlimited, main storage and external-page storage capacities limit the maximum number of virtual storage address spaces in an installation. Virtual storage address space has to exist in either of two places, namely main storage or external page storage. The total capacity of these two has a direct bearing on the amount of virtual storage space that an installation can have. Currently, the maximum number of address spaces supported in MVS is 1,635.

2.2 VIRTUAL STORAGE CONCEPTS IN MVS

In MVS a virtual storage address space (figure 2.6) is divided into 256 segments. The size of each segment is 64K. Each segment is further divided

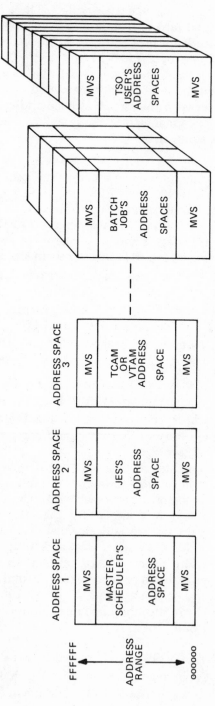

Figure 2.5 Multiple virtual storage.

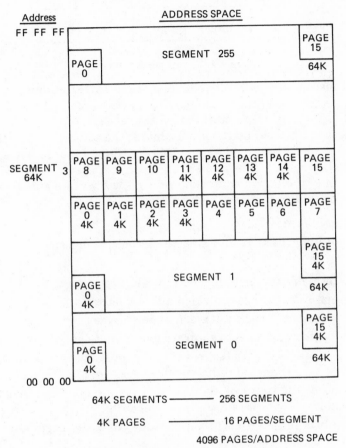

Figure 2.6 MVS virtual storage space.

into 4K pages. Now we can define a *page:* 4K (4,096 bytes) of data or instructions in an address space.

2.2.1 Virtual Storage Addressing

A virtual address (figure 2.7), when loaded into a general register, is 32 bits long. But only the last 24 bits in a register are used for virtual address generation; so, bits 0 through 7 are ignored by the system when it is working with addresses. The next 8 bits (bits 8 through 15) are used to index into the segment of virtual storage we want to address. Remember that there are 256 segments in a virtual storage address space. The 8 bits can represent 256 (2^8) different possibilities or segment numbers in a virtual storage addressing-scheme.

Since each segment is divided into 16 pages, the next 4 bits point to a page within a segment. We have defined a page in MVS as a 4K unit of

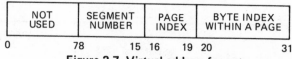

Figure 2.7 Virtual address format.

data and instructions within an address space. After finding a segment and a page within a segment, the next thing we want to know, to address any data, is the displacement of data within the given page.

This is accomplished by the last 12 bits of the address (bits 20 through 31). Twelve bits have an address range of 0 through 4,095 bytes, which happen to be the page size in MVS.

Thus, using the above addressing scheme, we will be able to address any location within a 16-meg address space.

2.2.2 Virtual Storage Terminology

The terminology used to describe the concepts presented thus far is summarized as follows:

- Real or main storage is divided into 4K *page frames.*
- External page storage is divided into 4K *page slots.*
- Only *active pages* of a job are in main storage.
- *Inactive pages* of an active job are *in external page storage* (EPS).
- If a job has been initiated and *swapped in*, active pages are in main storage page frames and the inactive pages are in EPS page slots.
- If none of the pages of an address space are in main storage, then that address space is said to be *swapped out.*
- If a job is initiated and swapped out, all of its pages are in EPS page slots.

2.2.3 Virtual Storage Management

In order for the system to keep track of pages in an address space, it has to know the following information:

- Is a segment or a page allocated?

   (At issue is whether a GETMAIN macro is issued for storage space. If a GETMAIN macro is issued for 4K of storage, a segment is allocated to that address space. Of that segment's 16 pages, one page is given to the requesting program.)
- Where is a page located—

   In a main storage frame?
   Or in an EPS slot?
- Is a particular page frame in main storage in use?

These pieces of information are stored in a complex management of tables known as page tables, external page tables, and segment tables.

2.2.4 Page Tables

To keep track of pages within a segment, the system has a page table for each segment. Since there are 256 segments with an address space, there are 256 page tables for an address space. Note: Page tables are only needed for allocated segments of virtual storage. If a segment is not allocated, there is no need for a page table for that segment.

Each page table consists of 16 entries, one for each page in that segment. These page table entries are called page table entries (PGTEs). The PGTE is 2 bytes long and PGTEs are contiguous. (See figure 2.8)

The first 12 bits of a PGTE points to the beginning of a page in *real storage* or *main storage*.

The twelfth bit is called *page invalid* (I) bit. This bit indicates where the page is located. If this bit is 0, the page is located in main storage. If this bit is 1, then the page is not valid, which means the page is not in main storage. But we don't know yet whether the page is allocated at all.

The answer to this is to examine the fifteenth bit, called *Getmained* bit or "G bit" for short. If this bit is a 1, the page is allocated. If the page is allocated but not in main storage, where is it? The answer is, Look in another table called the *external page table* (XPT). If G bit is 0, this indicates the page is not allocated.

2.2.5 External Page Tables

The external page table serves to locate an allocated page that is not in main storage. There are 16 entries in this table, and each entry is 12 bytes long. Each entry in this table is called an external page table entry (XPTE). (see figure 2.9.)

The address portion of the XPTE points to the slot address of the page in the external-page storage device. This external page storage is on a direct-access storage device, and the address is in cylinder, track, and record form. Each page table has a corresponding external-page table.

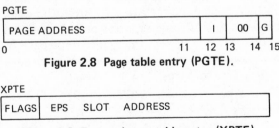

Figure 2.8 Page table entry (PGTE).

Figure 2.9 External page table entry (XPTE).

P ———— PAGE SEGMENT PROTECTION
C ———— COMMON SEGMENT
I ———— SEGMENT--INVALID BIT

Figure 2.10 Segment table entry (SGTE).

2.2.6 Segment Tables

The segment table (SGT) keeps track of the location of page tables and external-page tables. There is also an indicator to discern whether a segment is allocated or not. Since there are 256 segments in an address space, there are 256 entries in the segment table for an address space. Each entry in the segment table is called a *segment table entry* (SGTE). Each entry is 4 bytes long. (See figure 2.10.)

If I bit, which is the segment invalid bit, equals 1, the segment is invalid. If the segment is not allocated, no page table address exists for that segment.

If I bit equals 0, it means the segment is valid and a page table is built or exists for that segment. In that case the page table address points to the page table for that segment in real storage.

2.2.7 Control Registers

Since each address space has its own segment table, the system has to keep track of many segment tables. When an address space is active on a CPU, the location of the segment table for that address space is kept in a control register in the CPU called the *segment table origin register* (STOR). Control Register 1 is called the STOR register. The first 8 bits in the register (0 through 7) indicate the length of the segment table, and bits 8 through 25 point to the segment table address. (See figure 2.11.)

When an address space gets control of the CPU, Control Register 1 will point to the segment table for that address space. There are a maximum of 256 entries, one for each allocated segment. Each entry (SGTE) points to a page table for that segment. There are 16 pages in a segment. The pages can be either in main storage frames or in external page slots. The page table contains 16 entries, one for each page in that segment. This PGTE will point to a page in the real storage page frame. There are 16 entries in the external page table, one for each page in a segment; and these entries point to pages in external page slots.

Let us look very closely at the address pointers in some of the tables.

The PGTE address pointer is 12 bits long. This address, we said, should point to a page in real storage. Why only 12 bits? Because all the system needs to know is the beginning of a page. The other 12 bits of displacement are not necessary to locate a page. The generated address is not a

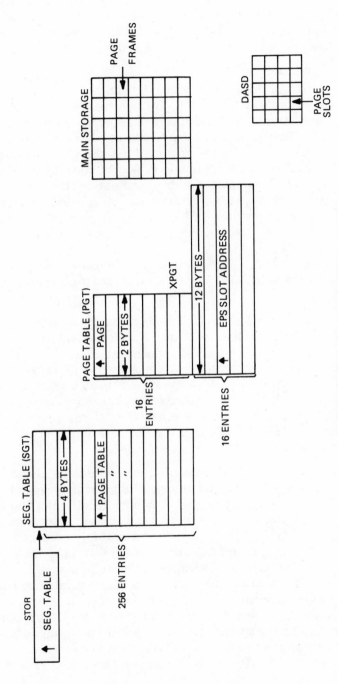

Figure 2.11 Relationship of virtual storage tables.

virtual storage address. It is the main-storage or real-storage address. The address pointer in SGTE is 21 bits long. The system appends three low-order 0s to make it a real-storage address. Three low-order 0s indicate that the address points to a doubleword aligned page table.

2.2.8 Dynamic Address Translation

Address translation is done by treating the addresses supplied by the program as logical or virtual addresses. These virtual addresses are translated by means of translation tables to real addresses to refer to main storage locations. Translation occurs in blocks of addresses called *pages*.

The address translation facility requires that the CPU be equipped with extended control or the EC-mode PSW. The sixth bit of the EC-mode PSW controls the dynamic address translation. If this bit is on, address translation occurs; virtual addresses are translated into real addresses that refer to main storage. When this bit is 0, no implicit dynamic address translation takes place; and logical addresses are used as real addresses to refer to main storage.

The process of dynamic address translation is depicted in figure 2.12. Using a virtual address of 10B158, the steps in the process are summarized as

- Before giving control of the CPU to a program in an address space, the MVS control program has to load the segment table origin register (control register 1) with the segment table address for that address space. Then the control program issues a LPSW instruction to load the program. This PSW's address translation bit (bit 5) will be turned on so that the virtual addresses can be resolved into the main storage location. Let us say the instruction address portion of the PSW contains 10B158, which is the first instruction in the application program.

- DAT hardware using the contents of control register 1 locates the segment table address in main storage. Note that the segment table origin address in control register 1 is only 18 bits. But the DAT appends six bits of 0s to generate the real address of the beginning of the segment table. Using the first eight bits of the address in PSW, DAT indexes the appropriate entry into segment table. In our case the seventeenth entry in the segment table. DAT can verify whether the segment index is out of range of the segment table by adding four 0s to the sgement index and comparing this value against the 8-bit segment table length in the control register 1. If it is outside the range, a segment translation is recognized and the unit of operation is nullified. Segment translation exceptions will generate a program interrupt code 10, and the program is terminated with 0C4.

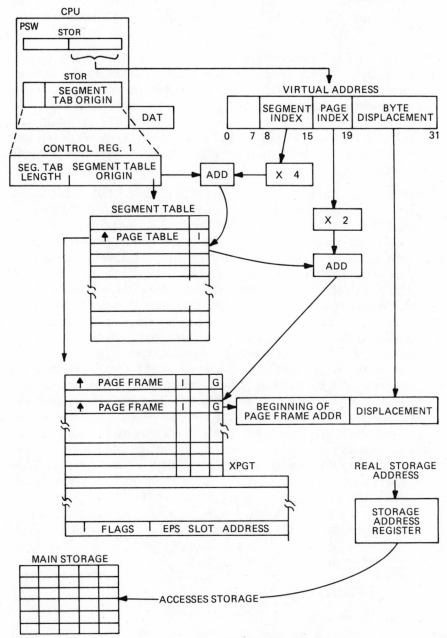

Figure 2.12 Dynamic address translation.

- DAT checks the segment invalid bit in that entry. If this bit is a 1, a segment invalid condition occurs. A segment translation exception is notified to the control program, and the unit of operation is nullified in DAT.

- If the segment invalid bit is off, DAT goes to the page table; and, using the next four bits in the PSW address (which is B in our case), indexes into the page table. In our case it is the 12 entry in the page table. Note: Page index from the virtual address is multiplied by 2 (because each entry in the page table is 2-bytes long). Adding this value to the beginning of the page table address (from the segment table) will generate the appropriate entry address in page table (study the diagram).

- In the page table entry DAT first checks the GETMAIN bit. If this bit is a 0, an exception condition occurs and a page translation exception is notified to the control program with a program interrupt code of 11, and the control program will terminate the unit of work with an abend code of 0C4. But if the bit is a 1, which means this page is allocated to the program, DAT proceeds to the next check, which is the page invalid bit. Two conditions can occur: (1) If I=0, this means the page we requested is in main storage. And the page address portion in the page table entry is extracted. The byte index portion of the virtual address is concatenated from page table entry to the page address, forming the main storage address. In our case, the requested address in main storage is 158 (hexdec) bytes into the page. (2) If I=1, the page we are looking for is not in main storage. So DAT informs the control program about this page translation exception. It also gives the external page storage slot address from the XPGT to the control program. The control program brings this page from the external page storage into a main storage frame. The control program then updates the page table entry to indicate that this page is in main storage by turning off the invalid bit and placing the address of real storage frame in the PGTE.

    When a page translation exception happens during an address translation, usually the program in control of the CPU loses the CPU control. But next time it gets control of the CPU, the DAT will find the page invalid bit off; and the byte index portion of the address in PSW will be concatenated to the page address (from PGTE) to form the main storage address.

2.2.9 Translation Lookaside Buffer (TLB)

The dynamic address translation we just described seems to be a time-consuming process. Since it is mostly done by the DAT hardware, the process is reasonably fast. In order to further speed up the translation processes, however, translation lookaside buffers (TLBs) are included in DAT processing. TLBs are also called associative array registers. The number of TLBs or registers are dependent on the type of the CPU model. The IBM System/370 model 168 and IBM 3033, for example, have up to 128 TLB entries. (See figure 2.13.) Addresses associated with up to 29 different address spaces can be contained in the TLB at any time. Segment table origin addresses for these address spaces are stored in a stack called STO-Stack, and each entry is identified by a number from 2 to 30.

In these buffers, the most recently used page frame addresses (real storage addresses) are stored along with the segment and page number. It also contains STO-Stack identification numbers for the corresponding address spaces so that conflicts in address generation can be resolved. When DAT recognizes an address translation, two parallel paths are taken for the real address resolution. One is through the segment page tables and the other is through the TLB. The segment and page index from the virtual address are compared against the segment and page number portion of all the TLBs instantaneously through hardware circuitry. If a match is found, the page frame location is used to generate the real storage address and the translation through tables is aborted.

If no match is found in the TLBs, normal dynamic address translation continues and the resultant value with the search argument is stored in the least recently used lookaside buffer (TLB). The LRU array bits in

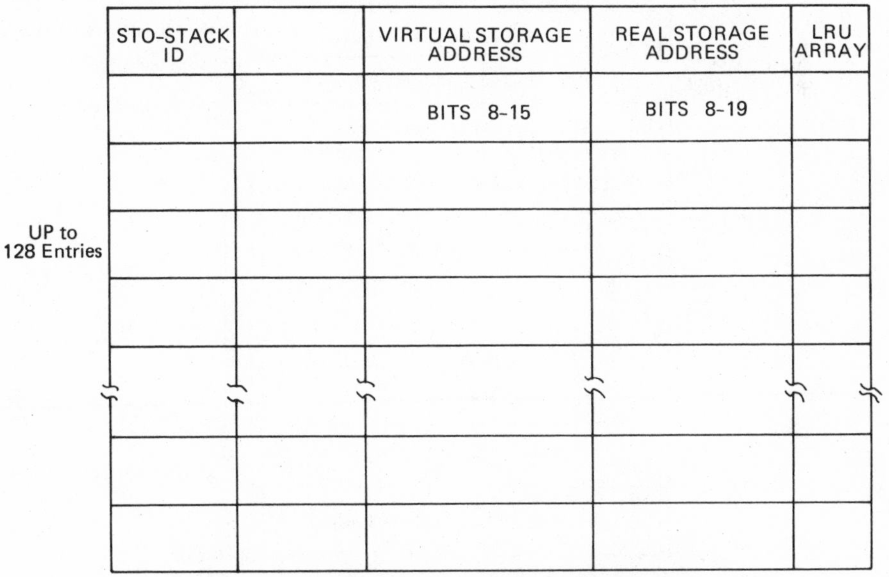

STO-STACK ID		VIRTUAL STORAGE ADDRESS	REAL STORAGE ADDRESS	LRU ARRAY
		BITS 8-15	BITS 8-19	

UP to 128 Entries

Figure 2.13 Translation lookaside buffer (TLB).

the TLB are used to find the least recently used buffer. Studies made by IBM claim that the hit ratio (in finding the real storage frame address in TLB) for translation through TLB is 90%.

By eliminating subsequent translation for the same address and its multiple real storage access for tables, TLB hardware speeds up the translation process considerably.

2.3 ORGANIZATION OF STORAGE IN MVS

The MVS virtual storage arrangement is conceptualized in figure 2.14. A virtual storage address space is divided into three major areas: the common area, the private area, and the system area.

2.3.1 System Area

The system area contains two parts. One is called *nucleus load module;* the other, *nucleus extension.* The nucleus load module part contains dispatcher, recovery support, and interruption handler code. It also contains system-wide tables such as the communication vector table and page frame table. The system area is depicted in figure 2.15. The unit control blocks that control every device in the system also reside in the nucleus.

The nucleus starts from address 0 of virtual storage. Nucleus extension contains fixed BLDL table, fixed link pack area, and other system wide information.

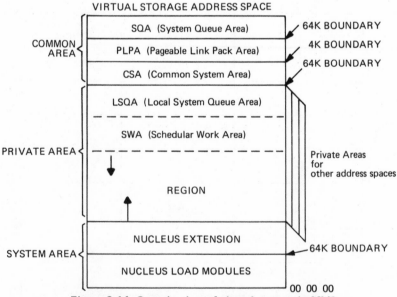

Figure 2.14 Organization of virtual storage in MVS.

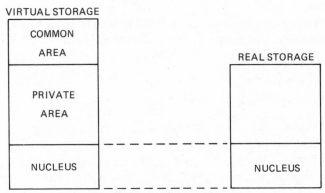

Figure 2.15 System area.

The nucleus is fixed in real storage, which means the virtual address of the system area is the same as the real address of this area in main storage. The address range of the system area is mapped one to one with real storage.

2.3.2 Private Area

This area should start on a 64K boundary after the nucleus. This area is for the users. This area will contain user programs and information about the user.

The amount of virtual storage a user gets from this region depends on the user's specifications. That is the region parameter in the job or the execution card in the JCL for a program. In order to keep track of what is going on in a private area, there are some system-related areas in the private area for a user. These are local system queue area (LSQA) and scheduler work area (SWA).

The LSQA of an address space contains control blocks and tables related to that address space. It is located at the high end of the private or user's region and extends downward. Subpools 253, 254, and 255 are located in LSQA. (Subpools are covered later.) LSQA contains segment and page tables for the address space.

SWA is the work area for the scheduler. This area contains subpools 236 and 237 and contains job queues for that address space. Subpools 0 through 127 and subpools 251 and 252 are allocated from the lower end of the private area extending upward.

The private area is addressable only to functions running in the user's address space with the user's segment table. All of the user's private area is pageable except LSQA.

When an address space is swapped in, the LSQA for that address space is fixed in real storage. Until the address space is swapped out, the LSQA pages will remain in main storage.

2.3.3 Common Area

Common area is common to all address spaces in the system. This area is divided in three parts: the system queue area (SQA), the pageable link pack area (PLPA), and the common system area (CSA).

System Queue Area

This part contains tables and queues relating to the entire system. This contains non-pageable system control blocks that relate to information for multiple private address spaces. This information cannot be in LSQA because LSQA can be paged out if an address space is swapped out. SQA is fixed at the high end of the virtual storage. SQA pages are fixed in real storage but their addresses have no one to one correspondence with virtual storage. SQA is built from the top end of the virtual storage extending downward.

Pageable Link Pack Area

This part contains SVC routines, access method routines, and other selected programs. These routines should be re-entrant. PLPA is not fixed in real storage and so it is pageable.

(Common System Area)

This part of common area is used to communicate between address spaces. System components like TCAM (Telecommunication Access Method) and JES (Job Entry Subsystem) have to communicate with other private address spaces for their operation. CSA contains subpools 231, 241, 227, 228, and 239. CSA is a pageable system data area.

The organization of virtual storage is further depicted in figure 2.16.

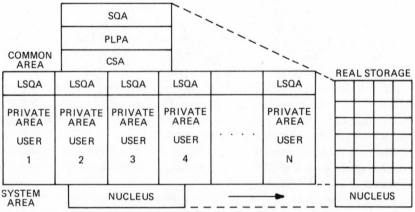

Figure 2.16 Organization of virtual storage in MVS.

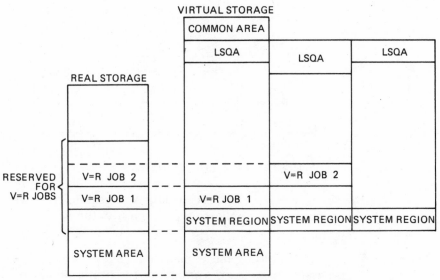

Figure 2.17 V=R regions in an MVS environment.

2.3.4 Table Location

One item that is immediately noticed is that there are common virtual storage areas for all address spaces. The system area and the common area are common to all virtual storage spaces. If we look at a segment table for any of these address spaces, we see some common page table entries for nucleus, SQA, PLPA, and CSA. The rest of the segment table entries point to private page tables that represent the private area for a user.

MVS designers put the common page tables in SQA so that they would avoid duplication of these tables in each of the private address spaces.

All the common page tables are located in SQA. The private page tables and segment tables for an address space are located in the LSQA of that address space.

2.3.5 Regions

In the private area for a user there can be two types of regions. One is called V=R region. This region of virtual storage is mapped one to one into real storage and is fixed in real storage. Some special applications which are time dependent use the V=R region. This region can be requested through JCL, but the V=R region is limited by an initial program load parameter called "VRREGN." Real storage up to the limit of V=R regions is reserved for all V=R jobs. Channel programs that modify themselves have to run on the V=R region. The V=R region is not subject to page faults. Figure 2.17 depicts V=R regions in an MVS environment.

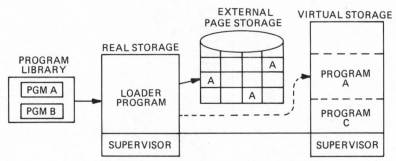

Figure 2.18 Program loading in MVS.

The other region of a private area is called the V=V region. This region is subject to page faults. Most application programs run the V=V region.

2.3.6 Program Loading

The concept of paging needs some explanation. Before paging is explained, it is necessary to see how a program stored in a library on a direct access device is loaded into virtual storage. This process is depicted in figure 2.18.

Before a job can execute, the program must be loaded into virtual storage. The address space for program A, for example, is in an auxiliary storage library, and its addresses are related to a 0 origin.

A system program called LOADER will relocate the program A's origin to the next available address in virtual storage, beginning at the private area. This is done by changing the base register value of program A as we demonstrated in our example of static relocation.

After the static relocation, a program's addresses will reflect virtual storage addresses. A loader program then starts to read program A from the auxiliary storage library to the main storage frames. Now a relationship between a page frame in memory and the virtual storage address of a job is established, and a segment table and page tables for that program is created. After completing entries in the appropriate tables, a program is considered to be loaded into virtual storage and is ready for execution. Only a program's most active pages (working set of a program) are kept in main storage. The rest of the pages for a program are in EPS. So the main storage contains active pages of all active jobs in the system. If, while executing a program, DAT finds a referenced page is not in main storage, a condition called *page fault* occurs. The referenced page has to be loaded into main storage from EPS. This operation of loading a page from EPS to main storage is called *page-in* or *demand paging.*

But what happens if there are no free page frames in main storage? Now it is time for the control program to find a page frame that was referenced the least number of times during the last interval of time.

Control program uses a table called PAGE FRAME TABLE (PFT). In this table there is an entry for each frame of main storage available to the system. Each entry contains an address space identifier identifying the owner address space for that frame along with the unreferenced interval count (UIC). The value in the UIC indicates how long the content of that main storage frame was inactive. (See figure 2.19.) After finding that page frame, the control program also checks whether the contents of that page frame were changed from the last page in operation. As we discussed in an earlier chapter, reference and change indicators are maintained for every 2K block of main storage by the hardware. If it has changed, that page has to be written out to external page storage before a page is brought into that page frame. This operation is called a *page-out*. If the content of the page is never changed (that means a true copy of the page exists somewhere in EPS), the control program can simply overlay the page frame with the new demanded page.

As we can see, it is through the concept of demand paging that new pages of a program are brought into storage when required. If a page is never referenced during executions, it will never be paged-in.

PAGE FRAME TABLE

STORAGE PROTECT
KEY OF FRAME

ADDRESS SPACE IDENTIFIER	SEGMENT & PAGE NUMBER	STATUS OF STORAGE FRAME	UIC		KEY	F	R	C

UIC   UNREFERENCED INTERVAL COUNT
F   FETCH PROTECT
R   REFERENCE BIT
C   CHANGE BIT

Figure 2.19 Page frame table.

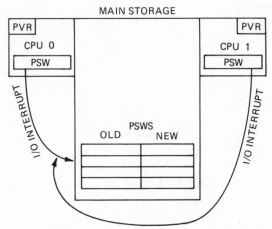

Figure 2.20 This diagram displays how without prefixing, old PSWs would be in conflict for the same type of interrupt from different CPUs.

2.3.7 Prefixing

When we talked about interrupts, we said that when an interrupt happens, the current PSW is stored in a fixed location of low storage. The same type of interrupt is prevented from happening by setting flags in the PSW and in the control register, so that the first level interruption handler has enough time to store the registers and PSW in the appropriate places in main storage and to notify the appropriate interruption handlers. Once the interruption handlers are notified and they are given the registers and PSW of the program, the disabled interruption flags can be reset to accept interrupts again.

But in the case of a multiprocessing system where two CPUs are sharing the main storage, the above technique will not work. Just disabling one CPU for a particular interrupt will not prevent the other CPU from taking an interrupt of the same type and overlaying the old PSW for that type of interrupt. This problem is suggested by figure 2.20.

This problem in a multiprocessing system is solved by giving each CPU its own copy of the first 4K (4,096) bytes of main storage called *prefix save area.* Thus neither CPU will access actual locations 0 through 4,095 for normal usage. The hardware term that enforces this technique is called *prefixing.* Absolute locations 0 through 4,095 are reserved for crisis and prevention usage only.

Two types of prefixing are done in the system: forward and backward.

Each CPU in a multiprocessing configuration has an internal register called prefix value register (PVR). This register is 12 bits long. A PVR entry is given in figure 2.21.

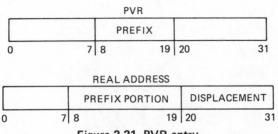

Figure 2.21 PVR entry.

A virtual address is given to the DAT box which, through its dynamic address translation feature, converts the virtual address into a real address. Prefixing hardware matches the bits 8 through 19 (called the *prefix portion*) of the real address against the content of the prefix value register for that CPU.

After the comparison, three possibilities exist:

1. Bits 8–19 (prefix portion) of the real address are 0s (address represented by real address falls within the locations 0 through 4,095 of fixed storage), and these bits are replaced with the PVR contents. Now, the prefixed address falls within the 4,096 bytes of system established area for that CPU called *prefix save area*. This type of prefixing is called *forward prefixing*.

2. If the prefix portion of the real address is not 0s and does not match the PVR value, the 24-bit real address is unchanged. The prefixing hardware has established that the real address neither falls into the 0–4,095 nor into the prefix save area for that CPU.

3. If bits 8–19 of the real address exactly match the PVR (address falls within the prefix save area), prefixing hardware alters the real address by replacing bits 8–19 of the address by 0s and thus forces an address in the absolute address range 0 through 4,095. This type of prefixing is called *reverse prefixing*. It is used in the system to store hardware-related information into a unique actual area that can be inspected by the other CPU.

Figure 2.22 represents address translation in a multiprocessing environment, and figure 2.23 conceptualizes prefixing in a multiprocessing environment.

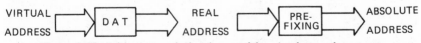

Figure 2.22 Address translation in a multiprocessing environment.

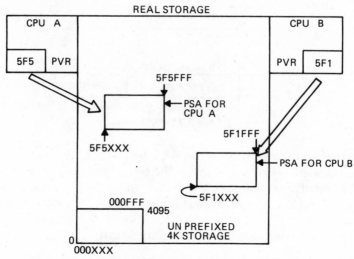

Figure 2.23 Prefixing.

3 Control Blocks

This chapter introduces the major MVS control blocks and their relation to one another. Knowledge of control blocks is useful in finding out vital information about the system and its status when a failure occurs.

3.1 BACKGROUND

In an MVT system the supervisor has only one queue representing units of work. For each unit of work a task control block (TCB) is created and chained to the system work queue. All the supervisor has to do is pick up the highest priority ready TCB from the work queue and dipatch the task. This amounts to loading the program status word in the CPU with the address stored in the task control block. In the case of a system like MVS and in a multiprocessing (tightly coupled) environment, the functions performed by the supervisor are more complex.

In an MVS system there are several address spaces, and in each address space there is normally more than one unit of work ready for execution. We can immediately see the need for two types of controls of the system. One type of control is to manage the units of work in an address space; the other is to manage the work of the system as a whole. Thus, the supervisor in MVS is divided into two parts called the *local* and *global* supervisors.

3.1.1 Local Supervisor Functions

Functions performed for a particular address space or for a particular user are grouped together and named *the local supervisor*. Local supervisor routines are coded re-entrantly so that only one copy of the routines is needed for all the address spaces. In a tightly coupled multiprocessing system, each of the CPUs may be executing the same local supervisor routine for different address spaces without any serialization. But within the same address space, execution of the local supervisor routine must be serialized.

Assume that there is a local supervisor routine to add a control block to the existing chain of similar control blocks in an address space and that this routine is called "ADDCB." In a conceptual MP system two CPUs are executing in two address spaces, namely A and B. Further assume that each CPUs is executing the ADDCB routine for its respective address space.

Since each address space has its own segment and page tables, they cannot access the private area of the other. Thus if our control block

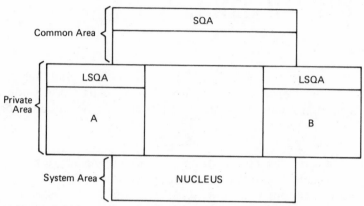

Figure 3.1 **Storage organization in a multiprocessing environment.**

queue for the local supervisor is in each address space's private area or local system queue area, the same local supervisor routine can be executed concurrently in different address spaces without any serialization. Figure 3.1 depicts storage organization in a multiprocessing environment.

In order for our ADDCB routine to add a new control block in between control blocks 2 and 3, the pointer in Control Block 2 (CB2) has to change the point to the new control block (CBX) and a pointer from the new control block (CBX) to control block 3 (CB3). (See figure 3.2.) If an interrupt happens while doing the chaining between the new control block (CBX) and control block 3 (CB3), the CPU control is switched from the current task to the interruption-handling routine. The control block chain is incomplete at this point. Suppose there is another high priority task ready for execution in the same address space. When the CPU is returned to the address space, the high priority task gets the CPU. If this task wants to execute the same ADDCB routine to add another control block (CBZ) to the end of the same chain of control blocks, it will update the pointer in CBX with the address of CBZ. The control block CB3 is now permanently lost.

In order to avoid such problems, the local supervisor function has to serialize when executing in the same address space, which means the CPU control should not be given to another task in the same address space until the original task completes the local supervisor function.

The technique of serializing is done through a software locking mechanism. This is covered in a later chapter.

3.1.2 Global Supervisor Functions

Functions logically associated with more than one address space and which are system-wide are collectively called the *global supervisor*. Global supervisor functions must *serialize* across address spaces or else the same type of problem covered above will happen in the common area rather than in the private area as in the case of the local supervisor.

Control blocks that could be isolated for each user are put into the local system queue area or in the scheduler work area of the user's private area, and the system-wide control blocks are put into the common area. Thus two categories of control blocks can be identified. One category represents the control blocks for the overall operation of MVS and the other category the operation of individual address space. This split is necessary to swap as much information as possible about an address space along with it and to keep only system-wide information about address spaces in the common area.

3.2 SYSTEM CONTROL BLOCKS

System control blocks are concerned with the overall operation of the hardware and software systems. While system control blocks contain user-related information, there is no specific orientation to a particular unit of work.

3.2.1 Common System Data Area (CSD)

This control block contains information about the various CPUs in the system. This control block keeps track of up to 16 CPUs on the system. Currently there are only two CPUs in an MP tightly coupled system. (Note: IBM 3084 MP has four CPUs connected to it.) CPU numbers are assigned 0 through F. Some of the fields of interest are CSDCPUOL at

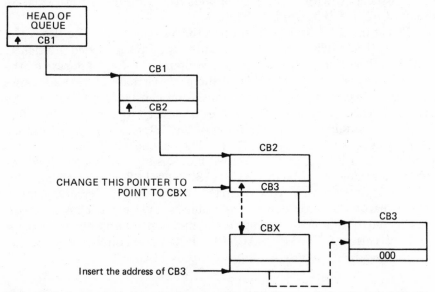

Figure 3.2 Conceptual view of adding a control block to a chain of control blocks.

offset X'A' and CSDSCFL1 at offset X'C'. CSDCPUOL identifies the number of CPUs currently active in the system. MVS accesses this field to determine whether the system is in unit processor or in (Multiprocessor) mode. There is a bit mask at offset X'8' called "CSDCPUAL," which will tell which CPUs are on-line. If a bit is 1, then the corresponding CPU is on-line.

This control block is in subpool 245, which is in the system queue area. This control block is pointed to by another control block called *Communication Vector Table.*

3.2.2 Communication Vector Table (CVT)

CVT is the major control block in the system. It resides in the nucleus and contains addresses of other control blocks and tables used by the control program routines. Almost all other control blocks can be chased through the pointers provided in the CVT. Even though the CVT can be anywhere in the nucleus, its address can be found in fixed locations of storage. Location X'10' and X'4C' of main storage will point to the CVT. Location X'4C' is more reliable in determining the address of the CVT, because in some circumstances location X'10' will be overlayed by the status of the system or by the DUMP program. Figure 3.3 gives a dump of the CVT.

3.2.3 Physical Configuration-Communication Area (PCCA)

The PCCA contains information about the physical facilities associated with each CPU in the system. For each CPU there is a corresponding PCCA associated with it. PCCA contains hardware related information about a CPU and is located in the SQA.

At location X'18' in PCCA, there is the *Virtual Address* of the Prefix Save Area (PSA). We have seen how and why a PSA is needed in a tightly coupled MP system. The PCCA also contains the *Real Address* of the PSA at location X'1C'. The reason there are virtual and real addresses for PSA is that dynamic address translation can be turned off. So, by giving the real address to prefixing, the absolute address can be generated. The PCCA contains the serial number of the CPU and its physical address in the system (such as 0, 1, 2, . . . , F). The channel check handler stores information in PCCA, so this control block is a good place to look for channel and device problems. At X'118' the field PCCACHUB contains the address of the device in use when the channel detected error occurred. General hardware error conditions, such as CPU error, channel error, storage control unit error, storage error, and control unit error, are registered at location X'11D' (PCCACHBL). PCCA also contains the channel availability table. The PCCA is pointed to by PCCAVT.

3.2.4 Physical Configuration-Communication Area Vector Table (PCCAVT)

PCCAVT contains a processor array that contains slots for 16 CPUs. Each slot contains the PCCA address of the corresponding CPU. This control block is in SQA and is pointed by CVTPCCAT field of the CVT at offset X'2FC'. In the formatted CVT dump (figure 3.3), the label is "PCCAT" and an address of 00FFCEA8 is given.

3.2.5 Logical Configuration-Communication Area (LCCA)

This is the logical counterpart of PCCA and contains information needed by the software about the CPU. The First Level Interrupt Handler saves information such as registers when handling interrupts. The LCCA also contains time of day clock values and mode indicators to distinguish whether the CPU is processing a task or a service request. The LCCACPUA field in LCCA contains logical CPU address. Why a logical address? The software has a different meaning when a fullword contains all binary 0s. When we talk about locks, this will become clear. So if the physical CPU-addresses 0 through F are assigned as logical addresses, the software will not be able to recognize the meaning of all binary 0s as a CPU address. So the designers of MVS decided to give the logical CPU addresses as 40, 41, etc. up to 4F for physical CPU-addresses 0 through F, respectively. The LCCA is pointed to by LCCAVT.

3.2.6 Logical Configuration-Communication Area Vector Table (LCCAVT)

The control block LCCAVT contains addresses of LCCA tables for 16 CPUs. The LCCAVT is pointed to by the CVTLCCAT field of CVT and is located in the SQA. (See the label "LCCAT" in the CVT dump.)

3.2.7 Prefixed Save Area (PSA)

When prefixing was introduced, it was mentioned that each CPU has its own 4K of fixed storage. Absolute locations 0–4,095 also are called a "PSA." But this PSA is the unprefixed PSA and resides in the nucleus. Important fields in PSA include the physical and logical address of the CPU that this PSA is associated with and the virtual and real address of the PCCA and the LCCA for the same CPU. PSA also contains the address space that is active on the CPU and the current task within the address space.

3.2.8 Relationship of System Control Blocks

Figure 3.4 gives the relationship of the system control blocks, which are chained together as indicated. From formatted dumps of the PSAs,

**** C O M M U N I C A T I O N   V E C T O R   T A B L E ****

CVT 024A88

```
-18 VERID 40404040 40404040 40404040 40404040   MDL  00003081   RELNO F0F3F840   XAPG  0002F954
+0  TCBP  00000218   LINK  0002485C   RESV  00000000   BUF   00000000   XTLER 00042950
+18 OVL00 000050F0   PRLTV 00038378   ILK1  00019454   ILK2  00019596   XITP  000248C8
+30 SYSAD 00000000   DATE  0083286F   MSLT  00043A30   ZDTAB 00043B08   TPC   00024864
+48 RESV  00000000   EXIT  0A03       BRET  07FE       SVDCB 00024864   STB   0004127C
+5C RESV  00000000   CUCB  0003CB0    QTE00 00041262   QTD00 00109588   ODS   00109588
+74 DCB   13644630   IXAVL 00027B20   NUCB  00110000   FBOSV 00109588   RESV  00000000
+8C ILCH  0001A658   MSER  00043A30   OPT01 00030700   RESV  00000000           OPTA EB
+A4 MZ00  00FFFFFF   QOCR  00043A30   QMNR  80FDD458   SNCTR 00024F78   USER  00025040   OPTB 20
+B8 QCDSR 00034A9A   ENFCT 00046D18   SMCA  80FDD458   ABEND 00024F78   RMS   00025040
+D0 MDLDS 00034898   LNKSC 0A06       TSCE  00000000   PATCH 00046D48   SAF   00000000
+E4 RESV  007AE620   GTF   00046960   AQAVT C095AE10   VOLM2 80007300   DMSR  00CEF000
+FC EXT1  00024EE4   PURG  00000000   AMFF  80000000   QMSG  00047318   JESCT 00048528
+114 SFR  00047538   REAL  00234000   PTRV  00048478   RESV  00048482   LKRM  00048590
+12C RESV 0003D052   MCHPR 00000000   EORM  01FFFFFF   PTRV3 D5D6D5C1   RESV  D4C54040
+144 APF  80B809E0   HJES  00024EF0   RESV  00000000   RESV  00049690   PSAE0 0004969A
+15C GETL 00034C5E   PVTP  00034C5E   LPDIA 08982000   PSAD0 08982000   RESV  0004A0D8
+174 SLIDA 00000000  RT03  00049A6A   VLDWT 00049B00   EXSLF 08931D38   EXSNR 0004A0D8
+18C EXSNL 00        APG 76  00       RESV  TRAC2 07FB RSCN  0003BB54   TAS   0004A898
+19C RESV 00000000   0VL01 007B0000   RESV  00047DB0   RMFPT 00E76000   GVT   0004A898
+1B4 ASCRF 00FC8780  PUTL  80B7FA80   SRBRT 004447B8   OLT0A 0004AB60   SMFEX 0004AB60
+1CC CSPIE 00A6DBE4  IOSPL 0000       DSSAC 0000       STCK  80B7E000   MAXMP 80B7E000
+1E0 SCAN 80A27A00   BLDCP 00FC83A8   GETCL 0004AFD0   FRECL 0004B148   DELCP 0004B148
+1F8 CRMN 0004B4D0   QSAS  0004B4CE   FRAS  0004B4D4   S1EE  00038568   PARS  00038568
+210 QUIS 0004BE98   OPTE  0003C488   SDRM  00C2927C   IOSCS 00000000   AQTOP 00000000
+228 VVMDI 00000761  GDA   00FBDE00   ASCBH 00023400   ASCBL 00F50CC0   RTMCT 00FCE288
+240 SV60 00C66344   SCBP  0004C8A0   SDBF  8097C000   RTMS  8097C000   TPIOS 0002BE34
+258 SIC  009AC110   EXPRO 000509C0   GSMQ  0002BE30   LSMQ  0002BE38   GSPL  00000000
+270 VWAIT 00FA6070  APFT  000447A0   QCS01 00346C8    FQCB  00346C8    LQCB  000312A0
+288 RENQ 00FA6070   LKRMA 00048A84   CSD   00FFCD30   DQIQE 00051200   RPOST 00052CD8
+2A0 062R1 0003ABBA  GLMN  000512B8   SPSA  00051AC0   WSAL  00052CB0   WSAG  00000000
+2B8 WSAC 00052D00   ASMVT 00052D38   IOBP  00053C58   SPOST 00031300   RSTIWD 80B91E68
+2D0 FETCH 00109588  PERFM 00038980   DAIR  80D71000   EHDEF 80B91600   EHCIR 00FFCEA8
+2E8 SSAP 00000000   IPCDS 00FD6058   IPCRI 00053C70   IPCRP 00053F90   PCCAT 00DC0000
+300 LCCAT 00FFCE68  XSTKS 000544B8   XSTKN 00054560   XUNSS 00054459C  PWI   00054B28
+318 PVBP 00DC1640   MFRTR 80E97D10   VPSIB 0002CEEC   VSI   00055640   VFP   00055640
+330 XUNSN 00054B5C  XEXTR 00FE1008   MSFRM 00056610   SCPIN 0FF6368    VIOP  0FF6368
+348 RMBR 00035908   GMBR  0003215A   OTC0A 00CF1000   RLSTG 00007E80   SPFRR 00007AD0
```

```
+360  VEMSO 00058288   SVT   0002BE10   IRECM 0CED33C8   DARCM 00D740F0   OPTO2 000307E8   STPRS 000586E8
+378  WTCB  00023B50   VACR  00000000   QUIT  00000000   GTFR8 00472CC6   VSTOP 00059020   VPSA  0097F000
+390  RMPTT 00000000   RMPMT 00059118   EXP1  00050E80   CSDRL 00FFFD30   SSRB  0003BA94   RPT   00CE1000
+3A8  QV1   000590F8   QV2   0003E768   QV3   0005911E   GSDA  80FFC438   ADV   00059D48   TPIO  0003E3A0
+3C0  CRCA  00000000   EVENT 00000000   SSCR  0097A3F8   CBBR  000323C2   EFF02 80BAF000   LSCH  0002BB50
+3D8  CDEQ  00FE49E0   HSM   00000000   RAC   00000000   CGK   00059DD0   SRM   0005AAA0   OPTOE 000315BC
+3F0  OPTO3 00030AF0   TCASP 00000000   ASMRM 0005AAE0   JTERM 0005B868   RSUME 0005BCB4   TCTL  0005C3DA
+408  CDAL  00000000   T6SVC 00025FE4   SUSP  0005B310   IHASU 00025030   VDCCR 0005CA10   CST   00FF6740
+420  SMF83 00EDB000   SMFSP 0005E9A8   MSFCB 00025FE4   HID   00FF5648   PSXM  0002D546   RESV  0005F218
+438  TPUR  00000000   DPUR  00000000   RPOS  00000000   RESTX 0005FFF4   XCPCT 01F4       CALL  05EF
+450  VFIND 00060288   VFGET 00060BF0   VFMEM 00061788   VFCB  00000000

EXT1  024EE4   FACHN 0090FFB8   RESV 00000000
EXT2  024EF0

SYMPTOM STRING: AB/500C4 PIDS/5752TC221 RIDS/IEDGRC11 REGS/FE000MODULE IEAVTSDT   DATE 10/13/83   TIME 13.19.45   PAGE 0135

+0    DSSV F1000000   NUCLS F1000000   DEBVR 0003CFA8   CVAF  00978000   MMVT  00061868   RESV 00000000
+18   QID  00000000   OLTEP 00000000   RESV  00000000   RESV  00000000   CCVT  00000000   RESV 00000000
+30   ICB  00000000   RESV  00000000   RESV  00000000   RESV  00000000   ATCVT 00000000   RESV 00000000
+48   RESV 00000000   RESV  00000000   RESV  00000000   RESV  00000000   RESV  00000000   RESV 00000000
+60   RESV 00000000   RESV  00000000   RESV  00000000   RESV  00000000   RESV  00000000   RESV 00000000
+78   RESV 00000000   RESV  00000000   RESV  00000000   RESV  00000000   RESV  00000000   RESV 00000000
```

Figure 3.3 Dump of the communication vector table (CVT).

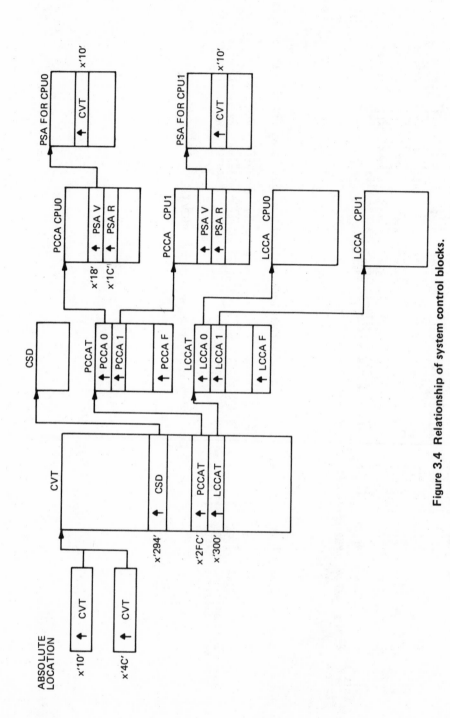

Figure 3.4 Relationship of system control blocks.

PCCAs, and LCCAs, it is possible to determine the location of the prefix value register (PVR) for each CPU. Prefixing is suggested by figure 3.5.

We have seen that each CPU has its own PCCA containing the physical facilities associated with it. In the PCCA we have the hardware CPU address as well as the virtual and real addresses of the PSA. Any addresses (real addresses) falling within the PSA will be reverse prefixed to the absolute locations 0 through 4,095. In the formatted listing of PCCA for CPU 0, the real address of PSA is FF0000. Prefixing compares the first 12 bits against the value in the prefix value register of CPU 0. If they are equal, reverse prefixing takes place and the first 12 bits are changed to 0s. Thus, looking at the real address of the prefixed save area and extracting the first 12 bits of that address, we get the PVR value for that CPU. Now try to find the PVR value for CPU 2.

3.3 ADDRESS SPACE CONTROL BLOCKS

There are three major control blocks associated with address spaces: ASCB, ASXB, and ASVT.

3.3.1 Address Space Control Block (ASCB)

Control block ASCB contains information and pointers needed for address space control. Each address space is represented by an ASCB in the system. ASCBs are located in the system queue area.

Several kinds of information describe an address space. *System-wide information* about an address space is stored in the ASCB, while the *user-related information* is stored in the ASXB. This technique will cut down the non-swappable storage requirement for ASCBs.

The reason that the ASCB is stored in the SQA is related to interrupt handling. When an I/O interrupt happens, CPU is switched away from the current address space to the interrupt handlers. Then its process dispatcher gets control of the CPU. The dispatcher's duty is to give the CPU to the highest-priority unit of work in the system. In order to find the highest-priority unit of work in an address space, the dispatcher has to scan through the ASCB chain. Thus we see the need for ASCBs to be visible to all address spaces in the system. The ASCB is not swappable. Information stored in ASCB includes the following:

- ASCB Identification Number at location X'24' in ASCB called "ASCBASID."
- Sequence number representing the ASCB's position on the dispatching queue (X'26' ASCBSEQN).
- Address of next ASCB on ASCB ready queue (X'4' (ASCBFWDP)).
- Whether the address space is swapped in or out.
- Dispatching priority of this address space.

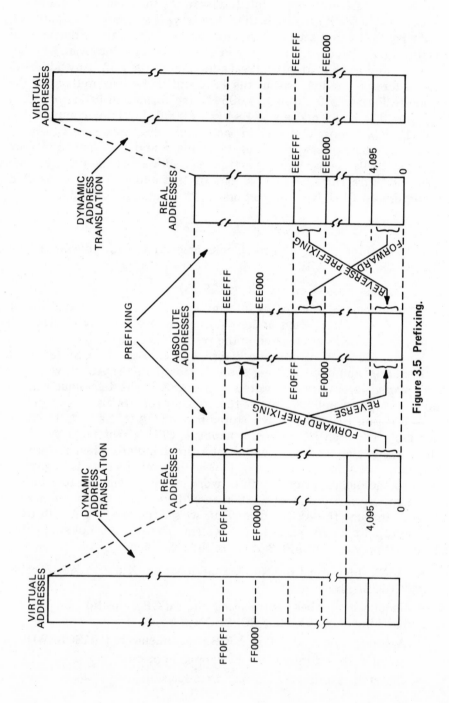

Figure 3.5 Prefixing.

- External page storage allocated for this address space.
- Real storage frames allocated to this address space.
- Number of Ready task control blocks in this address space.
- Pointer to Address Space Extension Block.
- Number of CPUs active in this memory. (It is possible that tasks from an address space are active in both CPUs of an MP system.)

The system resource manager (SRM) frequently checks the real storage frames available to the system. If it is over-utilized, SRM will swap out comparatively inactive address spaces or address spaces which are hogging the real storage frames. In order to determine this SRM uses the pointers in the ASCB for the EPS and real storage frame allocation for a particular address space.

3.3.2 Address Space Extension Block (ASXB)

This control block also contains information about an address space, but information of no particular interest to other address spaces or system components such as the dispatcher. The ASXB is located in the Local System Queue Area. It is swappable. Important pointers are:

- Number of TCBs in this address space.
- TCB dispatching queue for this address space.
- IHSA (Interrupt Handler Save Area) pointer.
- SRB dispatching queue for this address space.

3.3.3 Address Space Vector Table (ASVT)

Since there are many address spaces in a MVS system, it is necessary that there be a control block to keep track of all of the address spaces in the

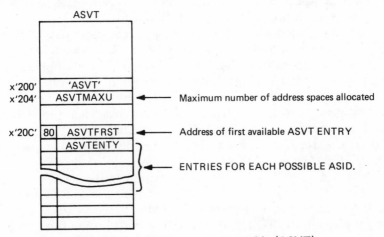

Figure 3.6 Address space vector table (ASVT).

system. Thus, the ASVT contains a list of all possible address space IDs, if assigned, with the address of the associated ASCB. Figure 3.6 depicts the ASVT.

ASVTFRST field points to the first available ASVT entry. Next to this field are the ASVT ENTRIES (ASVTENTY) for the system. These entries are 4-bytes long. If the first byte is hex 00, this means the corresponding ASID is assigned and the rest of the bytes point to the ASCB for that address space. But if the first byte is hex 80, then the corresponding ASID is not assigned to any address space and the entry contains either the address of the next available ASID or 0s if it is the last entry.

There is only one ASVT for the entire system and this control block is located in the system queue area. The maximum number of entries in ASVT is defined at system generation time. Each address space has an entry in ASVT, except the address space for the master scheduler. This address space is created before all other address spaces and has an ASID of 1. The master scheduler's ASCB is not located in SQA, but is hard coded in the system.

An address space is created for each started task and for LOG-ON and MOUNT commands. Examples of started tasks are the starting of initiators and system components such as JES2, RMF, TCAM, etc. MOUNT commands from a console also will create an address space. Every time a TSO user logs on to the system, an address space is created for the user. Thus the total number of address spaces in the system consists of started tasks, LOG-ONS and MOUNTS.

In order to find information about any address space, the control program locates the CVT. There is a pointer in CVT (CVTASVT) which points to ASVT. For every address space in the system there is an entry in the ASVT. This entry points to the ASCB for that address space. There is a pointer in ASCB to ASXB. Thus the supervisor or any component of MVS can find all information about an address space.

For all the swapped-in address spaces there is another pair of pointers in CVT. This pair of pointers identifies the ASCB dispatching queue. (See figure 3.7.) In earlier operating systems there was only one queue of dispatchable units of work. But in MVS there are multiple address spaces and multiple TCB queues for each. The dispatcher has to find the highest-priority ready ASCB (address space) first. This is done through the CVT pointers called "CVTASCBH" (ASCB head) and "CVTASCBL" (ASCB tail). After finding the address space, the dispatcher has to find the ready TCB. Again, in MVS there are other units of dispatchable work called *service request blocks.* (See the chapter on the service manager.)

Dispatching priority of an address space equals the DPRTY parameter in the EXEC Card that a user coded. In older systems such as MVT this priority is given in the TCB. If no DPRTY is coded, then the system will give a default value (already set up by system generation) to that address

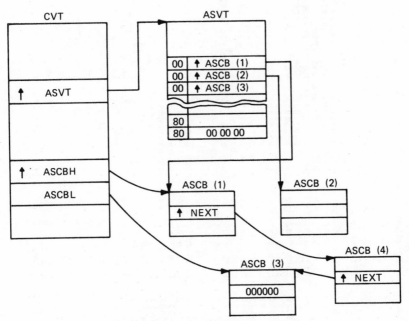

Figure 3.7 ASCB dispatching queue.

space. The TCBs in an address space will have the highest dispatching-priority (255), unless the user issues a CHAP macro or DPMOD or LPMOD parameter in ATTACH macro.

According to the dispatching priority of an address space, its ASCB is sequenced in the ASCB dispatching queue of the system. A corresponding sequence number is registered in the ASCB in a field called "ASCBSEQN."

Figure 3.8 gives a formatted listing of an ASCB and an ASXB.

3.4 OVERVIEW OF TASK-RELATED CONTROL BLOCKS

A task is a unit of work to the system and competes for system resources. Similar to the manner that an ASCB represents the idea of an address space, a TCB represents a task. There is one TCB per task in the system, and these TCBs are used as a means of monitoring the aspects of tasks. TCBs are located in the LSQA. There are pointers in the TCB pointing to other control blocks that are used by the program manager, task manager, and virtual storage manager for the execution and control of tasks within an address space.

By way of an overview, let us enumerate some significant pointers in the TCB.

1. TCB points to control blocks for SPIE macro. There is a field in TCB called "TCBPIE" which points to SPIE control area (SCA).

JOB *MASTER*

```
ASCB  023400
      +0    ASCB C1E2C3C2   FWDP 00FD8D48   BWDP 00000000   CMSF 00000000   SVRB 007A14F0   SYNC 0002E14B
      +18   IOSP 00000000   TNEW 007A00D0   CPUS 00000000   ASID 0001       SEQN 0001       IOSM 0000
      +2A   HLHI 01         DP   FF         RV00 00000000   LDA  007AEC68   RSM  C0023960   CSCB 00000000
      +3C   TSB  00000000   EJST 00000056   10F56200 EWST   9649A254 546CD260  JSTL 000141DD   ECB  00000000
      +58   UBET 00000000   TLCH 00000000   DUMP 0079FCB0   AFFN FFFF  RCTF 01  FLG1 00      TMCH 00000000
      +6C   ASXB 00023570   SWCT 4A08       DSP1 04         FLG2 C6  RESV 0000  SRBS 0000    VSC  0000
      +7A   NVSC 0127       RCTP 00000000   LOCK 00000000   LSQH 00000000   QECB 00000000   MECB 00000000
      +90   OUCB 00FE4878   OUXB 00FDE000   FMCT 002E       RESV 0000       XMPQ 00000000   IQEA 00000000
      +A4   RTMC 00000000   MCC  00000000   JBNI 00000000   JBNS 00024880   SRQ  00000000   VGTT 0076F38
      +BC   PCTT 00000000   SSRB 0000       SMCT 00         SRBM 07         SWTL 00000000
      +C8   SRBT 000000B4   8047AA00        LSMQ 00000000   LSPL 00000000   TCBS 00000000   TCBL 00000000
      +E0   WPRB 00023558   NDP  FF  TNDP   FF  NTSG FF     IODP FF         LOCI 00000000   CMLH 00000000
      +F0   CMLC 0000  LXR  SSOM 00000000   ASTE 00FBD010   LTOV 007AA000   ATOV 007ACC50   ETC  0000
      +106  ETCN 0000  LXR  0000  AXR 0000  STKH 00239C0    GQEL 00000000   LQEL 002B0D70   GSYN 00000000
      +11C  XTCB 007A3DE0   FW3  00000000   GXL  00979618   EATT 00000000   170D7400 INTS   9649EEE D3FE5040
      +138  FW4  00000000   RCMS 00000000   IOSC 00000285   PKML 8000       XCNT 01F3       NSQA 00000000
      +14C  ASM  00023990   RESV 00         RESV 000000     TCME 00000000


ASXB  023570
      +0    ASXB C1E2E7C2   FTCB 00023678   LTCB 007A00D0   TCBS 0017       RS00 0000       MPST 00000000
      +14   LWA  00000000   VFVT 00000000   BSAF 00000000   IHSA 00023D50
      +24   FLSA 00F91238   00F75510 0004462C  00044630 4002E9F0  00F754D0 000050F0  00FA0E1C 00000000
      +48          000044C  00FD2568 00000D08  00023594 9002F8B2  00010900 0002F30E  38000D08 400366AA
      +6C   FRWA 000240F0   SPSA 00067F28   RSMD 00000000   RCTD 00000000   RSV 00000000   OUSB 000247B8
      +84   RESV 00000000   PRG  40404040   40404040 40404040  40404040   PSWD 40404040   40404040
      +A0   SIRB 00023898   ETSK 00023678   FIQE 00000000   LIQE 00000000  FRQE 00000000   LRQE 00000000
      +B8   FSRB 00000000   LSRB 00000000   USER 00000000   000000 SECR 00  SENV 00000000  XSBA 007AE650
      +D0   RESV 007A0440   RESV 00000151   CASW 00000000   PTOE 00000000   RV24 00000000  JSVT 00000000
```

LOCAL SERVICE MANAGER QUEUE

QUEUE IS EMPTY

LOCAL SERVICE PRIORITY LIST

QUEUE IS EMPTY

REAL ADDRESS OF SEGMENT TABLE IS   FD7C00

PC NUM	AUTH KEY MASK	EXEC ASID	ENTRY ADDR	EXEC STATE	LATENT PARMS	EXEC KEY MASK
000000	FF00	0002	00115860	S	007ACC60	80000000
000001	FF00	0002	001161A8	S	007ACC68	80000000
000002	FF00	0002	00116E58	S	007ACC70	80000000
000003	FF00	0002	00117A80	S	007ACC78	80000000
000004	FF00	0002	00118178	S	007ACC80	80000000
000005	FF00	0002	001194A0	S	007ACC88	80000000
000006	FF00	0002	0011A318	S	007ACC90	80000000
000007	FF00	0002	0011A322	S	007ACC98	80000000
000008	FF00	0002	0011A32C	S	007ACCA0	80000000
000009	FF00	0002	0011B098	S	007ACCA8	80000000

Figure 3.8 Formatted listing of an ASCB and ASXB.

SCA contains the address of the program interrupt element (PIE) and the program mask at the time of SPIE initiation. PIE in turn points to Program Interrupt Control Area (PICA). PICA contains information such as the program mask to be used in the PSW, the user's SPIE exit routing address, and the interruption mask that identifies the program check interruptions that the user's SPIE exit routine will service.

2. For timer supervision there are control blocks such as timer queue element (TQE), pointed by the TCB.

3. For every open data-set for a task a data extent block (DEB) is created. DEB is an extension of the information in the DCB. Each DEB is associated with a DCB, and the two point to each other. DEB contains information about the physical characteristics of the data set and other information used by the control program. One important pointer in DEB is the input output block (IOB). Since IOB is the communication medium between a routine that requests an I/O operation and the I/O supervisor that executes the I/O operation, it is an important control block for debugging I/O related problems. DEBs are chained together and anchored in the TCB.*

4. TCB points to a save area where registers and PSW are saved by the control program.

5. The task input/output table (TIOT) contains the DD names and the corresponding I/O devices for a task and is pointed by TCB.

6. TCB also points to the data control block for JOB LIBRARY or STEP LIBRARY for programs that execute under this TCB.

7. There can be several load modules associated with a task. Each load module represents a level of control for that task. This level of control is represented by Request Blocks. Request blocks are chained together and used for task supervision.

8. Program manager uses content directory entry (CDE) for controlling the usage of a particular load module which is loaded into the private area of an address space. CDE points to XL (Extend List), which contains such properties of the load module as its length and its address in main storage.

9. All the load modules brought into the private area by LOAD macro are controlled by a control block called *Load List Element.* The program manager uses this load list element for the load and delete functions for a particular load module.

10. There is a set of control blocks for use by the virtual storage manager. TCB points to subpool queue element (SPQE), which describes the space in a particular subpool. SPQEs for different sub-

pools are chained together. Each SPQE points to description queue element (DQE), which describes 4K (4,096 bytes) of contiguous space held by that subpool. Some of this contiguous space may be in use and other may not be in use, so additional information is needed to describe the 4K of contiguous space. This is done through a control block called *free queue element*. Free queue element describes the contiguous free space in a subpool.

11. Partition queue element describes the space or virtual storage held by a region. This control block tells where the private area begins and how big it is. The free space segments in an address space are described by free block queue elements FBQEs chained from partition queue element.

> *NOTE:* A data set opened in one task cannot be closed in another task. The reason is that the task closing the data set will search only its DEB chain pointed by its TCB.

Figure 3.9 gives the relationship of the task-related control blocks covered here, and Figure 3.10 contains a formatted listing of the CSD, LCCA, PCCA and PSA control blocks for each of the CPUs in an MP system.

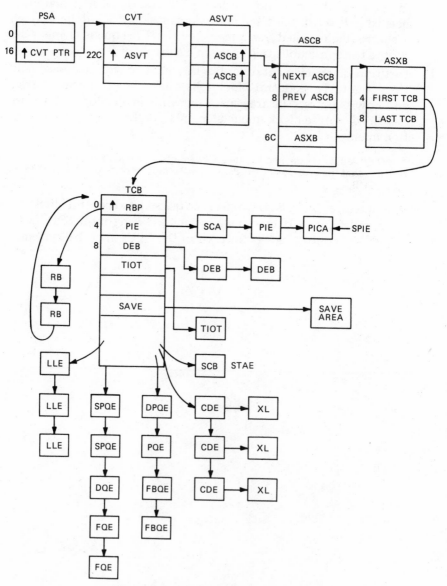

Figure 3.9 Task-related control blocks.

SYMPTOM STRING: AB/S00C4 PIDS/5752TC221 RIDS/IEDGRC11 REGS/FE000MODULE IEAVTSDT DATE 10/13/83 TIME 13.19.45 PAGE 0122

**** C P U   D A T A ****

```
CSD  FFCD30
           CSD        CPUJS A000    CHAD 000F     CPUAL A000    CPUDL 0002    SCFL1 40     SCFL2 00     SCFL3 00
                      RV043 00      MFICP 0000    ACR  00       FLAGS A0
+0    CSD   C3E2C440  00
+F    SCFL4 00000000  00000000      00000000      00000000      00000000      00000000     00000000     00000000
+18   MAFF  00000000  00000000      00000000      00000000      00000000      00000000     00000000     00000000
+40         0000      DDRCT 0001    GDCC 00000000 GDINT 0000    GDTOD 00000002 TCNT 00000000
+68   RV044 00000000  MASK 80004000 20000010      08000040      02000100      00080004     00020001
+7C   UCNT  00000000  00000000      00000000      00000000      00000000      00000000     00000000     00000001
+A0   RESV  00000000  00000000      00000000      00000000      00000000      00000000     00000000     00000000
+C8         00000000  00000000      00000000      00000000      00000000      00000000     00000000     00000000
+F0         00000000  00000000      00000000      00000000      00000000      00000000     00000000     00000000
+118        00000000
```

```
SVT  02BE10
              GSCH1 0002BC4E   GSCH2 0002BC6C   MSEEP 000582A8   MSDEP 00058288
              JSTEQ 00000000   DSREQ 00000000   GSMQ 00000000    GSPL 00000000
+00   ISECT   000CDB90
+14   RSCS    0005BCC8
+28   LSMQ    00000000   00000000   00000000   00000000   00000000   00000000   00000000   00000000
+2C   WAS     00000000   00000000   00000000   00000000   00000000   00000000   00000000   00000000
+4C           00000000   00000000   00000000   00000000   00000000   00000000   00000000   00000000
+6C   DACTV   00000000   XASCB 00FC8628   XMD 007A9E08   WAIT 4000000    GSPH 00248A0   XEPM 000CDFF0
+8C   ISECR   00000000   LASCB 00CE7BE    CMCKM 80000000 CMST1 000CE2E8  CMRT1 000CE3AE
+A0   BBR     00000000   CMSTR 000CE668   CMSBR 000CE6E2 CDSPE 000CE7F4  CDSPD 000CE7FC
+B4   CMRT2   00000000   SRBRS 000CE9E8   AFFST 0009AE38 AFFOB 0009AE86  SRBG 0009AE10
+C8   SRBSV   00009AE22   SRBF 00000000   SRBS 00007ED2   SRBA 00007CD1
+DC   SRBRG   00020001   SSRBE 00050002   SSRBS 00007ED2  SRBA 00FC5090
+F0   SRBE    0005BCD4   RSCA 0005BCE0    SUSQ 00077008   SVT E2E5E340
+104  RSUA    C0000000   DSPC 000461B8    AFTV 007AC000   RSTD 00077614
+118  FWI     000248B8   SSTSV 00000394   TRCO 000830EC   SSEM 000CF510
+12C  ISSAT   000CE9F4   RSV23 00000000   NSLX 000A       MDLQ 00000000  SLWLN 00000000
+140  SRBMD                                                SET1 0003C352  EXP2 00050810
```

```
LCCA FF3210
             LCCA D3C3C3C1   CPUA 0042     OCPU 0000
+0    LCCA   D3C3C3C1        00000000      00000000      00000000     00000000     00000000     00000000     00000000
+8    PGR1   00000001        007B0D50      007B0FF8      00000D08     00F4F000     8004F218     007B0D50
+28   PGR2   00000008        50C8F948      007B1000      00001000     00F4F000     50C8FBB4     4003025E
+48                          070C0000      007B0D50      PINT 00020011 PVAD        MCR1 0FFD7C00 CR0
+68   PPSW   00C8FAA6
+88   PGR3   00000000        00000000      00000000      00000000     00000000     00000000     00008931
+A0          00000000        00FF3210      00FFC1F0      00000000     00FF44A0     00053F90     00000000
+C0   XGR2   AD040264        50080C5C      00FFCEA8      00FCD308     00080F64     40080D86     00000000
+E0          00000000        00000000      00000000      00000000     00000000     00000000     00000000
+100  XGR3   00000000        00000000      00000000      00000000     00000000     00000000     00000000
+120         00000000
+140
```

Figure 3.10 Formatted listing of CSD, LCCA, PCCA, and PSA control blocks for each of the CPUs in an MP system.

```
+160  RSGR 00000000  00000000  00000000  00000000  00000000  00000000  00000000  00000000
+180                  00000000  00000000  00000000  00000000  00000000  00000000  00000000
+1A0  RIR2-7 00FDF678 00FF6740 00FE6D98 00024A88 00000000 0000BFA8
+1B8  PX1K 0000  PX1S 0000  PX1A 0000  PX1P 0000  PX2K 8000  PX2S 0025
+1C4  PX2A 0000  PX2P 0025  PX3K 0000  PX3S 0000  PX3A 0000  PX3P 0000
+1D0  RESV 00000000  PSW3 00000000 00000000
+1E0  INGR 00FF5B88  00FF5B88  00FD5ED0  000504A8  00FE1008  0004FAC0  00F4B8A0  00024908
+200  SCR0 00000000  MCR0 00000000  IHR1 00  IHR2 00  IHR3 00  IHR4 00
+20C  SPN1 00  SPN2 00  SPN3 00  SPN4 00  ESSA 0002556A  ASCP 00000000
+218  CPUS 00FEAD68 DSF1 00  DSF2 00  PSMK 00  RV68 00
+220  DSR2-5 400584BA 00FFC1F0 00054308 00000000   RPR2-5 0003D672 F002F7A6 007ACD90 007AC968
```

```
+240  RESV 00000000 00000000 00000000 00000000  TCR0 00000000  RESV 00000000
+258  TFP0     000051B4 4EE90600  TFP2 00000000  WTIM 000051B5  E5D4A000
+270  DSS1 00000000 00000000 00000000  DSS2 00000000 00000000 00000000  DSS3 00000000 00000000
+294  DSSC 00000000 00000000 00000000  DSSR 00000000 00000000 00000000  DCPU 00000000  RCPU 00000000
+2AC  CRLC 00000000  LCR0 DD84EE40  CRFL 00  CREX 00  LKFG 00  RV88 00
+2B8  PINV 0000  SLIP 00000000  LWTM 00000000  ICR0 DD84EE40  ECSA 0002556A
+2D0  SAFN 0000  PGTA 0025007A CD90  RV89 00000000  RV90 00000000
+2E0  IRT  00108100  07140000  00005238  0001A680  00FF384C
+300       00000000  00FF3130  007AF324  5002F2C4  00FF3D38  90285E4
+320       80027E58  90296AC   80005040  80027E50  0001A4FA  800292DC
+340       80029880  00005040  40027434  8002A520  0001A678  00000D28
+360  SMQJ 00000000  SPLJ 00000000  ESS2 00000000  FSSJ 00000000  ADRTI 00000000 00000000
+378  ADRT2 00000000 00000000
+380  SGPR 80000000  80878000  00000FFF  00024A88  007AF548  00000000  00000CC0  00000CE0
+3A0       00000000  90032C18  00000FF8  00001284  00000002  000334C8  80032AFE  0004731C
+3C0  R167 0000 PERC 0000  PERA 00000000
+3C8  XXM2 00000001 00010001  XXM3 00000000 00000000  RXMR 00000000  SXMR 0080003D 0000003D
+3E8  LKG1 80000025 00000025  00000000  00FF8AD34 0095AEF4  00F8AD34 0096F860  00FF35F8 600B1DE8
+430  LKG2 00F8AD34 0095AEF4  00FF3210 00C42F26  000B1C62 00FE2A10  00B1BB2 00FF35F8
+450       00F447B8 00C42F26  00000042 0002BE10  00000C00 00FE2A10  00F8AD34 00FF3210
+470  ELKP 070C0000  00C42F36  500B1C86  500B1C86  40C42F36  00C42F26
+478  STG1 00000000  00000000  00000000  00000000  00000000  00000000
+49C  00000000
+4C0  SCSA 0011B1EB 00315020 50171lEC 00FD0988 007A7000  00000000
+4D4  SREG 0079CA28 00C95F9A 40EB8572 0079CDC0 0079CB40  00030000  80000005  00FCF000
+4F4       40EB85A0 40EB8592 00FE1538 00E80000  SMSK 04  RSMK 07  PGMM 40  TCFB 00
+50C  RES1 60C2B49A 00FF3210 00F464A0 500777BA 8005BCEC  C0000042 00000001
+528  RES2 08000051 00000051 007A82B8
+534  R300 00000000  R301 00000000   PRMT 00000000  PTCB 00000000  PRTN 00044C14  CDXM 8000003B 0000003B
```

Figure 3.10 *continued*

```
+550  SRXM  80000025  00000025  00000000  R203 00000000  IOSS 00FA00B0  IOC3 80000025  IOC4 00000025
+568  BBRC  00000000  00000000  00000000  007AE550  8004C276  007ADA68  9004C3D4  00000C00  00F50CC0
+56C  CDSV  0000D000  80000000  6004BEBC  6004BEBC  00000004  00000000  6004C3FA  00FF3210
+5AC  SLSA  00000000  00000000  00000000  00000000  00000000  00000000  00000000  00000000
+5CC        00000000  00000000  00000000  00000000  00000000  00000000  00000000  00000000


PCCA FF44A0

+0    PCCA D7C3C3C1   CPID F2F3F2F2   F0F4F1F5 F3F0F8F1   CPUA 0002        CAFM 2000        TQEP 00024908
+18   PSAV 00FE9000   PSAR 00FEC000   RV81 00000000       RV82 00000000    RV83 00000000    RV84 00000000
+30   RV85 00000000   RV86 00000000   RV87 00000000       RV88 00000000    RV89 00000000    RV90 00000000
+48   RV91 00000000   RV92 00000000   RV93 00000000       RV94 00000000    RV95 00000000    RV96 00000000
+60   RV97 00000000   RV98 00000000   RV99 00000000       RV9A 00000000    RV9B 00000000    RV9C 00000000
+78   RV9D 00000000   RV9E 00000000   TMFL 80             TODE 00          CCE 00           INTE 00
+84   RPB 00000000    RISP 00         EMS2 00             EMS3 00          RMSB 00          EMSP 00
+90   EMSE 00080F64   EMSA 00FFC1F0   PWAV 00FC8788       PWAR 00FB4788    LRBV 00FC8260    LRBR 00FDF678
+A8   ELAD 00FC81A8   ELBA 00FC8158   CCHM 00FC8118       SRB 00000000     00FC8260         LRBR 00FB4260
+C4   CCHI 00000000   00000000        00000000            00000000         CHAN 00          SRBL 00
+E2   0000 RESV       00000000        00000000            00000000         00000000         00000000
+108  CHUB 0000B310   CHPF 00         CHBL 00             CHVA 10          CHTS 07          CHS1 00
+118  CHS2 00         CHRB 00         IOSI 00             CHW1 00000000    CHW2 00000000    LOGL 0000
+121  00              LGP1 00         LGP2 00             CHPB 00          RESV 00          CHF1 00
+12E  CELL 0070       CHF3 00         CHF4 00             CHSV 00000000    00000000         00000000
+135  CHF2 00
+144  CHID 00000000   00000000        LOGA 00000000       RV54 00000000    RV55 00000000    RV56 00000000
+15C  RV57 00000000   RV58 00000000   RV59 00000000       RV60 00000000    RV61 00000000    RV62 00000000
```

SYMPTOM STRING: AB/S00C4 PIDS/5752TC221 RIDS/IEDGRC11 REGS/FE00 MODULE IEAVTSDT DATE 10/13/83 TIME 13.19.45 PAGE 0124

```
+174  RV63 00000000   ATTR 00         RV01 00             RV35 0000        RV36 00000000    00000000   00000000
+180  RESV 00000000   00000000        00000000            00000000         00000000         00000000   00000000
+1A8  00000000        00000000        00000000            00000000         00000000         00000000   00000000
+1D0  00000000        00000000        00000000            00000000         00000000         00000000   00000000
+1F8  00000000        00000000        00000000            00000000         00000000         00000000   00000000
+200  00000000        00000000        00000000            00000000         00000000         00000000   00000000
+228  00000000        00000000        00000000            00000000         00000000         00000000   00000000
```

```
*****  PSW - REGISTERS FOR CPU 0002  *****

PSW        00000000 00000000   00000000 00000000

GPRS 0-7   00000000 00000100 00000000 00000000 00000000 00F8CCDC 401076C6 40107668 00F8CC88
GPRS 8-15  00000000 00000000 00000000 00000000 00000000 00000013 00000000 00107FBB 007AE5A0
```

Figure 3.10 continued

```
CTRS 0-7    DD84EE40  0FE92C00  FFFFFFFF  80000025  00000025  80FC5000  00000000  0FE92C00
CTRS 8-15   00000000  00000000  00000000  00000000  00000000  00000000  EFC80FCD  00FB43A8

FPRS 0-2    00000000  00000000  00000000  00000000
FPRS 4-6    00000000  00000000


PSA  000000

     +0   RNPSW 040C0000 00000000 00023298  ROPSW 00000000 00000000  CVT   00024A88  RESV  00000000
     +18  EOPSW 070E0000 00000000 00000000  SOPSW 070C2000 00C850D6  POPSW 070C3000 00C85000
     +30  MOPSW 00000000 00000000 IOPSW 070C0000 00152BC0  CSW   00000000 04000000
     +4C  CVT2  00024A88  TIMER 70CCC1FF    TRACE 00FBEDC0  ENPSW 040C0000 000250D8    CAW  FFFFFFFF
     +60  SNPSW 040C0000 000259D8  PNPSW 000C0000 00026370  MNPSW 00000000 00026CA8
     +78  INPSW 040C0000 000273B8  EPARM 00FEC000           SPAD  0000  EICOD 1202  RESV 00
     +89  SVILC 02      SVCN 0001  RESV 00  PIILC 02  RV049 00  PICOD 11
     +90  TEA   00C85000           MCNUM 00 RESV 00  PERCD 00  RESV 00   PER  00000000
     +9C  RESV  00      MTRCD 000000  RESV 00000000  MPL   00027760  CHNID 00000000
     +AC  IOEL  00FB41A8  LCL FFFFFFFF  RESV 0000  RESV 00    RESV  00   IOA  0000051E
     +BC  RESV  00000000 00000000 00000000 0000000000  RESV 00  0000000000
     +E0  RESV  00000000           MCIC 00000000 0000000000
     +F0  RESV  00000000  MEDC 00  RESV 00    RGNCD 00000000
     +100 RESV  00000000 00000000 00000000 00000000   FSA  00000000  00000000
     +120 FLA   FFFFFFFF FFFFFFFF FFFFFFFF FFFFFFFF    FFFFFFFF FFFFFFFF
     +140 FFFFFFFF 00000000 00000000 00000000 00000000 00000000 FFFFFFFF
     +160 FPSAV 00000000 00000000 82000170 00000000   00DBF68  00000000
     +180 GRSAV 00000000 00000000 00000000 00000000   00000000 00000000
     +1A0 00000000 00000000 00000000 00000000 00000000 00000000 00000000
     +1C0 CRSAV 00000000 00000000 00000000 00000000   00000000 00000000
     +1E0 00000000 00000000 00000000 00000000 00000000 00000000
     +200 PSA   D7E2C140  CPUPA 0002  CPULA 0042   PCCAV 00FF44A0  PCCAR 00FF74A0
     +210 LCCAV 00FF3210  LCCAR 00FF6210  TNEW 007ACD90  TOLD 007ACD90  ANEW 00F8CC88
     +224 AOLD  00F8CC88  SUPI 00  SUP2 00  SUP3 00    SUP4 00
     +22C GPREG 80000025 00000000 00000000 RSREG 00000000  RV103 00000000  EXPS1 070C0000 00C42F26
     +248 EXPS2 050C1000 00054236 MPSW 040C0000 00C42F36  MCHEX 040C0000 000A84AA
     +260 IPCR  AD040264  IPCRM 04  IPCD AD00026C  IPCDM 00  IPCC3 00  RESV 0000
     +270 IPCSA 00FFC1F0  RECUR 00  DSSGO 00  SNSM2 04  RTM1S 04  SRSA 00000000
     +280 DISPL 000277A8  SALCL 000277B0  IOSSL 00000000  IOSCL 00000000
     +294 IOSUL 000277B0  TPNCL 00000000  TPDNL 00000000  TPACL 00000000
     +2A8 OPTL  000277B8  CMSL 00000000  LOCAL 00000000  RLOCK 00000000
```

SYMPTOM STRING: AB/S00C4 PIDS/5752TC221 RIDS/IEDGRC11 REGS/FE00MODULE IEAVTSDT   DATE 10/13/83   TIME 13.19.45   PAGE 0125

```
+2B8  MSORG 00000009 0002BE10 007AED28 00000D28 00000028 007AF324 800582B4  RESV 00000000 00000000 00000000
+2DC  00000000 00000000 00000000 00000000 00000000 00000000  CMSLK 000277E0  LCPUA 00000042
```

Figure 3.10 *continued*

```
+2F8  HLHI  00000001  LITA  00027800  SVPSW 070C0000  00152BC0         CRO   DD84C000
+30C  MCHFL 00        SYMSK 04        ACTCD 0002      MCHIC 00         WKRAP 00000000
+314  WKVAP 00000000  VSTAP 0000      CPUSA 0002      STOR  0FFD7C00   DSSRS 00000000
+324  DSSR2 00000000  DSSR3 00000000  DSSWK 00000000  DSSF4 00         00000000 00000000
+340                  DSSF1 00        DSSF2 FF        DSSF3 00         DSSFW 00000000
+348  DSSRP 00000000  00000000 DSSPP 00000000         DSSI4 00000000   RV042 00000000
+360  DSSPR 00000000  RV025 00000000  RV040 00000000  RV041 00000000   NSTK  00000C00
+374  RESV  00000000  0000 RET 07FE   RETCD 47FFE000  CSTK  00000C00   PSTK  00FE6C30
+388  SSTK  00FE6030  SSAV  00000C00  MSTK  00FE6720  MSAV  00FE7A10   ESAV2 00FE7320
+39C  PSAV  00000C00  ESTK1 00FE7320  ESAV1 00FE6030  ESTK2 00FE7A10   SRPSW 00000000
+3B0  ESTK3 00FE7F20  ESAV3 00000000  RSTK  00FE8430  RSAV  00000000   STOP  07FE0000
+3C8  RSPSW 00000000  00000000 START 07FE0000  00000000                INTE  00
+3E8                  SFACC 8007D000  LSFCC 581003F0  SVC13 0A0D  TRACE 00
+3FC  RTMIR AD07027B  PCPSW 078C2000  00A2D4D6 ATCVT 00000000   CDAL  00000000 00000000
+414  CSID  0001      RV100 0000      SCPSW 040C0000 6008C782    SMPSW 070C0000 000366A8
+428  GSAV  00F8AD34  00F8AD34        00F8AD34       00F8AD34 00FF3210
+448        0095AEF4  00FE2A10 500B1C86 000B1BB2 40C42F36 00C42F26
+468  PSWSV 070C2000  00C42F26 0002BE10  00FFFFFF FEB78000 PCFUN 00000000 PCPS2 0000  PCPS3 0000
+480  PCGR8 00FEC454  00C85DD6 CPUT     PCGRA 00000000 PCGRB 00000000
+490  SCRGI 00000000  SCRG2 9008BECE    PCPS4 0000 RV071 0000  0000  MODE 00
+4A0  RV072 0000 MODES 00  STNSM 07     LKJW 00000000 MODEW 000000 RESV 00000000
+4B0  LKJW2 00000001  LCR10 00000000
+4B8  SLSA  00000001  LCR11 00000000 9649A243 7877B240 400258E2 00001202 00024A88 400250E6 00000000
+4DC                  00023400  00000000 00000000 00000000 00000000
+500  LKSA  00000000  0002556A  00000000 00000000 000422D3 00FE7448 00000000
+520                  00041238  000B1E0C 000B16CC 900414D0 00FEAD68
+540  RSMSW 040C0000  00030216
+548        00700000 0007E118 00000000 4002E9F0 00F92DE0 00000008
+568  RSMGR 00F34054  0002FBA6 0074D050 00F34568 00F92D50 007AF324 6007E4C6 00000000
+588  HWFB  C0        CROCB 10  00000000 RV090 0000 CROSV DD84EE40
+590  PCCRO 00000000  RCRO  00000000  TKN 0000  ASD 0000  SEL 00000000
+5A0  SKPSW 070C0000  SKPS2 00117620
+5A8  GXMSV 00010001  00010001  RV160 00000000 00000000       SCFB  00000000
+5BC  XMCRO 00000000  XMCR1 00000000  XMCR3 00000000 XMCR4 00000000 XMCR5 00000000
+5D0  XMCR7 00000000  XMCR9 00000000  XMCRA 00000000 XMCRB 00000000 XMCRC 00000000
+5E8  XMGRS 00000000  00000000  00000000 00000000 00000000
+608            00000000  00000000 00000000 00000000
+628  XMPSW 078D2000  0070A39E XMFB1 00  0007E118 00000000 XMILC 0002  XMPIC 0001
+638  XMTEA 00785010  XMPEF 00 RV135 00  RV128 00 XMRA1 00 XMRA2 00 XMPSS 0001 XMPSL 00000000
+648  XMETE 00000000  RV148 00000000  RV149 00000000 TIME 00000000 FFFFFF FFFFF000
+660  SRSAV 00FAA000  RV148 00000000 007B0FFF 00F9DA00 00F9FC90 007B0D7B RV151 80000025 RV152 00000025
+678  GGRSV 007BD077  007B0D77 0007E118 00048B38 00F902C8 000447B8 00C42F26
+698            007B0D77 000277BD DTSAV 00FFFFFF FFFFF000        XMCRE EFC80FCD
+6B8  DCR3  80000025  DCR4  00000025
```

Figure 3.10 *continued*

```
          STORAGE KEY IS 00 FOR STORAGE BEGINNING AT 000006C0
000006C0 00 00FFFFFF FFFFF000 00000000 00000000 00000000 00000000 00000000 00000000   *................*
000006E0 00 00000000 00000000 00000000 00000000                                        *................*
00000700 TO NEXT LINE ADDRESS SAME AS ABOVE
00000800 00 9004C3D4 00000000 00000011 FFFFFFEF 00000000 00000000 00000000 00000000   *...CM...........*
00000820 00 00000000 00000000 00000000 00000000                                        *................*
00000840 TO NEXT LINE ADDRESS SAME AS ABOVE
00000AE0 00 00000000 00000000 00000000 00000000 00000000 00000000 00000000 00000000   *................*
         +B00 IOEP1 000273E8  IOEP2 000275A8  IOEP3 0027650  IOSRC 000291D2  IOEP4 000276A0  IOEP5 000275A8   *
         +B18 IOEP6 000275A8  IOEP7 000275A8  IOEP8 000275A8  IOEP9 000275A8  IOEPA 000275A8  IOEPB 000275A8

SYMPTOM STRING: AB/S00C4 PIDS/5752TC221 RIDS/IEDGRC11 REGS/FE00MODULE IEAVTSDT   DATE 10/13/83   TIME 13.19.45   PAGE 0127

LCCA FFBC00
   +0   LCCA  D3C3C3C1   CPUA 0040      OCPU 0002
   +8   PGR1  00000000   00000000       00000000       00000000       00000000       00000000       00000000
   +28  PGR2  00000030   00000000       00000000       008D321A       003C0074       008D3DF0       008D3DF0
   +48        008D321A   008D2268       00725A00       0090D298       0047D038       4047EB20       00725A00
   +68  PPSW  076C1000   0047D108       0090D298       095AF28        00788010       MCR1 0FFD7C00  CR0
   +88  PGR3  00000000   0047D108       PINT 00040004  PVAD  00000000 00000000       00000000       00000000
   +A0        00000000   00000000       00000000       00000046       00000000       00000000       00000000
   +C0  XGR2  00000000   00FF5B88       00FF5B88       00024A88       00030000       000B1938       500B1730
   +E0        00000000   00000000       00000002       000277B8       000B16CC       A0AA0896       00FF7C98
   +100 XGR3  00000000   00000000       00000002       00000004       00000000       00000000       00000000
   +120       00000000   00000000       00000000       00000000       00000000       00000000       00000000
   +140 RSGR  00000000   00000000       00000000       00000000       00000000       00000000       00000000
   +160       00000000   00000000       00000000       00000000       00000000       00000000       00000000
   +180 RIR?-7 00FFCEA8  00048B38  00FFBC00 00000000 007A40EC 007A4018
   +1A0 PX1K  0000       PX1S 0000  PX1A 0000  PX2K 0200  PX2S 0025
   +1B8 PX2A  0025       PX2P 0025  PX3K 0000  PX3A 0000  PX3P 0000  003C0074  008D3F0
   +1C4 RESV  00000000   00000000  PSW3 00000000 00000000  4047EB20  00000000
   +1D0 INGR  0004FF70   0004FAC0  00FFA068  00F8F480  00F6E1B0
   +1E0 SCR0  00000000   MCR0 00000000  IHR1 00  IHR2 00  IHR3 00  IHR4 00  00000000
   +200 SPN1  00         SPN2 00    SPN3 00    SPN4 00    ESSA 002556A  ASCP  00000000
   +20C CPUS  00FF6998   DSF1 00    DSF2 00    PSMK 00    RV68 00
   +218 DSR2-5 400584BA  00FF4440  00054308  00000000  RPR2-5 0003672  F002F7A6 007ACD90 007AC968
   +220 RESV  00000000   00000000  00000000  TCR0 00000000  RESV  40000000
   +240 TFP0  0005621  A57FE400  TFP2  00FFFFFF FFF61200 WTIM  00005621  AB7F2400
   +258 DSS1  00000000   00000000  DSS2 00000000  SRBJ 00000000  DSS3 00000000  00000000  00000000
   +270 DSSC  00000000   DSSR 00000000  SRBJ 00000000  DCPU 00000000  RCPU  00000000
   +294 CRLC  00000000   LCR0 DD84EE40  CREL 00  CREX 00  LKFG 00  RV88 00
   +2AC PINV  00000000   SLIP 00000000  LWTM 00000000  00000000  ICR0 DD84EE40  ECSA 002556A
   +2B8 SAFN  00004000   PGTA 0025007A  CD90  RV89 00000000  RV90 00000000  FFFFFFFF  00FF3F2C
   +2D0 IRT   00000000   00FF6650  00000000  0005238  0001A680  0001A3C4  00028248  80029ADC
   +300                  07140000  00000000  00000000  50029ABA  5002F2C4  00028248
```

Figure 3.10 *continued*

```
+320        800292E0  800296AC  40029A4   00000000  A002A5B6  0001A432  00000000  00FF8D58
+340        80029380  00005040  00046080  8002A520  0001A658  00010000  00000000  00000000
+360  SMQJ  00000000  SPLJ 00000000  ESS2 00000000  FSSJ 00000000  ADRT1 000001F6 35516220
+378  ADRT2 00000000
+380  SGPR  88000000  80878000  00000FFF  00000FF8  007AF548  00000C00  00000CE0
+3A0        000324C8  90032C18  00000000  00001194  00000002  80032AFE  0004731C
+3C0  R167  0000 PERC 0000 PERA  00000000
+3C8  XXM2  8000005D  XXM3 00000000  RXMR 00000000  00000000  SXMR 0080003D 0000003D
+3E8  LKG1  80000005  00010005  00120001  00120001  500B2708  807ADA68  807AD270
+40C        00000000  00F9C150  00000000  007ADA68  007AD270  0009F040  00FFBFE8 600B2ACC
+430  LKG2  00000001  007A7558  00000D08  8009F2D6  002C42E0  0009EF10  0FD3C60
+450        00FBC0A0  0004A898  007ADA68  0009F040  000B26A0  0009F040  00000000
+470  ELKP  070C0000  000B2564
+478  STG1  00000000  00000000  00000000  007A7000  00000000  00000000
+490        00000000  00000000  00000000  00000000  00000000  00000000
+4C0  SCSA  00181EB   00315020  5011 71EC 00FDD988  00975FB8  00020000  00FCE590
+4D4  SREG  007A0700  00D1B464  00000001  007A2D78  00975FB8  80000001  RSMK 00 PGMM 40 TCFB 00
+4F4        40054588  00000000  00000000  00000000  SMSK 04  80000040
+50C  RES1  60C2B49A  00FFBC00  00F69398  C00777CC  8005BCEC  C0000040
+528  RES2  00800058  00800058  007810C0
+534  R300  R301 00000000  PRMT 00000000  PTCB 00000000  PRTN 00044C14 CDXM 80000046 00000046
+550  SRXM  00000001  00010001  R203 0000000  IOSS 00F90018  IOC3 00000001 IOC4 00010001
+568  BBRC  00000000
+56C  CDSV  00000000  00000000  007AE550  8004C276  007ADA68  9004C3D4  00000C00  00F75EA0


SYMPTOM STRING: AB/S00C4 PIDS/5752TC221 RIDS/IEDGRC11 REGS/FE00MODULE IEAVTSDT  DATE 10/13/83  TIME 13.19.45  PAGE 0128

+58C  SLSA  00000D00  80000000  6004BEBC  00000000  00000000  00000000  6004C3FA  00FFBC00
+5AC        00000000  00000000  00000000  00000000  00000000  00000000  00000000
+5CC        00000000  00000000  00000000  00000000  00000000  00000000


PCCA  FFC1F0
+0    PCCA  D7C3C3C1  CPID F2F3F0F2 F0F4F1F5 F3F0F8F1  CPUA 0000  CAFM 8000  TQEP 00024920
+18   PSAV  00FED000  PSAR 00FF0000  RV81 00000000  RV82 00000000  RV83 00000000 RV84 00000000
+30   RV85  00000000  RV86 00000000  RV87 00000000  RV88 00000000  RV89 00000000 RV90 00000000
+48   RV91  00000000  RV92 00000000  RV93 00000000  RV94 00000000  RV95 00000000 RV96 00000000
+60   RV97  00000000  RV98 00000000  RV99 00000000  RV9A 00000000  RV9B 00000000 RV9C 00000000
+78   RV9D  00000000  RV9E 00000000  TMFL 80  TODE 00  CCE 00  INTE 00
+84   RPB   00000000  RISP 00  TMFL2 00  EMS2 00  EMS3 00  RMSB 00  EMSP 00
+90   EMSE  0009B9E4  EMSA 00FF44A0  PWAV 00FCA018  PWAR 00FB6018  LRBV 00FC8EB8 LRBR 00FB4EB8
+A8   ELAD  00FC8E00  ELBA 00FC8DB0  CCHM 00FC8D70  PWAR SRB  00000000  00000000
+C4         00000000  RESV 00000000  00000000  00000000  00000000  CHAN 00  SRBL 00
+E2   00000000  00000000  00000000  00000000  00000000  00000000  00000000
+108  CCHI  00000000  00000000  00000000  00000000  00000000  00000000  00000000
```

Figure 3.10 *continued*

```
      CHUB 000073D0   CHPF 40      CHBL 09      CHVA 1F      CHTS 82       CHS1 00
+118  CHS2 00         CHRB 40      IOSI 14      CHW1 0000051F CHW2 00000000 LOGL 0000
+121  CELL 0070       LGP1 00      LGP2 00      CHPB 00      RESV 00       CHF1 84
+12E  CHF2 7D         CHF3 00      CHF4 40      CHSV 00000000 800654F2     00FF7BB0
+135  CHID F0F0F0F2   LOGA 00000000 RV54 00000000 RV55 00000000 RV56 00000000
+144  RV57 00000000   RV58 0000    RV59 00000000 RV60 00000000 RV61 00000000 RV62 00000000
+15C  RV63 00000000   ATTR 40      RV01 00      RV35 0000    RV36 00000000
+174
+180                  00000000     00000000     00000000     00000000     00000000     00000000
+1A8                  00000000     00000000     00000000     00000000     00000000     00000000
+1D0                  00000000     00000000     00000000     00000000     00000000     00000000
+1F8                  00000000     00000000     00000000     00000000     00000000
+200                  00000000     00000000     00000000     00000000     00000000     00000000
+228                  00000000     00000000     00000000     00000000     00000000     00000000


PSA   FED000

+0    RNPSW 040C0000  ROPSW 00000000  00000000   00DBBA20  CVT  00024A88  RESV 00000000
+18   EOPSW 070E0000  SOPSW 00000000  070C1000   00DBBA20  POPSW 076C1000 0047D108
+30   MOPSW 00000000  IOPSW 070E0000  070E0000             CSW  00DD7A40  0C000000   CAW 001C738
+4C   CVT2 00024A88   TIMER 70BF98FF  TRACE 00C0000        ENPSW 040C0000 00025D08
+60   SNPSW 040C0000  PNPSW 00000000  00C00000             MNPSW 00080000 00026CA8
+78   INPSW 040C0000  EPARM 000273B8  00026370             SPAD 0002   EICOD 1202  RESV 00
+89   SVILC 02        SVCN 0001       RESV 001             PIILC 04   EICOD 1202  RESV 00
+90   TEA 00788010    RESV 00         MCNUM 00             RV049 04   RV049 00    PICOD 04
+9C   RESV 00         MTRCD 000000    RESV 00              PERCD 04   RESV 00     PER 00000000
+AC   IOEL 00FB4E00   LCL FFFFFFFF    RESV 0000            MPL 00027760 CHNID 1000008
+BC   RESV            00000000        RESV 0000            RESV 00    RESV 00     IOA 00C00187
+E0   RESV            00000000        MCIC                 RESV       00000000    00000000
+F0   RESV 00000000   MEDC 00         RESV                 FSA  00000000 RGNCD 00000000
+100  RESV 00000000                  00000000             FFFFFFFF   00000000    FFFFFFFF
+120  FLA  FFFFFFFF   FFFFFFFF        00000000             FFFFFFFF   FFFFFFFF    FFFFFFFF
+140                  FFFFFFFF        00000000             00000000   00000000    00000000
+160  FPSAV 00000000  00000000        82000170            00DBF68    000DBF68    00000000
+180  GRSAV 00000000  00000000        00000000            00000000   00000000    00000000
+1A0                  00000000        00000000            00000000   00000000    00000000
+1C0  CRSAV 00000000  00000000        00000000            00000000   00000000    00000000
+1E0                  00000000        00000000            00000000   00000000    00000000
+200  PSA  D7E2C140   CPUPA 0000      CPULA 0040          PCCAV 00FFC1F0 PCCAR 00FFF1F0
+210  LCCAV 00FFBC00  LCCAR 00FFEC00  TNEW 00000000       TOLD 00000000 ANEW 00F702F0
+224  AOLD 00F8CC88   SUP1 04         SUP2 00             SUP3 00    SUP4 00
```

SYMPTOM STRING: AB/S00C4 PIDS/5752TC221 RIDS/IEDGRC11 REGS/FE000MODULE IEAVTSDT   DATE 10/13/83   TIME 13.19.45   PAGE 0129

```
+22C  GPREG 00000000 00000000 00000000 00000000 RSREG 00000000 RVI03 00000000 EXPS1 070C0000 00036AA8
+248  EXPS2 050C1000 000B19E8 MPSW 040C0000 00B2564 MCHEX 040C0000 001EAEE6
```

Figure 3.10 continued

```
        IPCR  AD070264   IPCRM 04                   RESV  000000         IPCD  AD07026C   IPCDM 04                   IPCC3 04   RESV 0000
+260    IPCR  AD070264   IPCRM 04                   RESV  000000         IPCD  AD07026C   IPCDM 04
+270    IPCSA 00FF44A0   HLHIS 00000000             RECUR 00             DSSGO 00         SNSM2 04   RTM1S 04   SRSA 00000000
+280    DISPL 000277A8   ASML  00000000             SALCL 000277B0       IOSSL 00000000   IOSCL 00000000
+294    IOSUL 00000000   IOSLL 00000000             TPNCL 00000000       TPDNL 00000000   TPACL 00000000
+2A8    OPTL  000277B8   CMSL  00000000             LOCAL 00000000       RLOCK 00000000
+2B8    MSORG 00FDD988   00FE272C 007AED28          00000D28 007AF324 800582B4   RESV 00000000 00000000 00000000
+2DC    00000000         00000000 00000000          00000000             00000000         CMSLK 000277E0   LCPUA 00000000
+2F8    HLHI  00000000   LITA  00027800             SVPSW 070C0000       000420D2         CRQ   DD84C000
+30C    MCHFL 00         SYMSK 06                   ACTCD 00             MCHIC 00          WKRAP 00000000
+314    WKVAP 00000000   VSTAP 0000                 CPUSA 0000           STOR  0FFD7C00   DSSRS 00000000   00000000
+324    DSSR2 00000000   DSSR3 00000000             DSSWK 00000000       DSSTS 00000000
+340                     DSSF1 00                   DSSF2 FF             DSSF3 00          DSSF4 00
+348    DSSRP 00000000   DSSPP 00000000             RV040 00000000       DSS14 00000000   DSSFW 00000000
+360    DSSPR 00000000   RV025 00000000             RV040 00000000       RV041 00000000   RV042 00000000
+374    RESV  00000000   0000  RET 07FE             RETCD 47FFE000       CSTK  00FF8C30   NSTK  00000C00
+388    SSTK  00FF8C30   SSAV  00000C00             MSTK  00FF9320       MSAV  00FF9320   PSTK  00FF9830
+39C    PSAV  00000C00   ESTK1 00FF9F20             ESAV1 00FF8C30       ESTK2 00FFA610   ESAV2 00FF9F20
+3B0    ESTK3 00FFAB20   ESAV3 00000000             RSTK  00FFB030       RSAV  00000000   SRPSW 00000000
+3C8    RSPSW 00000000   00000000                   07FE0000 00000000    00000000 00000000  STOP 07FE0000
+3E8                     SFACC 8007D000             LSFCC 581003F0       SVC13 0A0D        TRACE 00   INTE 00
+3FC    RTM1R AD07027B   PCPSW 071C1000             00CFC128 ATCVT 00000000   WTCOD CDAL 00000000
+414    CSID  0000       RV100 0000                 SCPSW 040C0000 40030CAA    SMPSW 070C0000 00366A8
+428    GSAV  00000000   00000000 00000000          5002BD38 0003C488 00230004 0076DA88   00000040
+448    50045D72         00F8C488 0002BCB0          000457B9 00FFBC00 00FE2A10 000447BA 0002BE10
+468    PSWSV 070E0000   CPUT  00000000             00FFFFFF FFF5DE00 PCFUN 00000000 PCPS2 0000   PCPS3 0000
+480    PCGR8 00000000   PCGR9 00000000             PCGRA 00000000       PCGRB 00000000
+490    SCRG1 00FF7BB0   SCRG2 00F90F6C             PCPS4 0000 RV071 0000   MODEW 000000   MODE 04
+4A0    RV072 00FF7BB0   MODES 08                   STNSM 07             LKJW  00000000   FZERO 00000000   RESV 00000000
+4B0    LKJW2 00000000   LCR10 00000000
+4B8    SLSA  00000000   00000001 9649A243          78605040 400258E2    00001202   00024A88 400250E6 0047E308
+4DC    00000000         00023400 0002556A          00FF6BE8 00000000    000422D3   00FFA048 00000000
+500    LKSA  00000000   000412D4 00041238          000B1E0C 00000400    000B16CC 900414D0   00FF6998
+520    00000000         0007E4C6
+540    RSMSW 040C0000   80F34030 00000000          0007E118 00000000    0FA08B0 00F34030   4002E9F0 00F910B8 00000008
+548    00F90F6C         00F34030 0074D050                                007AF324 5007E8AA 00000000
+568    RSMGR 00F90F6C   0002FBA6 00000000          RV090 0000           CROSV DD84EE40
+588    HWFB  C0         CROCB 10                   TKN 0000             ASD              SEL 00000000
+590    PCCR0 00000000   RCR0  00000000
+5A0    SKPSW 070C0000   SKPS2 00117620             RV160 00000000 00000000 00000000 00000000
+5A8    GXMSV 00010001   XMCR1 00000000             XMCR3 00000000       XMCR4 00000000   SCFB  00000000
+5BC    XMCR0 00000000   XMCR9 00000000             XMCRA 00000000       XMCRB 00000000   XMCR5 00000000
+5D0    XMCR7 00000000   XMCR9 00000000             XMCRA 00000000       XMCRC 00000000
+5E8    XMGRS 00000000   00000000                   00000000             00000000         XMCRE EFC80FCD
```

Figure 3.10 *continued*

```
+608  XMPSW  00000000 00000000 00000000 00000000 00000000 00000000
+628         078D0000 00000004 XMFB1 00 RV128 00000 XMILC 0002 XMPIC 0001
+638  XMTEA 00793010 XMPEF 00 RV135 00 XMRA1 00 XMRA2 00 XMPSS 00000000 XMPSL 00000000
+648  XMETE 00000000 00000000 00000000 TIME 00FFFFFF FFFFF000
+660  SRSAV 00000000 RV148 00000000 RV149 00000000 RV150 00000000 RV151 80000001 RV152 00000001
+678  GGRSV 00000000 00FE2700 0010EAE8 80010000 0078F8B0 007AD040 80000000 00FF5658
+698         00024A88 0010DFFC 007AD100 000277A8 00000000 000447B8 00042CD2
+6B8  DCR3 80000025 DCR4 00000025 DTSAV 00FFFFFF FFFFF000

                   STORAGE KEY IS 00 FOR STORAGE BEGINNING AT 00FED6C0
00FED6C0 00 00FFFFFF FFFFF000 00000000 00000000 00000000 00000000 00000000   *......0......*
00FED6E0 00 00000000 00000000 00000000 00000000 00000000 00000000 00000000   *.............*

SYMPTOM STRING: AB/S00C4 PIDS/5752TC221 RIDS/IEDGRC11 REGS/FE000MODULE IEAVTSDT   DATE 10/13/83   TIME 13.19.45   PAGE 0130

00FED700 TO NEXT LINE ADDRESS SAME AS ABOVE
00FED800 00 9004C3D4 00000000 00000011 FFFFFFEF 00000000 00000000 00000000 00000000   *..CM.........*
00FED820 00 00000000 00000000 00000000 00000000 00000000 00000000 00000000 00000000   *.............*
00FED840 TO NEXT LINE ADDRESS SAME AS ABOVE
00FEDAE0 00 00000000 00000000 00000000 00000000 00000000 00000000 00000000 00000000   *.............*

+B00  IOEP1 000273E8 IOEP2 000275A8 IOEP3 00027650 IOSRC 000291D2 IOEP4 000276A0 IOEP5 000275A8
+B18  IOEP6 000275A8 IOEP7 000275A8 IOEP8 000275A8 IOEP9 000275A8 IOEPA 000275A8 IOEPB 000275A8
+B30  IOEPC 000275A8 IOEPD 000275A8 IOEPE 000275A8 IOEPF 000275A8 IOSLH 000275A8 LSCH1 0002BB50
+B48  LSCH2 0002BB70 SVT 0002BE10 WTPSW 070E7000 00000000 WTR15 00010001 WTR0 00000000
+B60  WTR1 00000000 TWCPU 0000 TASID 0000 WTTCB 00023B50 STMP 4371B310
+B70  00000000 00000000 00000000 00000000 00000000 00000000 00000000 00000000
+B90  00000000 00000000 00000000 00000000 00000000 00000000 00000078 00000000
+BB0  00000000 00000000 00000000 00000000 00000000 00000000 00000000 00000000
+BD0  00000000 00000000 00000000 00000000 00000000 00000000 00000000 00000000
+BF0  00000000 00000000 00000000 00000000 00000000 00000000

+C00  STAK 00000CE0 00000CE0 00000020 00000CE0 00000D00 00000080 00FE2700
+C20  80FE2700 0000F503 00000104 00000030 007259D8 008D321A 00000000
+C40  008D31F0 008D2268 008D2268 008D321A 0090D298 0095AF28 0047D038
+C60  00725958 4047EB20 0047ED68 0047EB20 02000025 20000025 0047D038
+C80  80000005 80000006A 00010000 00000025 00000025 0080006A 00000007
+CA0  0080006A 00000006A 00000000 00000000 0080006A 00000000 00000006A
+CC0  00000000 00000000 00000000 00000000 00000000 00000000 00000000
+CE0  000374E4 00000000 00000000 00000000 00000000 000447B8 00000000
+D00  000B9426 00000008 8000000B 00F90F40 00F90F40 000447B8 00000000
+D20  000B9426 00000008 FF7ACD90 FFACD90 00F90F40 50000502 007AF324
+D40  00A8640 00000008 00000000 00088000 40036786 00020000 00000000
+D60  00DA999B 00000080 50000000 4DA8032 4DA8032 00088000 0097D408
+D80  000A8640 00000080 00100000 40100000 0097D1D0 0097D1D0 0097D408
+DA0  00080FC6 00000000 00000000 00FCD200 00FCD160 0005A48 0FF810C
+DC0  00000000 00000000 00000000 00000000 00000000 00000000 00000000
```

Figure 3.10 *continued*

```
                      00000000 00000000 00000000 00000000 00000000 00000000 00000000 00000000
+DE0                  00000000 00000000 00000000 00000000 00000000 00000000 00000000 00000000
+E00                  00000000 00000000 00000000 00000000 00000000 00000000 00000000 00000000
+E20                  00000000 00000000 00000000 00000000 00000000 00000000 00000000 00000000
+E40                  00000000 00000000 00000000 00000000 00000000 00000000 00000000 00000000
+E60                  00000000 00000000 00000000 00000000 00000000 00000000 00000000 00000000
+E80                  00000000 00000000 00000000 00000000 00000000 00000000 00000000 00000000
+EA0                  00000000 00000000 00000000 00000000 00000000 00000000 00000000 00000000
+EC0                  00000000 00000000 00000000 00000000 00000000 00000000 00000000 00000000
+EE0                  00000000 00000000 00000000 00000000 00000000 00000000 00000000 00000000

00FEDF00  00 00000000 00000000 00000000 00000000 00000000 00000000 00000000 00000000    *..............*
00FEDF20  TO NEXT LINE ADDRESS SAME AS ABOVE
00FEDFE0  00 00000000 00000000 00000000 00000000 00000000 00000000 00000000 00000000    *..............*

STORAGE KEY IS 00  FOR STORAGE BEGINNING AT 00FEDF00
```

HOME ASID 0025   PRIMARY ASID 0025   SECONDARY ASID 0025   CML ASID NOT HELD

SYMPTOM STRING: AB/S00C4 PIDS/5752TC221 RIDS/IEDGRC11 REGS/FE00MODULE IEAVTSDT   DATE 10/13/83   TIME 13.19.45   PAGE 0131

***** UNPREFIXED 0-4K STORAGE *****

```
PSA   FE9000
+0    RNPSW 040E0000  00023298  ROPSW 00000000 00000000  CVT   0024A88  RESV 00000000
+18   EOPSW 01002401  100DF49C  SOPSW 00000000 00000000  POPSW 0000005  800E11EE  CAW FFFFFFFF
+30   MOPSW 00000000  00000000  IOPSW 00000000 00000000  CSW   000E1AA8  0C000000
+4C   CVT2  0024A88   TIMER FFDEA4FF  TRACE 80FBEDC0      ENPSW 040E0000  001250D8
+60   SNPSW 040E0000  00025A20  PNPSW 000E0000 00026370  MNPSW 00020000  001E35BE
+78   INPSW 040E0000  000273B8  EPARM 00FEC000            SPAD  0000      EICOD 0000  RESV 00
+89   SVILC 00        SVCN 0000       RESV 00             PIILC 00        RV049 00    PICOD 00
+90   TEA   00000000  MCNUM 00        PERCD 00            RESV  00        PER 00000000
+9C   RESV  00000000  MTRCD 000000    MPL 00027760        CHNID 0000000
+AC   IOEL  00000000  LCL 00000000    RESV 0000  RESV 00  RESV  00        IOA 00000000
+BC   RESV  00000000  00000000 00000000  00000000 00000000  00000000 00000000
+E0                   MCIC 00000000
+F0   RESV  00000000  MEDC 00         RESV 00000000       FSA   00000000  RGNCD 00000000
+100        00000000  00000000        00000000            00000000        00000000
+120        00000000  00000000        00000000            00000000        00000000
+140        00000000  00000000        82000170            00000000        00000000
+160  FPSAV 00000000  00000000        00000000            000DBF68        00000000
+180  GRSAV 00000000  00000000        00000000            00000000        00000000
```

Figure 3.10 continued

```
+1A0          00000000 00000000 00000000 00000000 00000000 00000000 00000000 00000000
+1C0  CRSAV   00000000 00000000 00000000 00000000 00000000 00000000 00000000 00000000
+1E0          00000000 00000000 00000000 00000000
+200  PSA     D7E2C140        CPUPA 0002   CPULA 0042        PCCAV 00FF44A0  PCCAR 00FF74A0
+210  LCCAV   00FF3210  LCCAR 00FF6210  TNEW 00000000  TOLD 00000000  ANEW 00000000
+224  AOLD    00FF0000  SUP1 00         SUP2 00        SUP3 00        SUP4 00
+22C  GPREG   00000000         MPSW 00C0000   RSREG 00000000  RV103 00000000  EXPS1 00000000  00000000
+248  EXPS2   00000000  MCHEX 00000000  AD00026C
+260  IPCR    AD000264  IPCRM 00  IPCD AD00026C         IPCDM 00  IPCC3 00  RESV 0000
+270  IPCSA   00000000  HLHIS 00000000  RECUR 00000000  RESV 000000  DSSGO 00  SNSM2 00  RTM1S 00  SRSA 00000000
+280  DISPL   000277A8  ASML 00000000  SALCL 00000000  DSSSL 00000000  IOSSL 00000000  IOSCL 00000000
+294  IOSUL   000277B8  IOSLL 00000000  TPNCL 000277B0  TPDNL 00000000  TPACL 00000000
+2A8  OPTL    000277B8  CMSL 00000000  LOCAL 00000000  RLOCK 00000000
+2B8  MSORG   00000000  00000000 00000000 00000000 00000000 00000000  RESV 00000000 00000000 00000000
+2DC          00000000                        CMSLK 000277E0  LCPUA 00000042
+2F8  HLHI    00000000  LITA 00027800  SVPSW 00027800  CRO 00000000
+30C  MCHFL   00        SYMSK 00  ACTCD 000  MCHIC 00  WKRAP 00000000
+314  WKVAP   00000000  VSTAP 00  CPUSA 0002  STOR 0FFD7C00  DSSRS 00000000
+324  DSSR2   00000000  DSSR3 00000000  DSSWK 00000000  DSSTS 00000000  00000000  00000000
+340          00000000  DSSF1 00  DSSF2 FF  DSSF3 00  DSSF4 00
+348  DSSRP   00000000  DSSPP 00000000  RV040 00000000  RV041 00000000  RV042 00000000
+360  DSSPR   00000000  RV025 00000000  RETCD 47FFE000  CSTK 0000C00  NSTK 0000C00
+374  RESV    00FE6030  0000 RET 07FE  07FE  MSAV 00000000  PSTK 00FE6C30
+388  SSTK    00FE6030  SSAV 00FE6030  MSTK 00FE6720
+39C  PSAV    00000000  ESTK1 00FE7320  ESAV1 00000000  ESTK2 00FE7A10  ESAV2 00000000
+3B0  ESTK3   00FE7F20  ESAV3 00FE7F20  RSTK 00FE8430  RSAV 00FE8430  SRPSW 00000000
+3C8  RSPSW   00000000  00000000 00000000  START 07FE0000  STOP 07FE0000  TRACE 00  INTE 00
+3E8          00000000  SFACC 8007D000  LSFCC 581003F0  SVC13 0A0D  TRACE 00  CDAL 00000000
+3FC  RTMIR   AD00027B  PCPSW 00000000  SCPSW 00000000  ATCVT 00000000  WTCOD 00000000  SMPSW 070C0000
+414  CSID    0001      RV100 0001  RV071 0000
+428  GSAV    00000000  00000000 00000000 00000000 00000000 00000000 00000000 00000000
+448          00000000  CPUT 00000000  PCFUN 00000000  PCGRA 00000000  PCGRB 00000000
+468  PSWSV   00000000  PCGR9 00000000  CPUT 00000000  PCPS2 0000  PCPS3 0000
+480  PCGR8   00000000  PCPS4 00000000
+490  SCRG1   00000000  SCRG2 00000000  MODEW 000000  MODE 00
```

Figure 3.10 *continued*

4 Task Management

The key to effectiveness of MVS as a general purpose operating system is the generality with which tasks are managed within the system. One task may invoke another task and that task can invoke yet another task. Storage, scheduling, and resource control are managed on a dynamic basis.

4.1 TASK CONTROL

There can be several load modules associated with a task in MVS. These load modules represent levels of control for that task and are represented in the system by request blocks (RBs).

4.1.1 Request Blocks

When executing a program A, i.e.,

/ /STEP EXEC PGM = A

the initiator gives control to this program by an ATTACH macro. The load module containing the program to be given control is brought into virtual storage, if a usable copy is not available in virtual storage. The program manager who processes the ATTACH routine will create a TCB for this task. The load module brought in is a level of control for the task and is represented by an RB. (See figure 4.1.) Since this is the only load module for this task, there will be only one RB pointed to by the TCB. Program A is active, and the CPU is executing instructions in A, and it reaches a LINK macro for another program B. As far as the logic of Program A is concerned, the control of CPU is passing to another load module called B. The LINK macro issues an SVC instruction and requests the control program to find a copy of the load module B; it then passes control to the designated entry point. Now the RB structure has to be changed because of the new level of control by the load module B. This activity is conceptualized in figure 4.2. Figure 4.3 shows the request blocks chained to the task control block for the previous example. TCBRBP field in the TCB will always point to the current RB or the current level of control. Thus our TCB will point to the RB for load module B. RB_b will point to RB for A (RB_a). The last RB in the RB chain will always point back to the TCB.

Now let us say program B issues a LOAD macro for program C. The control program searches for load module C and, if found, loads the program into virtual storage. Control program returns in register 0 the virtual storage address of load module C. But control of CPU is not given

85

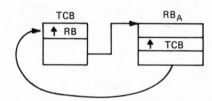

Figure 4.1 Request block chained to a task control block.

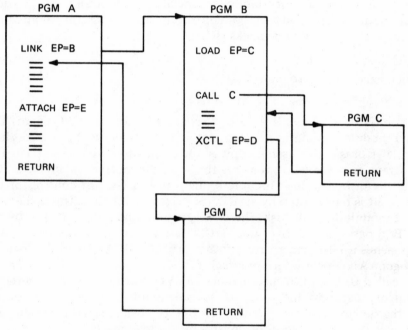

Figure 4.2 Example of task control.

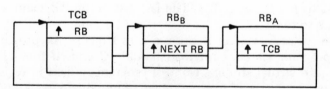

Figure 4.3 Request blocks chained to the TCB.

to C. Since there is no new level of control, LOAD does not create an RB. Even though there are three load modules in our address space, namely A, B, and C, only two RBs exist in our RB chain.

We can issue a CALL macro for C by specifying the virtual address returned from the previous LOAD macro. The net effect of a CALL macro is a branch and link instruction (BALR 14, 15). Register 15 should contain the entry point address of program C, and register 14 contains the return address back to program B. Even though load module C is active, it is under the level of control of load module B, namely RB_b. This is possible because CALL does not evoke the supervisor and hence the supervisor is unaware of the new level of control by load module C. (See figure 4.4.)

Control is returned from program C when the CPU executed the RETURN macro. This RETURN macro generates a branch instruction (BR 14). This branch instruction will give control of the CPU back to program B at the instruction after the CALL macro. This return will do nothing to the existing RB chain.

Now let us say we issued a XCTL macro specifying load module D. To a certain extent XCTL does similar functions as LINK does. It loads the load module D into virtual storage and control is given to D. XCTL indicates to the control program that the use of the load module containing the XCTL macro instruction, namely load module B, is completed. The control program removes the current level of control, namely $RB_{b/c}$, and adds the new level of control for load module D. TCB pointer for the current RB points to RB_d (figure 4.5).

When a RETURN is issued in program D, conceptually the control is given to load module A at the instruction after the LINK macro. Since we finished one level of control, the control program removes RB_d from the RB chain.

4.1.2 Multitasking

Suppose in A we issue an ATTACH macro with an entry point E; a subtask is created. This subtask is a new unit of work that competes with

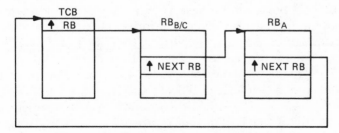

Figure 4.4 Request blocks after a CALL macro.

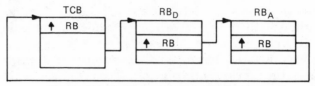

Figure 4.5 Task control after XCTL macro.

mother task A for the system resources such as the CPU, storage cycles, channels, etc. A new TCB is created for this unit of work and a level of control for load module E is chained to the TCB. Now we have two tasks in the same address space and levels of control for each of these tasks.

If more than one task is active in an address space, it is called *multi-tasking*. In an MP environment it is possible that two tasks from the same address space be active on both CPUs at the same time. Multitasking is depicted in figure 4.6.

4.1.3 Task Dispatching

Task dispatching priorities of the tasks in an address space do not affect the order of job selection for execution. This is done through the address-space–dispatching priority. Once an address space is selected for dispatching, the highest-priority ready task is given control of the CPU. In an MP system, task priorities cannot guarantee the order in which the task will execute, so that any kind of synchronization through task priority is not possible.

4.2 TCB QUEUES

There is always more than one TCB associated with an address space. So, there is a need to keep track of them, and this is done through two TCB queues. One is called the *TCB dispatching queue* or *TCB ready queue*. The other queue is called *subtask queue* or *family queue*.

4.2.1 TCB Dispatching Queue

The TCB dispatching queue can be located in the ASXB. The ASXBFTCB field in the ASXB points to the first TCB on the TCB dispatching queue and ASXBLTCB points to the last TCB on this queue. Pointers within the TCB point to the next highest priority TCB on this queue. This pointer field within the TCB is called "TCBTCB field." The TCBs are also chained backwards through a field called "TCBBACK." In order to find this TCB queue of an active address space, the dispatcher goes to the PSA and from a field called "PSAAOLD" (at offset X'224') gets the address of the ASCB. The ASCB then points to ASXB which contains the head and tail of the TCB queue. Figure 4.7 shows a TCB dispatching queue. All the TCBs in an address space, irrespective of their dispatching status, are chained together on this queue.

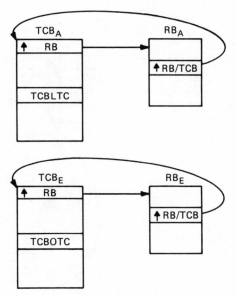

Figure 4.6 Example of multiple tasks in an address space.

4.2.2 Subtask Queue

The subtask queue can be considered a family queue. The relationship between TCBs or the hierarchy of TCBs are represented by this queue.

A submitted job gets control of the CPU by an INITIATOR task which is active in an address space. The initiator gets information about a job from the JCL submitted. In order to give control of the CPU to a job, INITIATOR issues an ATTACH macro specifying the program name that was given in the EXEC card of the JCL. As a result of this macro, a TCB is created. The TCB attached by the initiator is called a *Jobstep TCB* (JST). Since the initiator is the creator of JST, we can consider the initiator as a mother and the subtask as a daughter. These relational pointers are stored in the TCB in the following fields:

- TCBJST
  This field points to the jobstep TCB.

- TCBOTC
  This field points to the task that attached this task. In our analogy this field points to the mother TCB.

- TCBLTC
  This is a pointer to the TCB for a task last attached by this task. This field can be considered pointing to another (last) daughter TCB.

- TCBNTC
  According to definition, this field points to the TCB for the task previously attached by the task that attached this task.

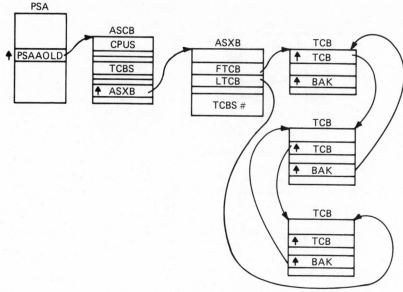

Figure 4.7 TCB dispatching queue.

Let us try to understand these four pointers in the TCB through examples. If initiator attaches a task S, the family queue pointers in the TCB for S will look like this:

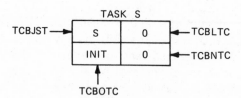

Since the initiator attached this task, the TCB for S is called a jobsteb TCB and is pointed by the field JSTCB. The mother of S is the initiator, so the TCBOTC field contains the initiator's TCB address. The other two fields TCBLTC and TCBNTC are 0 since S does not attach another subtask and the initiator did not attach a task previous to attaching the jobstep task, namely S.

Note: For a jobstep task, the TCBNTC field in the TCB will always be zero because this is the only task created by the initiator in an address space. After creating this jobstep task, the intiator goes into a wait state.

Now let us assume that S attached a subtask A. Now the family queue points in the TCBs of S and A will look like this:

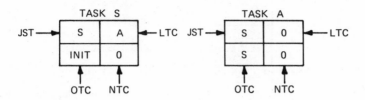

If S attaches another subtask B, the pointers will be:

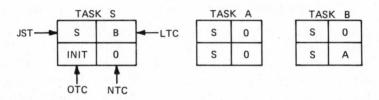

4.3 STATES OF A TASK

A task can be in any of three states: active, ready, or waiting. The state of a task can be determined through the use of control blocks, presented previously.

4.3.1 Active

An active task can be found in two ways. At offset X'114' in the TCB, there is a field called "TCBFBYT1." Within this field, there is a bit called "TCBACTIV bit." If this bit is a 1, it means this TCB is active on a CPU. In the formatted TCB, look at the field TCBFBYT1 and try to analyze this field using *OS/VS2 SYSTEM PROGRAMMING LIBRARY: Debugging Handbook, Volume 3.*

Another way to find the active task on a CPU is to go the the PSA for that CPU and get the TCB address from the PSATOLD field, as shown in figure 4.8. A task can be said to be *active* when the CPU fetches and executes instructions for that task.

4.3.2 Waiting

The waiting state of a task means the dispatcher cannot dispatch this task for the control of the CPU. A waiting state is caused by two reasons:

1. A WAIT macro is issued within the program for the completion of some events in the system.

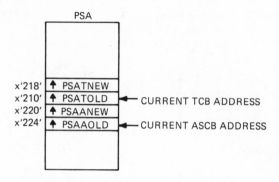

KEY: ↑ means "pointer to"

Figure 4.8 Determination of an active task through the PSA.

2. A non-dispatchability bit is set in the TCB (TCBFLG4/5) by some routines which do not want this task to be dispatched. If the non-dispatchability bit is set, it does not mean that the task is in a wait state, but rather it is said to be non-dispatchable. In either case, when the task is waiting for an event to occur or the non-dispatchability bit is on in the TCB, the dispatcher will not dispatch the task.

The way to find out whether a task is in a wait state due to a WAIT macro is to check the RB wait count field (RBWCF) of the current RB pointed by the TCB. If the RBWCF is greater than 0, then the task is waiting due to a WAIT macro issued in a program for that task.

4.3.3 Ready

A ready task can be defined as a task that is not active and not waiting. Ready tasks can be dispatched by the dispatcher when they become the highest priority TCB in the highest priority address space.

4.4 TASK DISPATCHING

The process of assigning a CPU to a task is referred to as *dispatching*. The assignment is performed by a module called the *dispatcher*.

4.4.1 Dispatcher

The dispatcher dispatches a task according to the status of the task namely, ready, active, or waiting. In order to select the highest-priority work in the system, the dispatcher first selects the highest-priority address space. This is done by searching through the ASCB dispatching chain. We have seen that there are fields in every ASCB indicating its priority and its position on the ASCB dispatching queue. Once the ASCB is selected, the dispatcher can now go to the ASXB and pick up the TCB dispatching queue for that address space. The first TCB in this queue is the highest-priority task in that address space. By looking at the TCB flags, the dispatcher knows whether this task is dispatchable or not. If dispatchable according to the flags in the TCB, the dispatcher finds the current level of control or the current RB, by checking the RBWCF field. If this field is 0, that means this task is not in a wait state and the dispatcher does the last check on the TCB. This last check is to find out whether this task is already active on the other CPU in an MP system. If not, the dispatcher dispatches this task. If any of the above tests fails, the dispatcher goes to the next-highest-priority TCB in the chain and repeats the tests for selection.

4.4.2 TCB Structure

The nature of the TCB structure in an address space is dependent upon the operational function performed by that address space. For example master scheduler's TCB structure is different from INITIATOR's or JES's TCB structure. This is due to the fact that each of these system components perform a different type of function and has different levels of control. TCB structure will also be different for tasks started from a console by a START command or a TSO task started due to a LOG-ON or a task started by a batch INITIATOR. The structure we are going to look at is the TCB structure for a batch job.

There will be at least five TCBs in an address space created for a batch job. If we look at the ASXB control block for a batch address space, we see the highest priority TCB address (figure 4.9). The first TCB in an address space is called the *region control task* (RCT) TCB. The functions of this control task are to

- perform initialization functions for an address space;

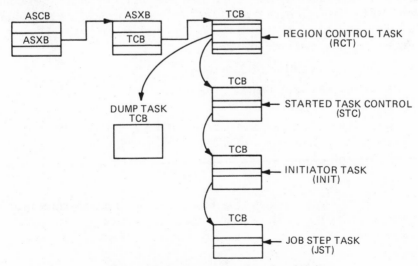

Figure 4.9 Task structure for a batch job.

- prepare an address space to be swapped out;
- prepare an address space for execution after it has been swapped out (pre-swap in).

The RCT's TCB is hard coded. When an address space is created by the memory create routine, ASCB, ASXB, and a TCB for RCT are initialized by the routine. This is similar to the situation where the first address space's (master scheduler's) ASCB is hard coded into the nucleus of the system. (Somewhere something has to get started!) In the region control task's TCB, pointers are set so that, when the dispatcher comes down to a newly created empty address space, it finds a ready TCB and dispatches it. Thus the region control task does the initialization functions for that address space. After that, RCT attaches a dump task.

The dump task is a permanent task in each address space. This task initiates the dumping of the content of an address space directly into a data set(s), namely SYS1.DUMP00 (01, etc.). Supervisor issues a SDUMP macro to do the dumping of an address space.

The next task the region control task will attach is the started task control (STC) task. The functions of the STC task are:

- determine which command was issued to create this address space (START, MOUNT or LOG-ON);
- according to the command, attach the appropriate task.

In the case of a START INIT command, an initiator task is attached. For a LOG-ON, a terminal monitor program (TMP) task is created. A mount command gives control to the mount processor. For all the other types of start, a started system task is created. Examples of other start commands can be start F, where F is a PROC (procedure) in SYS1 PROC library. When we start a task like this, this task does not use an initiator.

Functions of an initiator task are to

- oversee the allocation of data sets;
- open catalogs and libraries;
- attach jobstep task;
- notify the system resource manager (SRM) that a job has been selected. INITIATOR uses SYSEVENT macro to do this;
- termination of job.

4.4.3 TCB Priority

When we talk about priorities of tasks in a system, there are three priorities associated with it: address space, task, and subtask.

Address Space Priority

The control program assigns a dispatching priority for an address space at address space creation time and will change or alter this priority to achieve maximum load balance in the system. But if coded DPRTY= (V1, V2) in the EXEC statement in JCL, the system will calculate the dispatching priority for that address space as follows:

Address Space Dispatching Priority = (V1 x 16) + V2.

Once a priority is given to an address space, it can only be altered by the system. But if there is another jobstep with another DPRTY value in the EXEC statement, the address space priority will be changed to the new value specified at step execution time.

Task Priority

The second priority associated with a task is the task priority. There are two priorities associated with task priority: the dispatching priority and the limiting priority. Limiting priority is the highest priority a task can have. The control program assigns these priorities at step initiation time, and it is usually set to the highest value, namely 255.

Subtask Priority

The third type of priority associated with a task is the subtask priority. If a task attaches a subtask without specifying any priorities through LPMOD and DPMOD parameters of the ATTACH macro, dispatching and limiting priorities of the subtask will be the same as the mother task, or else priorities are calculated and given to the subtask TCB. Priorities of a subtask can also be changed through CHAP macro. The dispatching priority of a subtask can be raised above its own limit priority but not above the limit priority of the mother task. When the dispatching priority of a subtask is raised above its own limit priority, the subtasks's limit priority is raised automatically to the dispatching priority.

5 Service Management

The operational environment for MVS is sufficiently complex to warrant special tasks that execute on behalf of the system as a whole. These tasks are generally classed as service routines, which are covered in this chapter.

5.1 INTRODUCTION TO SERVICE REQUESTS

Since there are multiple virtual storages in MVS, there is a need for the supervisor to communicate with different address spaces. But from one address space it is not possible to communicate directly with the other address space. For each address space is only addressable through its own segment and page tables, and the STOR register should be loaded with the segment table origin address before address translation can proceed.

Another function that contributes to the need for special MVS facilities is the processing of interrupts. The control program usually disables the CPU and all other interrupts until the interrupt processing is completed. This occurs since serialization of system resources is needed. In the case of a multiprocessing system, both CPUs have to be serialized to accomplish this. In order to reduce the CPU time wasted due to serialization, a new unit of work called *service request* is introduced into the system. We will see later how this service request accomplishes CPU parallelism.

5.1.1 Subsystems

The MVS system requires functional support from tasks running in the system which are named *subsystems*. One subsystem defined at system generation time is the "MASTER subsystem." This master (MSTR) subsystem starts other subsystems such as the job entry subsystem (JES). JES is called the *primary subsystem*. It is the duty of the subsystem to read, execute, print, and punch jobs. It also performs additional functions such as console message processing, operator command processing, remote job entry, TSO interface processing, and SMF accounting.

A subsystem is implemented as a single system task under which the subsystem dispatches its own unit of work. Because the operating system is only aware of the system task for the subsystem and not of the units generated by the subsystem, it cannot dispatch the subsystem to more than one CPU at a time in a multiprocessing environment. Through the service request units, the system is made aware of the subsystem's units of work and can dispatch in parallel on both CPUs.

Thus, in an MVS system, a unit of work is divided into tasks represented by TCBs and service requests represented by service request blocks (SRBs) as suggested by figure 5.1.

5.1.2 Need for Service Requests

In order to create a task, the first thing to do is issue an ATTACH macro. The ATTACH macro expands into machine instructions, the last of which will be a supervisor call instruction (SVC 42). This instruction causes an SVC interrupt and goes through the processing of interrupt handling that we described previously. When an interrupt happens, some of the common functions to be performed are analyzing the interrupt, performing the required functions, and giving control of the CPU to the dispatcher.

We see the enormous amount of work done by the control program just to create a task. If the created task does very little work, it is not cost-justifiable to create one. In these circumstances, service requests are made to perform functions.

5.1.3 Properties of Service Requests

A service request is characterized as follows:

- Relatively short in duration.
- Performs special functions for IOS, SRM, ASM, interrupt handlers, etc.
- Represents a service request with a greatly simplified version of TCB called service request block.

As a TCB represents a task, an SRB control block (figure 5.2) represents a service request; and this notifies the dispatcher of the existence of a work unit.

Suppose we have an address space consisting of several tasks and one or more service requests.

The manner in which TCBs and SRBs are dispatched for execution requires special consideration.

Once a highest-priority address space has gained control of the CPU, all SRBs associated with that address space are dispatched before any TCBs. SRBs within an address space are said to be on the LOCAL SRB

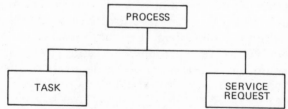

Figure 5.1 A unit of work is represented by a task or a service request.

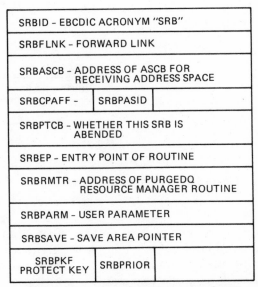

SRBID - EBCDIC ACRONYM "SRB"		
SRBFLNK - FORWARD LINK		
SRBASCB - ADDRESS OF ASCB FOR RECEIVING ADDRESS SPACE		
SRBCPAFF -	SRBPASID	
SRBPTCB - WHETHER THIS SRB IS ABENDED		
SRBEP - ENTRY POINT OF ROUTINE		
SRBRMTR - ADDRESS OF PURGEDQ RESOURCE MANAGER ROUTINE		
SRBPARM - USER PARAMETER		
SRBSAVE - SAVE AREA POINTER		
SRBPKF PROTECT KEY	SRBPRIOR	

Figure 5.2 A service request block (SRB).

queue. If the performance of a unit of work is so important that it has an effect on the performance of the whole system, then these units of work are classified as GLOBAL SRBs. Suppose this kind of "can't wait" type of work has to be dispatched in an address space, but the address space priority is low in the ASCB chain. The dispatcher cannot dispatch this unit of work. As we know, the dispatcher only selects the highest-priority address space and dispatches the LOCAL SRBs first. So, an important unit of work is defined as a GLOBAL SRB.

Some service requests are so important that they must be the next process dispatched. These SRBs are placed on a special dispatching queue called the "GLOBAL SRB queue." As soon as the dispatcher performs its next function, it gives CPU control to each SRB in the GLOBAL SRB queue before dispatching any address space.

Local SRBs are given a priority equal to that of the address space in which they will be dispatched but higher than that of any task within that address space. GLOBAL SRBs are given priority above that of any address space in the system, regardless of the actual address space in which they are dispatched.

So we have one GLOBAL SRB queue for the entire system and one LOCAL SRB queue for each address space, as depicted in figure 5.3.

5.2 UTILIZATION OF SERVICE REQUEST BLOCKS

This section gives examples of how SRBs are used.

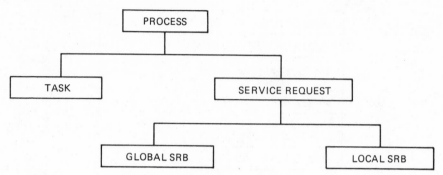

Figure 5.3 Delineation of service requests.

5.2.1 Local SRBs

An I/O interrupt, as we know, does not occur when an I/O request is made, but when an I/O operation is completed. By that time the address space requested by the I/O operation may not be active; most probably the address space will be in the wait state.

Let us see what happens when we issue a GET for data. Access method routines will make available the data if the data is in main storage. Or else the access method will request the I/O Supervisor to get the data from the external storage specified. When the channel and device become available, IOS brings the data into the main storage. But it may take some time for the IOS to do this function, due to other high-priority requests or unavailability of the data path. So the access method (AM) issues a WAIT macro to put the requesting task in a WAIT state until the data becomes available in main storage. Due to the WAIT processing, the RBWCF for the current RB associated with the task (TCB) is incremented by 1 and finally the dispatcher is given control.

The dispatcher selects the high-priority address space and checks for a ready unit of work. If none, it goes to the next ASCB in the chain, repeats the same process until it finds a ready unit of work and dispatches it. Let us assume that our address space has lost the CPU control due to the above processes.

When the channel finishes transferring our requested data from an external device to main storage, the system is notified through an I/O interrupt. But notice that the I/O interrupt happened in another address space than the one which requested the I/O operation. This necessitates a mechanism for address space communication so that the waiting address space can be informed of the availability of data in main storage, as in our case. This type of communication or service is provided through service requests.

In our case the I/O interrupt handler collects the necessary information about the interrupt and schedules an SRB. At this point the interrupt handler can start any I/O request waiting for a channel and accept any additional pending interrupts. The interrupt handler has done only a minimal amount of interrupt processing, and the rest of the processing of the interrupt is scheduled for a later time. This type of SRB scheduling has the following advantages:

- Faster re-use of channels by delaying complete processing of the interrupt.
- The ability to process the interrupt except where specific serialization is needed.
- The ability to complete the interrupt in any CPU, not just the one that took the interrupt. An SRB can be dispatched on any CPU.
- The ability to switch from the random address space where the interrupt was taken to the address space which requested I/O. This provides the I/O interrupt handler (IOH) routine the ability to address the user's control blocks (such as the event control block), which are necessary to complete the IOH processing.

5.2.2 Global SRB

Every so often the system resource manager (SRM) checks the available frame count of main storage. If this count is low, there is a possibility of system degradation due to excessive nonproductive paging, called *thrashing*. Before this situation arises, the SRM notifies the real storage manager (RSM) to 'steal' pages (take away page frames that are not used frequently) from address spaces.

There is a table in the nucleus called the *page frame table* (PFT). This table contains information about the real storage page frames. Some of the information stored is the ASID of the address space to which this frame is assigned, its corresponding virtual storage block number, forward and backward pointers for all the frames associated with that address space, and also a counter called unreferenced interval count (UIC). If a page frame is not used or referenced within a specified time period, UIC for that page frame is incremented by 1. A high UIC value means a relatively inactive page frame. Using this PFT, the SRM determines the page frames to be "stolen" from an address space and schedules a global SRB to run in that address space.

Let us think for a while why we need to schedule an SRB to do this? Even though the PFT is in the nucleus and is addressable to the SRM after the page stealing, the respective address space has to be notified about the change in its page frames. If you recall, page tables of an address space contain information about whether the page is in real storage frames or in external page storage slots. These page tables are located in the LSQA of the address space and are not addressable from another address space. This is the reason an SRB is needed to switch control from one address space to another.

5.3 PROCESSING OF SERVICE REQUESTS

In order to process a service request, the first thing that MVS does is create an SRB control block, which is 44 bytes long and resides in fixed addressable storage. MVS does a GETMAIN for 44 bytes from the appropriate subpool and initializes the 44 bytes into an SRB format. Then it places the SRB into the system LOCAL or GLOBAL SRB queues.

One of the properties of a service request is the relatively short duration of execution time. If we introduce SRB through an SVC interruption, it is like defeating the purpose of the existence of an SRB. So IBM came up with a SCHEDULE macro. This macro will not generate an SVC instruction but it will place an SRB on the appropriate queues. Later we will see how this macro does this. Some of the information needed within the SRB at the time of SCHEDULE is the following:

- SRBASCB—This field contains the address of the ASCB to which the asynchronous routine will be dispatched. This is the only way the dispatcher knows to which address space the routine should be dispatched.

- SRBPKF—High-order 4 bits in this field indicate the protect key the routine will assume.

- SRBEP—This field contains the entry point of the routine. SRB is like a TCB which executes load modules or routines. The routine to be executed under an SRB should be in the nucleus or in the linkpack area.

- SRBPARM—It contains the address of a parameter list to be passed to the service routine.

- SRBPRIOR—This field indicates the priority level associated with this SRB when scheduled. This field is not to distinguish an SRB as LOCAL or GLOBAL but for a unique situation where an SRB has to continue its process even though all other SRBs associated with an address space have stopped. One of the priority levels is for normal systems operation, while the other is for specialized functions necessary to perform quiesce functions for SRBs. This level of priority is known as the nonquiesceable level.

5.3.1 SCHEDULE Macro

The format of the SCHEDULE macro is simple:

$$\text{SCHEDULE SRB = SRB address, SCOPE} = \begin{Bmatrix} \text{GLOBAL} \\ \text{LOCAL} \end{Bmatrix}$$

General characteristics of the SCHEDULE macro are the following:

- Generates in line code, no SVC instructions.
- Picks up addresses for Q headers from CVT.

- Uses compare and swapp (CS) instructions to update the SRB chain.

When an SRB control block is built, there is nothing to identify whether this SRB is a local or a global one. That is why we need a SCOPE parameter in the SCHEDULE macro. According to this parameter, the SCHEDULE macro generates Q header labels in CVT as CVTLSMQ (for local) or CVTGSMQ (for global). The expansion of the SCHEDULE macro is given in figure 5.4. Figure 5.5 suggests what the SCHEDULE macro does. The first generated instruction loads the address of the SRB into Register 1. Next Register 15 is loaded with the CVT address. The next instruction finds the displacement between two labels, namely CVTLSMQ and CVTMAP within the CVT, and loads Register 15 with a full word. This full word is a pointer to the head of the local service manager queue. (We could have used the instruction L R15,CVTLSMQ and achieved the same result—providing addressability to the CVTLSMQ. But this will tie up one base register.)

The next load instruction will load the content of the full word pointed to by Register 15 into Register 0. This full word initially contains 0s; but once there is work in the system represented by SRBs, this full word will point to an SRB, which will point to the next SRB, and so on down the SRB chain.

The next instruction stores Register 0 into the new SRB's forward link field. What is the system doing here? The system is trying to add our new SRB into an appropriate SRB queue, depending on the scope specified in the SCHEDULE macro. How is the system doing this?

The system takes the contents of the queue head which points to an SRB in the chain and places this pointer into the forward link field of the new SRB. Now the system has introduced an SRB into the chain. Updating of the queue with the address of the new SRB is done through compare and swap (CS) instruction.

```
SCHEDULE  SRB = SRBADR, SCOPE = LOCAL

+ LA      R1,SRBADR
+ L       R15,16
+ L       R15,CVTLSMQ - CVTMAP(R15)
+ L       R0,0(R15)
+ ST      R0,SRBFLNK - SRBSECT(R1)
+ CS      R0,R1,0(R15)
+ BNE     * - 8
```

Figure 5.4 Expansion of the SCHEDULE macro.

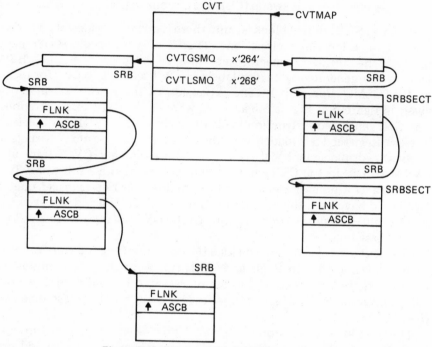

Figure 5.5 Result of the SCHEDULE macro.

Let us try to understand why we need a compare and swap instruction rather than a store instruction. Consider a hypothetical situation in which two CPUs in a multiprocessing environment try to add SRBs onto the same SRB chain at the same time. The process may be as follows:

1. Queue head is pointing to SRB3 initially.
2. CPU 0 tries to add SRB1 onto the Q.

    Content of head is placed in forward link field of SRB1. So SRB1 points to SRB3. But queue head still points to SRB3.

3. An interrupt happens on CPU 0, and CPU 0 is switched away from this process.
4. CPU 1 comes along and tries to add SRB2 on the same queue.

    Content of head is placed in the forward link field of SRB2. Now SRB2 points to SRB3.

    Places the address of SRB2 into the queue head, thus completing the addition of a new SRB onto the chain.

    Keeps executing instructions.

5. CPU 0 gains control of the interrupted processes of adding SRB1 onto the chain. It tries to finish the execution before updating the interrupt SRB1 forward link fields pointing to SRB3.

Next thing after the interrupt is to change the queue head field with the address of SRB1. So CPU 1 places the address of SRB1 into the queue head, overlaying the address of SRB2.

6. Now effectively the system has lost SRB2.

This illustrates the need for a serialization technique in a situation where two CPUs are accessing the same storage locations at the same time.

In a uniprocessor mode, a CPU is not aware of the other CPU and is not affected by the other. Normal sequence of fetching instructions—decoding, fetching operands, and execution—is done in a proper sequence. But in the case of a multiprocessing system (tightly coupled) where two CPUs share the same main storage, serialization of CPUs is needed and is accomplished by a hardware mechanism called *interlocking*. This hardware mechanism prevents simultaneous access of a storage area from more than one CPU.

Compare and swap (CS) instructions provide interlocking between CPUs. During a CS instruction, execution of a CPU operation is interlocked to eliminate the possibility of the word which is being examined from being altered by the other CPU.

OR IMMEDIATE (OI) instructions do not interlock storage and therefore provide no protection from the other CPU. OI instruction execution consists of fetching the first operand from main storage into the arithmetic and logic unit (ALU), ORes the bits specified in the second operand to the first, and storing the first operand back into main storage.

Between a fetch cycle and a store cycle, the other CPU could have changed the storage locations since there is no interlocking of CPUs.

Let us illustrate this through an example. Two CPUs want to update a common flag field through OI instruction. CPU 0 wants to OI with X'01', and CPU 1 with X'80'. After the execution we expect a X'81' in the flag field. But see what can happen:

CPU 0	FLAG	CPU 1
	x'00'	
1) Fetches flag and flag contains 00	x'00'	2) Fetches flag and also gets flag as 00
3) Does the OI instruction with x'01' and the result x'01' is still in ALU	x'00'	
4) Store cycle delayed due to some reason or another	x'00'	5) Does the OI instruction with x'80'
	x'80'	6) The result is stored back into flag
7) Stores the value in ALU into flag	x'01'	

Thus we get a wrong value in the flag. All instructions that fetch the storage modify the content in the ALU and stores back into the main storage can have the same problem. Add Packed (AP) is another instruction that has the same problem in an MP environment.

The solution is to use the CS instruction:

CS R0,R1,0(R15)

Action of this instruction is as follows: Contents of Register 0 is compared with a word in main storage addressed by 0(R15). Two conditions can happen and the condition code is set accordingly.

1. If condition code is 0, then it is an equal comparison. In this case the word in storage is replaced by the contents of Register 1.
2. If condition code is 1, then it is an unequal comparison. In this case Register 0 is loaded with the word in main storage.

Now let us see how this CS instruction can be used to solve our OI problem:

```
        CPU 0                      CPU 1

      LA  R6,x'01'              LA  R6,x'80'
      SLA R6,24                 SLA R6,24
       L  R5,WORD                L  R5,WORD
RETRY DS  OH             RETRY  DS  OH
      LR  R4,R5                 LR  R4,R5
      OR  R4,R6                 OR  R4,R6
      CS  R5,R4,WORD            CS  R5,R4,WORD
      BNE RETRY                 BNE RETRY
WORD  DS  F              WORD   DS  F
```

Let us see what I am doing here. I am loading Register 6 with the value to be ORed with; shifting the value to the left hand side of the register, assuming we want to OR to the first byte of the word; then loading into Register 5 the content of the word; next ORing the content of the word with the value in Register 6; and finally doing the compare and swapp instruction.

By using the CS instruction, we make sure the content of the word is the same as before we did the OR instruction. If the values in Register 5 and the storage location WORD are the same, it means the other CPU does not change the content of WORD. So using the Interlock hardware function, we store the ORed value in Register 4 into the mainstorage location WORD.

If the value in Register 5 and the main storage location WORD are not the same, then it means the other CPU has changed the location in main storage while we are doing the LR R4,R5 and OR R4,R6 instructions. The ORed value in Register 4 cannot be stored in this situation. So CS sets a condition code of 1 and loads Register 5 with the new value of WORD from main storage.

The next instruction BNE (branch not equal) will branch to RETRY, OR with the new value and do the CS instruction again. We will be in this loop until an equal comparison occurs and thus successfully stores the ORed value in storage location WORD.

Now back to the SCHEDULE macro. Adding SRBs into a chain by two CPUs can successfully be done by the CS instruction.

CS R0,R1,0(R15)

BNE * - 8

By doing the CS instruction, we make sure the other CPU has not changed the queue header and stores the new SRB value into the queue header. Otherwise, the new SRB address inserted by the other CPU is stored in Register 0 and a condition code of 1 is set. The next instruction, due to the unequal comparison, forces a branch to ST (STORE) instruction, which stores the new SRB address in our SRB forward link field and does the CS instruction again. On an equal comparison our SRB address stores into the queue header, and successfully chains our SRB into the queue.

5.3.2 Characteristics of Service Routines

- Registers on entry to routines.
  Register 0 contains the address of SRB. Register 1 contains the value in SRBPARM. Register 14 is the return address to the dispatcher. No clean up or status restoring is performed at this direct entry to dispatcher.
  Register 15 contains the entry point address of the service routine. Note that Register 13 does not point to a save area.

- Operating State
  Routines are entered in supervisor state, physically enabled for interrupts, unlocked, and the key as specified by SRBPKF.

- Service routine is responsible for freeing the SRB once the SRB is dispatched. Usually the first thing a service routine does is to free the main storage for the SRB. This is because after dispatching, the dispatcher will not keep track of SRBs.

- Service routine cannot issue SVC instructions. Then how does this routine FREEMAIN an SRB? The answer is that these routines use branch entries to system functions that do not use the current TCB pointer from PSA (PSATOLD). This restriction is due to the fact that when the CPU executes service requests, the TCB pointer in PSA, namely PSATOLD, will contain 0s.

- Order of scheduling may not equal the order of execution; no ordering can be assumed in these service routines.
- Routine should be in virtual storage.
- Routines run enabled and may be interrupted. But they will not be switched away until they voluntarily give up control of the CPU. Interrupts that occurred are processed; but any dispatchable unit of work made ready by the interrupt processing is ignored and control is returned directly to the service routine. This property is called NON PRE-EMPTIBLE. This is to reduce the overhead of status saving and restoring in between a short duration of the execution of the service request.
- Service routines can be suspended due to a page fault or an unconditional request for a suspend-type lock that is not available at that time. In these cases the routine cannot continue its execution, so a PRE-EMPT processing occurs.

The page fault handler or the lock manager—whoever made the PRE-EMPT decision—saves the full status in a special SRB called "SSRB." A GET CELL macro is issued to obtain the storage for SSRB and saves the status of the execution of the routine in there, such as general register, floating point registers, PSW, ASCB address, and the timer value.

When the page fault is resolved or lock becomes available, the service routine is made eligible for re-dispatching. This is done by scheduling the SSRB to the LOCAL SRB queue with a non-quiesceable level of priority.

When the dispatcher finds the special SRB by testing for SRBRMTR (Resource Manager Routine Pointer), it restores the status, releases SSRB via "free cell" and LPSW (Load PSW) from the SSRB to continue execution from the point of suspension.

5.3.3 Stop SRB Function

When an address space is to be swapped out or it is terminating, it is necessary to stop the SRBs. This stop SRB function prevents the dispatching of new SRBs but allows all service routines already dispatched to finish. We have seen that an SRB can be suspended due to a page fault or lock requirement. These suspended SRBs need to be re-dispatched when the resource becomes available so that even if the Stop SRB function is active, these are given control. Or else the address space of the suspended SRB will never get control of the CPU. Because the resume PSW for that address space is in the SSRB. This is the reason we have nonquiesceable priority level in the SRB.

6 Lock Management

In pre-MVS systems, resource serialization was accomplished by physical disablement of the CPU by setting bits in PSW for I/O and external interrupts and by an ENQ/DEQ technique, covered later. This technique can be used to serialize only one CPU and it will not be effective in an MP system where two CPUs share the same main storage and the devices. In MVS, serialization of resources is achieved through an operational technique known as *lock management*.

6.1 BACKGROUND

Some of the considerations made by the MVS architects to serialize functions in the control program that reference the same data or control blocks lead to the development of the lock manager. These considerations are

1. Serialization in a tightly-coupled MP system.
2. Serialization within an address space due to multitasking.
3. Serialization across address spaces for a common resource.

6.1.1 Lock Word

In order to implement the idea of locking or serialization through software, a designated storage location called *lock word* is set by a CPU before it uses any serially reusable resource. And the lock is released by the CPU after the execution involving the resource.

6.1.2 Utilization of a Lock Word

Before using a serially reusable resource, the CPU checks the lock word. If the lock word is 0, the processes that are using the CPU store its identification into the lock word and start using the resource. If the processor on the other CPU wants to look at this resource or to modify it, it cannot do it until the lock word becomes 0 again; the processor is said to be *spinning on the lock word.* The processor that holds the lock sets it to 0 just before enabling. This provides serialization of two CPUs in a way equivalent to disabling.

6.1.3 Interlocking

In an MP environment *two* CPUs may find that the lock word contains 0. And both will store their identification into the lock word and continue execution assuming that they own the serially reusable resource exclusively. In order to prevent this, a hardware feature called interlocking is implemented. The compare and swapp (CS) instruction uses inter-locking and can be used to store the CPU ID into the lock word.

6.2 PHILOSOPHY OF LOCK MANAGEMENT

Even though the locking technique provides serialization, it creates a system bottleneck. Since a large portion of the control program deals with manipulating system control blocks, a large percentage of the CPU power will be wasted if one CPU is executing while holding the lock and the other is spinning on the lock waiting to gain control of it and hence of the serially reusable resource. One solution to the above problem is to assign a lock for each resource item requiring serialization so that the probability of two CPUs contending for the same resource at the same time will be very, very small. MVS is a very large and complex operating system requiring hundreds of serially reusable resources. So the maintenance of such a large number of locks (one for each resource) will result in a huge CPU overhead. A compromise solution was to analyze the MVS system for components having a minimum of interaction be-tween them and assign a lock for each of them. A lock assigned to a component governs all serially reusable resource associated with that component. This will provide a significant reduction in wasted CPU time compared to a single lock approach or too many lock assignments as in the latter case.

6.2.1 Local Supervisor Functions

The first logical breakdown of the MVS system is by local and global supervisor functions. Local supervisor functions can be defined as those functions associated with a particular user or an address space. Examples of these functions are GETMAIN for a user subpool or ATTACH of a sub-task, etc. Queues associated with a particular user are placed in the local system queue area (LSQA) and scheduler work area (SWA) in the user's private area. All the other control block queues that are system-wide are placed in the common area of the address space.

The local supervisor can run in parallel with itself in different address spaces without any serialization. But it must serialize with other execu-tions in the same address space due to multitasking or SRBs running with TCBs in an address space.

6.2.2 Global Supervisor Functions

Global supervisor functions are those functions in the MVS control pro-gram that are logically associated with more than one user or address space. Examples of these types of functions are GETMAIN for the system queue area or a system-wide ENQ, etc.

Global supervisor functions must serialize across address spaces. This is because common area of the system is addressable by any segment and page tables so that there should be some sort of serialization for common area when accessed from different address spaces.

In the case of the local supervisor, most of the user-related control blocks are in LSWA or in SWA. These areas are only addressable to functions running in an address space with its segment and page tables, so that serialization is needed only for executions of tasks or SRBs running parallel in the same address space.

6.3 CLASSES OF LOCKS

Locks are divided into two classes: Local Locks and Global Locks.

6.3.1 Local Locks

A local lock provides serialization within an address space. Only one lock exists for each address space and is used by the local supervisor to serialize with other local supervisor functions in the same address space.

Local supervisor functions acquire the local lock before they use resources associated with the local supervisor. But these functions do not physically disable the CPU by setting bits in the PSW. Local supervisor functions are said to be logically disabled by the local lock but in a hardware-enabled state.

A number of supervisor functions that formerly ran disabled now run enabled with the local lock. Type 1 SVC routines in MVT run physically disabled, which means no interrupts are allowed until the execution of the routine finishes. According to the type of interrupt, they may be pending or get lost when interrupts happen during CPU disablement. In MVS Type 1 SVCs like GETMAIN and WAITS are run logically disabled but physically enabled. In other words Type 1 SVCs request the local lock and get the lock before it starts executing the Type 1 SVC routine but in a physically enabled state.

Since interrupts are allowed while holding a local lock, a special save area is provided into which status could be saved if an interrupt occurred. This save area is called the interrupt handler save area (IHSA) and is in subpool 255 (LSQA). Let us say we don't have the local lock; and, in taking an interrupt, our registers will be saved some place by the interrupt. But if we hold the local lock and get interrupted, we cannot save the registers in the same place as in the case of a task that doesn't hold the local lock. The reason is that some of the register slots where registers are saved cannot be overlayed by the new values in registers. When we talk about interrupt handling, we will see what registers cannot be overlayed and why IHSA is pointed by a pointer in ASXB called "ASXBIHSA."

When the local lock is held in an address space, the dispatcher does not dispatch any other TCB in the address space. Let us say a task requesting a local lock gets the local lock; but the task is interrupted and the CPU control is switched away from it. After the interrupt processing, the dispatcher gets control of the CPU and tries to dispatch the highest-priority task in the highest-priority address space. But if a task in an address space holds the local lock, the dispatcher will not dispatch any tasks in the same address space, regardless of how high the priority of the task may be.

If another CPU is already executing work in the same address space when the local lock is obtained, the other CPU will continue execution of the task until it is interrupted and the CPU is switched away from it. When the dispatcher gets control, it will not dispatch any task in this address space since the local lock is held by a task in the address space.

Local locks are classified depending upon how a CPU responds when an unconditional request is made for a lock that is held by the other CPU. The two types are the spin lock and the suspend lock.

Spin Lock

The requesting CPU enters a loop in the Compare and Swap (CS) instruction until the lock is cleared by the other CPU.

Suspend Lock

The requester is queued and the requesting CPU passes on to work in another address space. When the lock is released, the highest-priority requester gets control of the CPU.

Combining the class and types of locks, a local lock is said to be an *enabled suspend lock*. *Enabled* means the holder to the lock is executing physically enabled for interrupts. And *suspend* means the request for the lock is queued if the lock is not available and the requesting CPU goes to do other work.

There can be only one local lock in an address space since the local supervisor is defined as a process which owns the local lock and resides in the address space. Local supervisor functions could be subdivided and could have assigned different locks. But it is not necessary because the local lock holder runs enabled and serializes functions within an address space; any other request for the local lock is suspended and the request is queued for later processing (this will not tie up the CPU). The local supervisor functions can continue executing in other address spaces because the local control blocks are within each private area of the address spaces and cannot be addressable from another address space.

6.3.2 Global Locks

Global supervisor functions that have a minimum of interaction between them can be divided into four classes:

- The dispatcher
- The storage manager

- The I/O supervisor
- Miscellaneous functions

Each of these functions is given one lock. Thus, the dispatcher lock is used to serialize the functions to change queues and control blocks used for dispatching. The storage management lock is used by the virtual, real, and auxiliary storage managers to serialize their resources. The I/O control blocks and queues are referenced by the I/O supervisor while holding the I/O supervisor lock. The rest of the functions within the global supervisor are performed by holding the miscellaneous lock.

Most of these global supervisor locks are disabled spin locks, which means the holder of the lock executes physically disabled and the other CPU requesting the lock spins in a disabled state until the lock is available. It is interesting to note what will happen if the CPU holding the global lock goes down and the other CPU is spinning in a disabled state for that global lock. While a CPU spins in a tight loop, every so often it is enabled for external interrupts.

The I/O supervisor and storage management functions cover a wide area and concern the "most wanted" resources. These functions are subdivided and given a lock each. This reduces the lock contention in these areas. The storage manager is divided into auxiliary storage manager (ASM) and space allocation functions. IOS is divided and given locks such as IOSYNCH, IOSCAT, IOSUCB, and IOSLCH. Three additional locks are assigned for teleprocessing functions and one for the System Resource Manager.

No page faults are allowed while the system is in a disabled state while holding the spin lock, which in turn affects the response of the system. Thus, an "enabled" global lock is defined and used to serialize across address spaces but in an enabled state. This also allowed certain functions to take page fault while holding a global lock. This lock is called the cross memory service (CMS) lock. The CMS lock is a global suspend lock. The set of MVS locks is summarized in Figure 6.1.

6.4 SUMMARY OF MVS LOCKS

The names, definitions, and hierarchy of MVS locks are listed as follows:

- DISP. Dispatcher lock is a disabled spin lock used to serialize functions associated with dispatcher queue. This lock is also used for other functions of supervisor that cannot be done under CMS lock. There is only one dispatcher lock in the system. This lock is located in a table called "IEAVESLA" at offset 0. All lock words for single system locks are located in this table. The dispatcher lock holds the highest position in the hierarchy of locks.
- ASM. Auxiliary storage manager lock serializes use of the global ASM

Global spin locks	Disabled	No page faults		SPIN if lock is unavailable
CMS suspend lock Local suspend lock	Enabled or disabled	Can take page faults if enabled	Cannot issue SVCs	SUSPEND if lock is unavailable

Figure 6.1 Summarization of the different types of locks.

control blocks. This is a global spin type lock. There is one ASM lock per address space. The total number of ASM locks are the total number of address spaces plus 4. ASM lock is located in the ASM Vector Table (ASMVT) at offset X'3C'. ASMVT is located in the system queue area. ASM lock is pointed by PSA+X'284'(PSAASML).

- SALLOC. This is the space allocation lock for real storage manager (RSM) and virtual storage manager (VSM). This global spin lock is used to serialize RSM and VSM functions. There is only one lock in the whole system, located in IEAVESLA+4. It is the third in the hierarchy of locks.

- IOSYNCH. IOS synchronization lock is a disabled global spin lock used to serialize the IOS purge function and other IOS global functions. Location of this lock is in IOCOM area at offset X'38'. This lock is pointed by an address in PSA at location X'28C'.

- IOSCAT. IOS channel availability table lock is used to serialize the selection of a channel by the I/O supervisor. There is one IOSCAT lock per CPU and this lock(s) is located in the IOCOM+X'30' and is pointed by PSAIOSCL (PSA+X'290').

- IOSUCB. This is a set of locks for IOS unit control blocks (IOSUCB). This lock is used to serialize the changing status of a unit control block (UCB). There is one lock for each UCB in the system. IOSUCB is a global spin type lock. Since there are multiple locks in the same level of lock hierarchy, these locks are categorized as class locks. These IOSUCB locks are located with the UCBs at offset '−8'. UCBs are located in the nucleus, and they describe the characteristics of devices attached to the system. When a CPU uses this lock, the lock address is placed in PSA called "PSAIOSUL" (PSA+X'294').

- IOSLCH. IOS logical channel queue lock serializes and updates to the IOS logical channel queues. There is one IOSLCH lock for each logical channel in the system. As in the case of IOSUCB locks, these IOSLCH locks are global spin types. These locks are located in the logical channel queue table at offset '+8'.

All devices in the system that are accessible on a common set of paths are members of a logical channel group. The LCH provides queueing control for the enqueueing and dequeueing of I/O request to devices that are members of a logical channel group. When a CPU actually holds any one of this class type lock, the lock address can be found in a field called PSAIOSLL (PSA+X'298') within the PSA of the CPU.

- TPNCB. This consists of a set of locks for VTAM node control blocks. These locks are global spin type locks and are used when scheduling work via node control blocks. PSATPNCL field in PSA (PSA+X'29C') points to one of this class locks when the CPU uses this type of lock.

- TPDNCB. These are locks for VTAM destination node control blocks. These node control blocks are used to schedule work in VTAM. There is one disabled global spin lock for each destination node control block. PSATPDNL field in PSA points to lock.

- TPACBDEB. This is a set of locks for VTAM access method control block DEBs and is used by VTAM to serialize feedback processing. There is one disabled spin lock per ASCBDEB. PSATPACL field in PSA (PSA+X'2A4') points to this type of lock held by the CPU.

- SRM. The system resource manager lock serializes the use of the SRM control blocks and associated data. This lock is a disabled spin lock and as all other single system locks it is located in a table called "IEAVESLA."

- CMS. The cross memory service lock serializes on more than one address space where this serialization is not provided by one or more of the other global locks. This is the only global lock that enables the CPU for interrupts. The CMS lock is a global suspend lock which provides global serialization when enablement is required. There is only one CMS lock in the system and it is located in IEAVESLA at offset X'C'.

- LOCAL. This local lock serializes the functions of local supervisor within an address space. There is one local enabled suspend lock per address space. These locks are located in each address space of the ASCBs at offset X'C'.

We have seen all the locks in the MVS system. Let us summarize what the objectives of locks are and the effect of locking. Figure 6.2 summarizes the MVS locks.

6.4.1 Object of Locking

1. To provide a means of serializing a resource on a CPU (or address space basis).
2. To increase control program parallelism (both disabled and enabled code).

6.4.2 Effect of Locking

1. Allows multilevels of serialization
2. Increased enabled time
3. Increased control program parallelism

There are certain rules to obtain a lock. For example, certain locks have to be held before requesting certain types of locks or locks have to be requested in a specific order. We learn about these rules in the next section. Before we go on to the next section, let us see how the CPU knows which locks it holds.

6.4.3 Lock Held Indicator

Locks held by a CPU are indicated by a bit string in its prefixed storage area. This bit map is called "PSAHLHI" (PSA Highest Lock Held Indicator) and is at offset X'2F8' into the PSA. In an MP environment there are 2 bit-maps, one for each CPU in the complex. In order to implement the locking rules, each CPU should know about the locks it holds. Another name for PSAHLHI is the *PSA current lock held string* or "PSACLHS." This string is 4 bytes long but the first 2 bytes are not used. The next 2 bytes or 16 bits are used as the bit string. Since we have only 13 different types of locks, the first 3 bits are ignored or contain 0s.

The rest of the 13 bits represent a particular lock. The bits are in the same order as the lock's hierarchy so that the high-order bit represents the DISP lock and the low-order bit represents the local lock. When a bit is on, it means the CPU holds that lock. In our lock chart the hierarchy column represents the bit pattern for each of these locks.

6.4.4 How to Find the Lockword

All single system locks such as DISP, SALLOC, SRM, and CMS are located in the nucleus at a label called "IEAVESLA."

A field in PSA called PSA lock interface table address (PSALITA) points to the lock interface table. The first word in this table points to the IEAVESLA.

Lock Name	Hierarchy	Class	Type	Number of Locks	Location of Locks	Add. of Lock When Held by a CPU	Description of Lock
DISP	1000	Global	Spin	1	IEAVESLA +0		Serializes all functions associated with dispatching
ASM	0800	Global	Spin	1 per add. space	ASVMT +x'3C'	PSA +x'284'	Serializes storage resources & global ASM control blocks
SALLOC	0400	Global	Spin	1	IEAVESLA +x'4'		RSM and VSM space allocation lock
IOSYNCH	0200	Global	Spin	1	IOCOM +x'38'	PSA +x'28C'	Serializes IOS global functions
IOSCAT	0100	Global	Spin	1 per CPU	IOCOM +x'30'	PSA +x'290'	Serializes access and updates of channel availability table
IOSUCB	0080	Global	Spin	1 per UCB	UCB -x'8'	PSA +x'294'	Serializes access and updates of UCB. Class lock.
IOSLCH	0040	Global	Spin	1 per LCH	LCH +x'8'	PSA +x'298'	Serializes the use of logical channel queue. Class lock.
SRM	0004	Global	Spin	1	IEAVESLA +x'8'		Serializes SRM control blocks and queues
CMS	0002	Global	Suspend	1	IEAVESLA +x'C'		Serializes cross memory services and functions
LOCAL	0001	Global	Suspend	1 per add. space	ASCB +x'C'		Serializes local supervisor functions within an address space

Figure 6.2 Locks Chart

The lock interface Figure 6.3 is used by the lock manager to indicate the type of setlock macro that was issued. For example, if a conditional request for a DISP lock is issued, the first entry in the Lock Interface Table (LIT) is used and the corresponding entry point (EP) into the lock manager routine is used. The index portion of LIT is used to ORs the bits into the PSA lock held string to show the new ownership of the lock. (Note the complement bit pattern for the release entries.)

A bit being on in PSACLHS indicates that a CPU holds a local lock but does not identify which local lock. There is one local lock for each address space, and there are lockwords for multiple class locks. Addresses of these locks are placed in the PSA for each CPU, and this table is called the CPU lock held table (PSACLHT X'280'). The requester of class locks provides a lockword, and the locking manager places the address of the lock in a corresponding slot in PSACLHT. If a bit corresponding to a class lock is on in PSACLHS, then there should be a class lock address entry in PSACLHT for that CPU.

6.4.5 Locking Hierarchy

Let us analyze why we need hierarchy rules for locking. Assume we are in a tightly coupled MP system and two CPUs are executing instructions simultaneously. The following events take place:

CPU 0	CPU 1
Events	
1. CPU 0 requests ASM lock and gets it	
2.	CPU 1 requests SRM lock and it gets SRM lock
3. CPU 0 holding the ASM lock requests SRM lock	
Note: Since CPU 1 has the SRM lock and SRM lock is a spin type global lock, CPU 0 spins till CPU 1 releases the SRM lock	
4.	CPU 1 executing instructions holding the SRM lock, requests the ASM lock
	Note: ASM lock is also a global spin type lock and since CPU 0 has it, CPU 1 starts spinning waiting for CPU 0 to release the ASM lock
5. Now both CPUs are spinning waiting for the other CPU to release a required lock. This situation is called a 'Dead Lock'.	

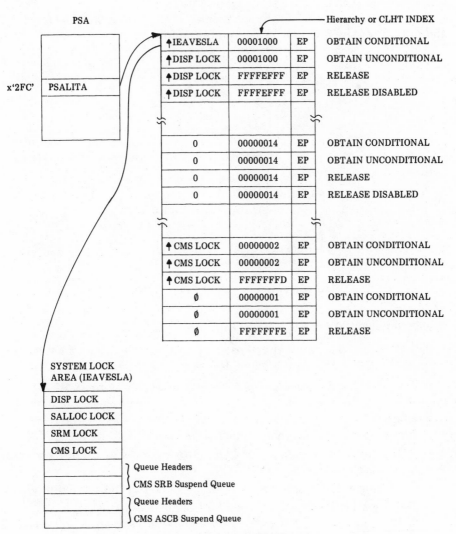

Figure 6.3 Lock Interfaces

This can happen only for an unconditional request for a LOCK. If the request were conditional, the locking manager will set a condition code and return control back to the requester, so that the requester can do some other processing until the lock becomes available.

The way to request a LOCK is through a SETLOCK macro. The format and options of the SETLOCK macro are the following:

SETLOCK OBTAIN

$$
TYPE = \begin{bmatrix} DISP \\ SALLOC \\ LOCAL, \end{bmatrix}
$$

[ADDR = (11)] ,

$$
MODE = \begin{bmatrix} COND \\ UNCOND \\ UNCOND,DISABLED \end{bmatrix}
$$

$$
\begin{bmatrix} REGS = \begin{matrix} SAVE , \\ USE \end{matrix} \end{bmatrix}
$$

RELATED = (info)

Special notes on SETLOCK MACRO:

- This macro does not expand to a SVC instruction; rather, a BRANCH AND LINK instruction is generated at the end of expansion.
- To use SETLOCK macro, the requester must be in supervision state with a protect key.
- RELATED is a required operand and is used to specify the relating functions or services that are performed while holding the LOCK.
- ADDR must be supplied for locks whose addresses are not known by the lock manager.
- Obtaining a global spin lock places the requester in disabled mode.
- Registers 11 through 1 are used by the macro expansion.
  SAVE - Registers 11-14 are saved in a 5-word save area pointed to by register 13.
  USE - Registers 11-13 are saved in registers 15, 0, 1.
  Register 14 will be used by the macro.
  None - Registers 11-14 are destroyed.
- DISABLED specifies that the caller is already disabled.
- COND specifies that the lock is to be obtained conditionally. If the lock is already held by the other CPU, the control of the CPU is

returned to the caller, indicating that the lock is not available. Register 15 contains the following condition codes:

Hex Code

00	the lock is obtained for the caller
04	the lock is already held by the caller
08	the obtain is unsuccessful

- UNCOND specifies that the lock is to be obtained unconditionally. If the lock is held by the other CPU, the requesting CPU will either spin on the lock until it is released or suspend the SETLOCK caller until the lock is released, depending on the type of lock requested. The way to release a lock is through the same SETLOC macro, but using the release option.

SETLOCK RELEASE

$$TYPE = \begin{Bmatrix} DISP \\ \cdot \\ \cdot \\ LOCAL \\ ALL \end{Bmatrix}$$

[ADDR =(11)],

[DISABLED],

[REGS= $\begin{Bmatrix} SAVE \\ USE \end{Bmatrix}$,]

RELATED=(INFO)

- Can use type operand to release all locks, all spin locks.
- Can indicate lock to be released in a register.
- Registers 11 through 1 are used by macro expansion.
- Disabled requests that control be returned to caller in disabled mode.
- ADDR must be supplied for locks where address is not known by lock manager.

In order to avoid the deadlock situation that we described previously, the first locking rule can be defined as follows:

1. The requester of a lock may only unconditionally request a lock higher in the hierarchical structure than the lock currently held by this CPU. In order to implement this rule we have a bit string specifying the highest lock held in the CPU. In the previous example, we violated this rule and hence got into a deadlock. CPU0

requested the SRM lock, which is lower than the ASM lock held by CPU0. It is not necessary to obtain all locks in the hierarchy up to the highest lock needed.

2. For global class locks, the requestor may only request locks of the type different from locks already held by the CPU. For example a requester may not request IOSUCB lock if he already holds a different IOSUCB lock.

3. When the CMS lock is being requested, the local lock must be held.

Two CPUs can hold two different locks of the same multiple class lock set. To find out if this is the case, let us see what happens if we request a CMS lock without holding the local lock.

Two tasks, Task A and Task B, from the same address space are executing on both CPUs. This situation is very common in a multitask programming environment. Let us consider the following events:

Events	Task A	Task B
1	Task A requests CMS lock and gets the CMS lock	
2	Task A is interrupted	
3		Task B requests local lock and gets it
4		Task B requests CMS lock
5	The whole address space is 'dead'	

Event #2 is possible because the CMS lock is a global enabled suspend lock.

When Task B requests the CMS lock, it cannot get the lock because Task A has the CMS lock. Since the CMS lock is a suspend type lock, the locking manager gives control of the CPU to the dispatcher so that it can dispatch work to other address spaces.

We have seen in previous chapters that the dispatcher will not dispatch a task in an address space if another task in the same address space holds the local lock. In our example, Task B holds the local lock and hence the dispatcher will not dispatch Task A. If the dispatcher will not dispatch Task A, it will never be able to release the CMS lock; and Task B, which is waiting for that lock, will also never get control. In effect, the address space of Task A and B will never be dispatched and this address space is said to be dead.

Let us summarize the lock hierarchy rules.

6.4.6 *Hierarchy Rules*

• Unconditional obtain must be for a lock higher than any currently owned.

- Conditional obtain can be for any lock regardless of hierarchy—except the CMS lock.
- CMS lock holder must own the local lock.
- Disabled routine must not unconditionally request the local or CMS lock.
- Only one lock can be held at any level by a requester.

6.4.7 Contents of Lockwords

Locks are represented by lockwords, and the lockwords define the availability and status of locks. Each lock or lockword is a 4-byte field. If the lockword is 0, it means the lock is available (or the lock is not owned) or else the lock is not available and the content of the lockword differs according to the type of lock.

6.4.8 Global Spin Lock

For the global spin lock, lockwords can have the following values:

1. x'00000000' – lock is available.
2. x'00000040' – in previous chapters we saw the logical address of a CPU. In an MP environment we have two CPUs and the logical addresses are 40 and 41. We mentioned that due to certain circumstances, we cannot use the physical address of CPU0 as binary 0s so that a logical address of 40 is assigned. If we used the physical address of CPU0 in a global spin lock it means the lock is available. This is one of the reasons why we need a logical address for CPUs. A hex value 40 in the lockword means the lock is held by CPU0.
3. x'00000041' – lock is held by CPU1.

6.4.9 Global Suspend Lock

There is only one lock under this type and it is the CMS lock.

1. x'00000000' – means CMS lock is available.
2. x'00xxxxxx' – where xxxxxx is the address of an ASCB, and that address space owns the CMS lock.

6.4.10 Local Suspend Lock

For the local lock the lockword can have the following values:

1. x'00000000' – lock is available.
2. x'00000040' – CPU0 owns the lock.
3. x'00000041' – CPU1 owns the lock.
4. x'7FFFFFFF' – a task or a SRB is suspended while holding the local lock due to (a) an unconditional request for the CMS lock while it is unavailable and (b) a page fault happened. At the time

of suspension, the CPU ID in the lockword is changed to a suspend ID (7FFFFFFF).

5. x'FFFFFFFF' – this value is called the interrupt ID and indicates to the dispatcher that a task or an SRB that was interrupted or suspended is now dispatchable due to the following reasons:

    1. A page fault for the locally locked task has been resolved. The last function performed in resolving a page fault is changing the suspend ID to an interrupt ID.

    2. The CMS lock is available now.

    3. Dispatcher dispatched a higher priority address space over this locked task.

6.4.11 How the Lock Manager Works

To obtain a lock, the requester issues a SETLOCK macro. The SETLOCK macro does not expand into an SVC instruction but into a BALR instruction. Depending on the type of lock and the type of request, the corresponding lock manager entry point is picked up from the lock interface table and is branched into to service the request.

1. The first thing the locking manager does is to save the registers at entry to the lock manager. The registers are saved in the PSA, and this area is called the *setlock register save area* (PSALKSA x'2B8').*

2. Next, the hierarchy check is performed to determine if there has been any violation to the hierarchy rule. In order to determine this, the lock manager compares the bit map generated by the SETLOCK macro to the current lock held string in the PSA. If the check fails, the requester is abended with a system abend.

3. If there is no violation of the hierarchy rule, the lock manager tries to get the lock. The lock manager examines the lockword to determine the availability of the lock through a compare and swapp instruction.

Note: the Setlock does not have to use a base register to get addressibility to PSA. All it does is to specify 0 as the base register.

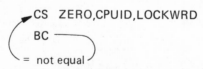

One register equated to 0 is loaded with 0s. The register equated to CPUID contains the CPU ID of the requester and the third operand reference, the lockword.

After the Compare and Swap instruction two situations arise:

1. *The lock manager obtains the lock for the requester.*

   This is the case where the comparison of register 0 is equal to the LOCKWRD content and the CPU ID is stored into the lockword (LOCKWRD).

   Turn on the appropriate bit in PSACLHS (PSA Current Lock Held String) by "oring" the value in the lock interface table.

   Sets up the address of the lockword in PSACLHT (PSA CPU Lock Held Table).

   Returns to the requester.

2. *The lock manager does not obtain the lock.*

   If the request for a lock was conditional, an appropriate condition code is set and the control is returned to the requester.

   If an unconditional request for a global spin lock cannot be satisfied, the CPU will spin on the CS instruction, continually testing for the availability of the lock.

   This disabled CPU loop is in IEAVELK. While in loop register 11, it contains the address of the requested global spin lock. Register 14 contains the address of the requester. (Figure 6.4)

In the case where a CPU holding the global spin lock fails while the other CPU is in a disabled spin loop for that lock, an interlock situation arises. To prevent this within the disabled spin loop, and EMS (emergency signal interrupt)/MFA (malfunction alert interrupt) window is provided.

Interrupts generated by the failing CPU, either by hardware (MFA) interrupt or by software (EMS) interrupt, are recognized through the EMS/MFA window. The CPU breaks away from the disabled spin loop and control is passed to alternate CPU recovery (ACR) routine. ACR now can recover the failing CPUs work and, using its PSACLHS, avoid interlock situations while dispatching work on the other CPU.

Unconditional request for a suspend lock. Type of processing for a suspend lock depends on the class of lock, namely CMS (GLOBAL suspend lock) or LOCAL Suspend lock and also will depend on the type of unit or work, namely a task (TCB) or a service request (SRB).

1. *Task asks for the local lock and cannot get it.*
   TCB and RB structure of the task may look like the following:

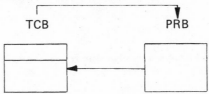

TCB   PRB

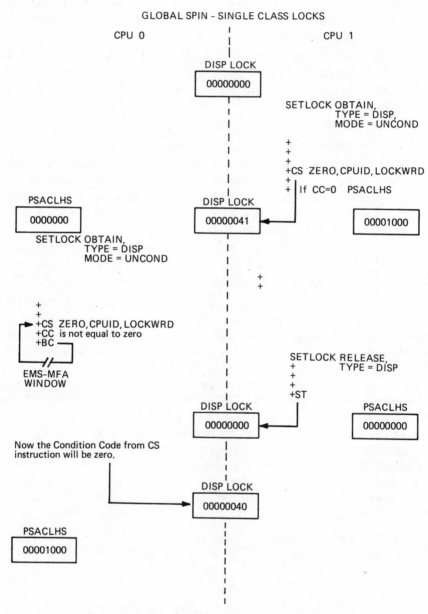

Figure 6.4 Global spin for dispatcher lock.

- Registers entry to lock manager, which are saved in PSA are moved into TCB register save area.
- Entry point to the locking manager is placed into the RBOPSW field in the PRB. RBOPSW is known as the resume PSW for this task. (Figure 6.5)
- Give control back to dispatcher.*

*NOTE: This is the technique used by the lock manager to suspend a task that is requesting an unavailable local lock. Since the dispatcher will never dispatch a task in an address space other than the one holding the local lock, the task just suspended will stay suspended until the local lock is released by the other task.

When the local lock is released and the suspended task becomes the highest-priority work, dispatcher will then dispatch this task.

2. *Service Request wants the local lock, but cannot get it.*
We have seen that when a service routine gets control, most of the time the first thing it does is release the SRB. While executing a service routine, the CPU can be said to be running wild without a controlling control block. So the process of suspending a service request is to recreate an SRB.

In order to do this, the lock manager obtains a special control block from subpool 245(SQA). This special control block is called "SSRB" (suspend SRB). In this special SSRB, lock manager saves the register at entry to SETLOC and the current FRR (functional recovery routine) stack. This FRR stack is used to recreate the process leading up to the point of SRB suspension.

This SSRB is then placed in a LOCAL lock suspend queue, anchored in the ASCB of the address space. ASCBFSLQ (ASCB+x'14') points to the first suspended SRB on the local lock suspend SRB Queue, and ASCBLSLQ (ASCB+x'18') points to the last suspended SRB on this queue. SSRBs within this local suspend queue are forward chained by the SRBFLNK (offset 4) field within the SSRB. SSRBs are similar to SRBs.

When the local lock is released, lock manager re-introduces suspended SRBs into the system by using the SCHEDULE macro. Dispatcher recognizes these special SRBs by testing for SRBRNTR (resource manager routine pointer); restores the status; and releases the SSRB via FREECELL and LPSW from SSRB to continue execution from the point of suspension.

3. *Task has local lock and requests CMS lock unconditionally, but cannot get it.*

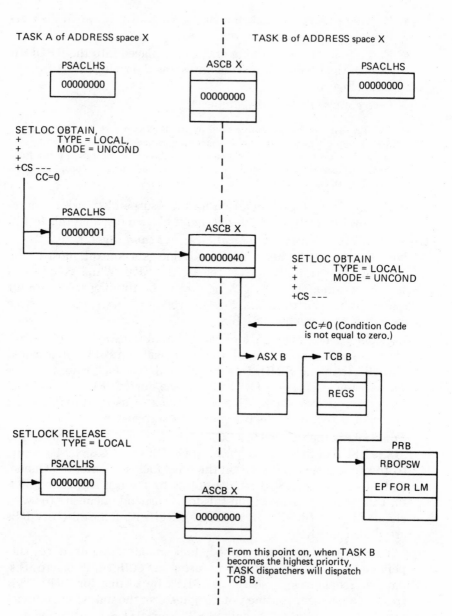

Figure 6.5 Task suspension for local lock.

Lock manager takes the register at entry to lock manager (from PSA) and moves them into IHSA interrupt handler save area (IHSA). ASXB+x'20' points to the interrupt handler's save area for locally locked interrupts.*

NOTE: In this particular case, the lock manager, while suspending a task, does not move the registers into the TCB. The reason for doing this is that there are valid registers in the TCB save area for locally locked tasks, and these values cannot be overlayed.

- Lock manager takes the OLD and NEW TCB pointers from the PSA (PSATOLD,PSATNEW) and moves it into IHSA.
- Lock manager takes the resume PSW which points to the entry to lock manager and places it in IHSA also.

By doing these, lock manager saves the status of the task in IHSA. We may ask why we need the TCB address in IHSA. This address enables dispatcher to identify the task that was holding the local lock while interrupted.

- Next thing the lock manager does is suspend the task. This is done by placing the ASCB of the task's address space on CMS lock suspend queue and by placing suspend ID (x'7FFFFFFF') into the local lockword, replacing the CPU ID. Lock interface table (LIT) points to IEAVESLA table. Offset x'18' onto this table is the queue header for CMS ASCB suspend queue. At offset x'IC' it is the pointer to the last element on this suspend queue.
- This completes the suspend process of a task, and the control is given to dispatcher.

4. *SRB has local lock and request CMSA lock but cannot get it.*
- Lock manager obtains an SSRB for SQA.
- Saves the registers and FRR stack in the SSRB.
- Places the SSRB on the CMS SRB suspend queue. This queue is in IEAVESLA at offset x'10'. The last element of this queue is at offset x'14'.
- Places the suspend ID (x'7FFFFFFF') into the local lockword that is in ASCB (ASCBLOCK) to indicate that this SRB had the local lock before it suspended.
- Go back to dispatcher.

RELEASE OF LOCKS

1. Release of local lock

   For suspended tasks nothing special has to be done, because lock manager has saved the registers in the TCB and the resume PSW in the PRB. This is the normal status of saving a task after an interrupt. When the dispatcher comes along and finds nobody holds the local lock, it will dispatch the highest-priority unit of work in that address space. Eventually this TCB will be dispatched.

   Suspended SSRBs on the local lock suspend queue are rescheduled by the lock manager. The first SSRB on the queue is given the local lock and is rescheduled. SSRB contains the register and PSW at entry to local lock manager routine.

2. Release of CMS lock

   Everything on the CMS suspended queues (SSRBs and ASCBs) are released. The lock manager releases ASCBs by placing interrupt IDs ('FFFFFFFF') into the local lockword (ASCBLOCK) and replacing the suspend ID in them. Also, ASCBs are removed from the CMS suspend queue.

   For suspended SSRBs, the lock manager traces back their ASCBs and changes the suspend IDs into interrupt IDs. Lock manager then reschedules these SSRBs onto the service manager queue.

   At the end of a CMS lock release, we have a whole bunch of ASCBs previously suspended, that now have interrupt IDs in their local lockword; a lot of SSRBs on the service manager queue due to rescheduling; and a lot of TCBs that were hanging around for CMS lock. After releasing the CMS lock, the control is given to dispatcher.

   Dispatcher first looks at the GLOBAL SRBs to be dispatched. Due to the release of CMS lock, we do not have any GLOBAL SRBs. We specify an SRB as *global* or *local* when we issue a SCHEDULE macro. Once the service request routine gets control, it releases the SRB, and thus there is no way to find whether the interrupted SRB is global or local. So lock manager, when it reschedules SSRB, will always use SCOPE = LOCAL in the schedule macro.

   Next, the dispatcher goes to the highest-priority address space and tries to dispatch local SRBs. Upon recognizing a special SSRB the dispatcher will restore the status (register and PSW from SSRB) and change the interrupt ID in the ASCBLOCK into CPUID. Dispatcher then releases the SSRB and does a LPSW. This will give control to the SRB at a CMS lock entry point in lock manager.

   If the highest-priority address space has no local SRBs but only TCBs, dispatcher examines the local lockword. If it contains an interrupt ID, it means a TCB, while holding the local lock, was interrupted, but is now dispatchable. Dispatcher now goes to the IHSA and restores the register and PSW. This will give control to the task at entry to lock manager. The key to dispatching of the locally locked task is the change of suspended ID into interrupt ID. If there is no interrupted locked task in an address space, dispatcher will give control to the highest-priority ready task in that address space.

7 Interrupt Handling

The interrupt mechanism is used in System 370 architecture to switch the status of the system within the supervisor state or from problem program to supervisor state. When an interrupt happens, an automatic machine action takes place. The current PSW, which is in the active CPU, is stored in a pre-assigned PSW slot in storage (called "OLD PSW") and a corresponding NEW PSW is brought into CPU as current PSW. This PSW will control the execution of the CPU. Address portion of this PSW points to an interrupt-handling routine for a specific type of interrupt.

7.1 FUNCTIONS OF THE INTERRUPT HANDLER

The first function of the interrupt handler is to save the environment of the system at the time of interrupt. This is done by saving the current PSW and the registers in the CPU to main-storage-save-area. Also, the interrupt handler isolates this interrupt-status–saving process from another interrupt. The next function of the interrupt handler is to give control to a routine to handle the specific interrupt.

7.2 SVC INTERRUPTIONS

When CPU executes an instruction of the type 0Ann, an SVC interruption occurs. An operation code of 0A denotes an SVC instruction and *nn* specifies the number of SVC routines that the requester wants. For example SVC 1 (0A01) is a WAIT SVC; SVC 8 (0A08) is for LOADING a module, etc. There can be up to 256 different SVCs in the system, and these SVCs are divided into different types according to their characteristics, such as size, lock requirements, and location. Types 1, 2, 3 and 4 are the most important ones. Type 5 and Type 6 are for some specialized cases. Table 7.1 summarizes the SVC programming-conventions.

7.2.1 SVC Types

Type 1 and Type 2 are link edited as part of nucleus and are fixed in nucleus. The names of these routines should be "IGC nnn," where *nnn* is the number of SVC.

Type 3 and Type 4 SVCs can be in the fixed link pack area or in a modified link pack area. Type 1 SVC always receives control with the LOCAL LOCK being held and should not release this lock until exiting from the SVC. Additional locks may be requested prior to entry to the routine or can be obtained dynamically while in the routine. For Types

133

TABLE 7.1 SVC Programming Conventions

CONVENTIONS	TYPE 1	TYPE 2	TYPE 3	TYPE 4
PART OF RESIDENT CONTROL PGM	YES	YES	NO	NO
SIZE IF ROUTINE	ANY	ANY	ANY	ANY
REENTERABLE ROUTINE	YES	YES	YES	YES
REFRESHABLE ROUTINE	NO	NO	YES	YES
LOCKING REQUIREMENTS	YES	NO	NO	NO
NAME OF ROUTINE IGC00nnn IGCssnnn	IGCnnn	IGCnnn	IGC00nnn NO SVRB	IGCssnnn
SVRB SIZE IF EXIST	NO SVRB EXIST	200	200	200
NUMBER OF USER SVC ROUTINE	Number of user SVC routine should be in descending order from 255 through 200.			
MAY ISSUE WAIT MACRO	NO	YES	YES	YES
MAY ISSUE XCTL MACRO	NO	NO	NO	YES
MAY ISSUE SVCs	NO	YES	YES	YES
EXIT FROM SVC ROUTINE	Branch Using Return Register 14			
RECOVERY	FRR	ESTAE OR FRR		

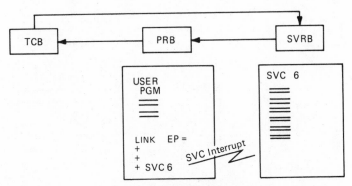

Figure 7.1 SVC execution.

3 and 4, the only lock that can be held on entry to routine is the local lock or the LOCAL and CMS lock combinations; but for Types 1 and 2, any number of locks can be held at entry to the routine.

Upon entry to an SVC routine, Registers 0, 1, 13 and 15 contains values at the time of SVC interrupt. These registers are used to pass parameters back and forth between the SVC routine and the calling program. Register 3 points to the CVT; Register 4 points to the TCB; Register 5 contains the address of the current RB at entry to the SVC routine; Register 6 contains the entry point of the SVC routine; Register 7 points to ASCB; Register 14 points to a routine called "EXIT PROLOG." The rest of the registers are unpredictable.

Type 1 SVC does not create a new level of control, which means it is executed under the current RB. But for all other SVCs an SVRB is created. The SVC routine will execute under this SVRB as depicted in Figure 7.1.

7.2.2 Methods of Abnormal Termination in SVC Routines

If an abnormal condition develops while executing a Type 1 SVC, the recovery termination manager (RTM) is given control at a special entry point called "RTM1." This routine is also activated if an SVC is issued while executing in a disabled code, in a locked state, or in the SRB mode. If another type of abnormal condition happens in a Type 1 SVC, RTM1 will try to recover from the error using the functional recovery routine (FRR) stack. RTM1 is entered via CALLRTM macro. Abnormal termination recovery from other types of SVCs is accomplished by STAE routines or FRR stack. If recovery is not possible, RTM is notified and RTM2 is entered. RTM2 performs normal and abnormal task termination for both system and problem program routines. RMT2 is evoked by issuing ABEND macro.

7.2.3 SVC Interruption Processing

Let us look at the values in CPU components just before an SVC interrupt happens. Registers contain values for the program. The Instruction reg-

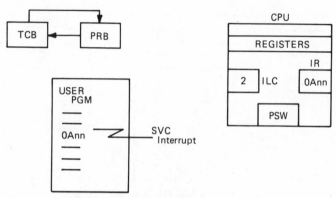

Figure 7.2 SVC interrupt processing.

ister (IR) contains the current instruction being executed (in our case the values will be 0Ann). The address portion of the PSW will point to an instruction after the SVC instruction. Instruction length code register (ILC) will contain an equivalent value of 2 since the length of the current SVC instruction is 2 bytes long (figure 7.2).

When the CPU executes the SVC instruction, an SVC interruption occurs. The hardware mechanism swaps the PSWs. Also the ILC and the interruption code (nn portion of SVC instruction) are saved in the PSA. After the swap, the current PSW points to SVC first level interrupt handler routine (SVC FLIH). See figure 7.3.

The SVC FLIH will execute physically disabled. This is to prevent other interruptions from occurring before the status is saved. Physical disablement is accomplished by setting appropriate bits in the PSW and in the control registers.

The first thing SVC FLIH does is save the registers in LCCA (LCCA-SGPR). Address of LCCA is obtained from PSA. Next, it checks for any SVC violations such as Type 1 issuing another SVC or an SVC issued while in SRB mode, disabled state, or locked mode. To check whether the system was executing a Type 1 SVC, the SVC FLIH will test a bit (ASCBTYP1) in ASCB. If this bit is on then SVC FLIH determines a violation, and the task is terminated with a system code of '0F8'.

An SRB mode is tested by checking the LCCADSF2/LCCASRBM bit in LCCA. If this SVC is issued under an SRB mode, the task is terminated with a system code of '0F8'.

To check whether any locks held while issuing an SVC instruction, the SVC FLIH issues a SETLOCK TEST, TYPE=ALL macro. The SETLOCK macro will load the PSA current lock-held string into a register, test it under a bit mask to determine any lock-held condition, and set a return code. The SVC FLIH will terminate the issuer of SVC if any locks were held. A system code of '0F8' is also issued.

By examining the SVC OLD PSW, the SVC FLIH can determine whether the system was in a disabled state while it issued this SVC. If yes, the task is terminated with a system code of '0F8'.

Note that SVC FLIH is running in a disabled state and it cannot issue an ABEND SVC (SVC 13). The way SVC FLIH terminates the violating task is by using a macro called "CALLRTM TYPE=SVCERR." CALLRTM macro generate a branch entry to RTM1. To terminate the task, RTM1 branches to RTM2, which is the code for SVC 13.

If the SVC FLIH determines the SVC instruction is valid, it does the following:

1. Get the TCB address from PSATOLD.

2. Get the address of RB from TCB.

3. From PSA, do status saving into the current RB.

    SVC OLDPSW is saved into RBOPSW.

    ILC is moved into RBINLNTH.

    Interruption code is stored in RBINTCOD.

4. Multiply SVC number by 8 to get the displacement into the SVC table. From this table, the entry point address of the SVC routine is determined, as shown in figure 7.4.

Each entry in the SVC table contains information for a particular SVC function, such as SVC entry point address, type, APF authorization, and lock requirement before the module execution. Even though SVC table can be located through the CVT, the SVC FLIH gets there by using an address constant in the nucleus.

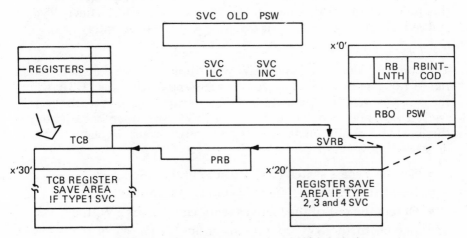

Figure 7.3 Status saving when an SVC is issued.

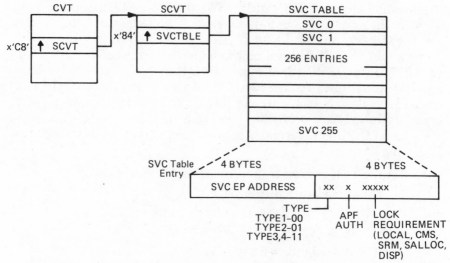

Figure 7.4 Determining the entry point address of an SVC routine.

Once the SVC FLIH finds the correct entry into the SVC table, it first checks whether any authorization is required to execute this SVC. This is tested by checking the APF bit in the SVC entry. If this bit is on, SVC FLIH issues a TESTAUTH macro to test the return code. If the return code is 0, the program is authorized and can use this routine. Otherwise, SVC FLIH loads a system code of '047' into Register 1 and issues:

CALLRTM TYPE=ABTERM, COMPCOD=(1).

NOTE: SVC FLIH cannot issue an SVC since it is executing in a disabled state.

The next thing SVC FLIH does is determine the type of SVC. From this point on the process depends on the type of SVC, namely Type 1 and rest of the types. So, let us examine each type separately.

7.2.4 Type 1 SVC

The control blocks for Type 1 SVC interrupt processing are depicted in figure 7.5. The SVC FLIH moves the register storage in the LCCA, where the registers were saved when the SVC interruption occurred, to the TCB register save area. Since this is a Type 1 SVC, the supervisor tries to get the local lock conditionally. If the local lock is available, the SVC FLIH does the following:

- Set the Type 1 switch (ASCBTYP1) in the ASCB.
- Enable the PSW for I/O and External interrupts.
- Obtain the rest of the locks as required from the SVC table.
- Branch to the SVC routine according to the entry point in the SVC table.

If the local lock is not available, SVC FLIH does the following:

- The instruction address portion of the PSW that was saved into the RB, is decremented by 2, so that the RBOPSW points back to the SVC instruction on the user program.
- Go to dispatcher.

Next time, when this task becomes the highest-priority ready task, the dispatcher will dispatch this task. Since this is not a locked task, the dispatcher will load the CPU register from TCB register save area and PSW from RBOPSW. This is where SVC FLIH saved the register and PSW. Since the PSW points to the SVC instruction, the task again issues the SVC and tries to obtain the local lock again. Figure 7.6 gives an overview of Type 1 SVC processing.

7.2.5 Type 2, Type 3, and Type 4 SVC FLIH Processing

Types 2 through 4 of SVC processing incorporates the following stages (Figure 7.7):

- Obtain storage for SVRB, by GETCELL. GETMAIN SVC cannot be issued because the process is still in SVC FLIH and in a disabled state.
- Registers at the time of interrupt are moved from LCCA to SVRB
- Chains SVRB on RB chain
- Enables for I/O and External interrupts
- Obtain needed locks according to SVC table entry
- Sets up registers 13,15,0,and 1 as they were at the time of interrupt.
- Register 14 is loaded with the address of EXIT PROLOG. EXIT PROLOG will do the clean up functions such as removing the SVRB and loading back the PSW and registers, so that the user program can continue from the next sequential instruction after the SVC instruction.
- Branch to SVC routine.

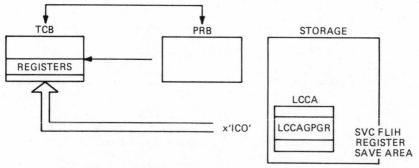

Figure 7.5 Control blocks for Type 1 SVC interrupt processing.

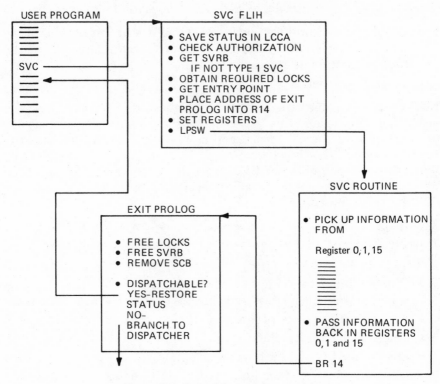

Figure 7.6 Type 1 interrupt processing.

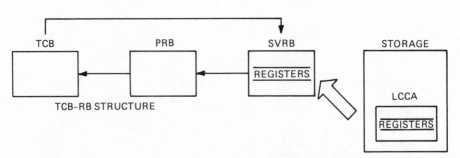

Figure 7.7 SVC processing and Types 2 and 3.

7.2.6 EXIT PROLOGUE Routine

After the SVC routine finishes processing, control is given to EXIT PRO-
LOGUE routine via a branch on Register 14 (BR 14) instruction. This
routine performs the exiting procedures for SVCs. There are two entry
points to this routine. One will force a dispatcher switch and control is
given to dispatcher and the other will give control back to the interrupted program.

When the EXIT PROLOGUE routine gets control, it saves the Registers
0, 1 and 15 from the CPU into the corresponding TCB register save slots.
These registers contain information from the SVC routine back to the
program that requested the service. For example, after a LOAD SVC
routine, it passes the module address in Register 0, the modules authorization code, and module length in Register 1. And usually return codes
are in Register 15.

Next EXIT PROLOG determines from what type of SVC routine it
is given control. This is because the TCB-RB structure is different for
TYPE 1 SVC and the rest of TYPES. For Type 1 SVC, registers are in
TCB, and the PSW at the time of SVC interrupt is in PRB. But for TYPE
2, 3, and 4, the registers are in the SVRB. The PSW at the time of interrupt is in the PRB. This process is depicted in Figure 7.8.

In the case of Type 1 SVCs, register slots 0, 1, and 15 in the TCB
are overlayed when EXIT PROLOG saves their registers from the CPU.
But for Type 2, 3, and 4, registers at the time of SVC interrupt are in
SVRB, so that saving of the above registers to TCB will not overlay the
values at the time of interrupt.

By examining ASCBTYP1 switch, EXIT PROLOGUE determines the
type of SVC. In the case of TYPE 1 SVC, EXIT PROLOG does the
following:

- Turns off TYPE 1 switch
- Disables I/O and External interrupts
- Frees any of locks held

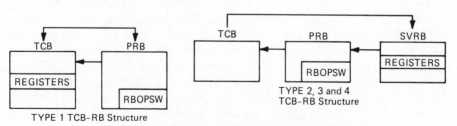

Figure 7.8 Register storage for SVC processing.

- Goes to the dispatcher if dispatcher force switch is on. Otherwise, goes to interrupted program. This logic is necessary because some SVC routines, such as POST and DEQ, will possibly make other high-priority work ready in the system. In this case, the dispatcher should be given control, so that dispatcher can dispatch the highest-priority work in the system.

In case of TYPE 2, 3, and 4 SVCs, EXIT PROLOG does the following:

- Releases all locks which are held for the execution of SVC routine.
- Gets the local lock, to manipulate the RB chain in the address space.
- Adjusts the RB chain
- Moves registers 2 through 14 to TCB
- Frees the SVRB (FREECELL)
- Disables the PSW for I/O and External interrupts*
- According to the dispatcher switch, goes to the DISPATCHER or to the interrupted program.

*NOTE: When LPSW instruction is executed to give control to the interrupted program, the I/O and external interrupts mask will be same as the time of SVC interrupt.

7.3 SPIE MACRO

Two major functions of program check interrupt handler are (1) handle interrupts such as monitor call (GTF), program event recording (DSS), page fault and program checks; (2) interface with user SPIE routine.

Let us first look at the "externals" and then the "internals" of specify program interruption exit (SPIE). This will help us understand the workings of program check interruption handler.

There are more than 20 different types of program interrupts in the system. See Table 7.2. Of these only four of them can be disabled by setting corresponding bits in the program mask field of the current PSW. These exceptions are fixed-point overflow, decimal overflow, exponent underflow, and significance. When disabled, these interrupt-causing events will be bypassed and the CPU will not be interrupted.

When a program check interruption happens, PCFLIH (program check first level interruption handler) gets control. PCFLIH makes a decision on whom to give control, either to control program EXIT routine or to a user-specified SPIE exit routine. Presence of a SPIE environment is reflected by a field in TCB (TCBPIE). If a SPIE environment exists, PCFLIH gives control to a SPIE EXIT routine specified. If no SPIE environment exists, then the control program EXIT routine is entered and this will produce a DUMP, (if specified through a SYSUDUMP or SYSABEND DD card) and terminate the process.

TABLE 7.2 Program Interruption Codes

CODES	MEANING
0001	OPERATION Exception
0002	PRIVILEGED OPERATION Exception
0003	EXECUTE Exeption
0004	PROTECTION Exception
0005	Addressing Exception
0006	Specification Exception
0007	Data Exception
0008	Fixed Point Overflow Exception
0009	Fixed Point Divide Exception
000A	Decimal Overflow Exception
000B	Decimal Divide Exception
000C	Exponent Overflow Exception
000D	Exponent Underflow Exception
000E	Significance Exception
000F	Floating Point Divide Exception
0010	Segment Translation Exception
0011	Page Translation Exception
0012	Translation Specification Exception
0013	Special Operation Exception
0040	Monitor Event
0080	Program Event

SPIE macro instruction creates a SPIE environment. Through this macro, address of the SPIE EXIT routine and types of interrupts to be "trapped" are specified. The format of SPIE macro is the following:

name SPIE exit address, (interrupts)

If the SPIE macro instruction specifies an exception for which an interruption has been disabled by the program masks in the PSW, these interrupts will be enabled by the control program when the SPIE routine (SVC 14) is executed.

It is possible to issue more than one SPIE macro with different interrupt specifications. In this case, each succeeding SPIE macro specification will override the previous ones.

7.3.1 Control Blocks Associated With SPIE

There are three major control blocks associated with SPIE processing:

1. Program interrupt control area PICA
2. Program interrupt element PIE
3. SPIE control area SCA

These three control blocks constitute a SPIE environment. A task is connected to this environment by a TCB pointer (TCBPIE). TCBPIE field points to SCA and SCA points to PIE and PIE in turn points to PICA.

LIST and STANDARD form of the SPIE macro expands into PICA and is initialized by the executable code provided by the expansion of the SPIE macro. PICA can be 6 or 8 bytes long depending on whether page translation exceptions have to be "trapped." The PICA entry is shown in figure 7.9.

The first four bits in PICA are 0. The next four bits are the new program MASK. SPIE routine (SVC 14) will place this program MASK in the current PSW.

The next three bytes are the address of a user-written SPIE exit routine. If the next bit (first bit in the fifth byte of PICA) is ON, this indicates the PICA is 8 bytes long. The extended bytes are used to trap special program check interrupts, such as segment translation exception, page translation exception, monitor event call, etc. The next 15 bits are used to indicate 15 possible program interrupts. When SPIE is issued, MVS returns the address of the previous PICA in Register 1. If no SPIE environment exists, Register 1 will contain 0s. If we issue SPIE macro with no operands, this will CANCEL the SPIE environment and will generate a PICA of all 0s. SPIE environment can be re-established by the use of execute form of the macro and points to a previous PICA.

7.3.2 Program Interrupt Element (PIE)

When SPIE macro is executed, the control program creates a 32-byte control block called "PIE" (figure 7.10). The only portion of this control block that is filled in is the PICA address. The rest of this control block is filled in when the program check interrupt occurs. At that time current PSW and register 12, 15, 0, 1 and 2 are stored in PIE. The current PSW is formatted as a BC mode PSW before storing in PIE.

PIE is freed on both CANCEL and ELIMINATE specifications. A PIE is created whenever a SPIE macro instruction is issued and no PIE exists.

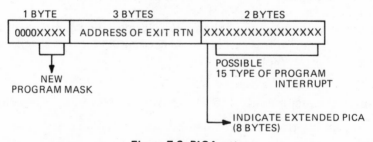

Figure 7.9 PICA entry.

0	PIE	
4	RESERVED	PICA ADDRESS
12	BC mode PSW at the time of PC interrupt	
16	Register 14	
20	Register 15	
24	Register 0	
28	Register 1	
32	Register 2	

Figure 7.10 PIE entry.

7.3.3 Register Contents Upon Entry to the SPIE Exit Routine

At entry to user EXIT routine, Register 1 contains the address of PIE and Register 13 contains the save area for the main program. This save area is not for the use of the EXIT routine. Registers 2 through 12 have the same value at the time of program interrupt, and Register 0 contains some control information. Register 14 contains return point to the supervisor. This entry point in supervisor is called "EXIT ROUTINE" (SVC 3). Register 15 has the address of the SPIE exit routine.

User-written SPIE exit routine should be in virtual storage when it is required. If a program interruption happens in the exit routine control program, EXIT is evoked to terminate the task. Within the user exit routine, registers 3–13 can be modified. Also, the address portion of the PSW in the PIE can be altered so that the routine can select any return point in the interrupted program. If the contents of Registers 14, 15, 0, 1, and 2 need to be modified, corrected values for these registers should be placed in PIE. This is due to the fact that when control is returned to the control program, it will restore these registers with the value found in PIE. To determine which type of interruption occurred, the exit routine can test bits 28 through 31 of the old program status word (BC mode) in the PIE and can take corrective action or ignore the exceptional condition. User's exit must return to an address specified in register 14.

7.3.4 SPIE Macro Internals

Before SPIE is issued, the TCB, RB relation is shown in figure 7.11. The TCB is active under control of a PRB, and CPU is executing instructions in the program. CPU contains the current PSW and the registers used by the program. Since we coded a SPIE macro (general form) in this program, it expanded into a control block called "PICA" and an SVC 14 instruction. PICA contains the new program mask, the exit routine address, and the program interrupts we want to trap.

When SPIE macro is executed, it causes an SVC interrupt. Since it is not a Type 1 SVC, an SVRB is created by the SVC FLIH. TCB-RB chain is depicted in figure 7.12.

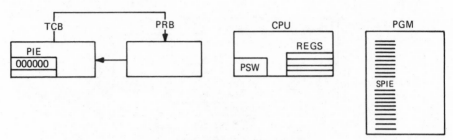

Figure 7.11 SPIE macro processing.

The address of the next sequential instruction in the program that is in PRBOPSW, and registers at the time of the SVC interrupt, is in the SVRB. Since there was no SPIE environment before, the TCBPIE field will contain 0s.

SPIE SVC routine (SVC 14) will perform a four-step logic:

Step 1 Is this request to eliminate SPIE environment?

The question is answered by testing Register 1. If it is 0, this is a request to eliminate SPIE. SCA and PIE are freed and the original program mask (from the TCBPMASK field in the TCB) is restored into the PSW. TCBPIE field is zeroed out, old PICA address is placed in Register 1 and RETURN.

If Register 1 at entry to the SVC routine is not 0 then do the next step.

Step 2 Is this a CANCEL SPIE?

This is determined by checking the PICA for 0s. If it is 0s then the SPIE environment is cancelled. Cancelling the SPIE environment has the same procedure described in Step 1. If not a CANCEL SPIE then go to Step 3.

Step 3 SCA and PIE should be created?

Check TCBPIE for 0. If it is 0, then the SPIE SVC routine has to create a SPIE environment. This routine issues GETMAIN for SCA and PIE, and places the address of SCA in TCB. It also places a pointer in SCA to PIE. Since there was no SPIE environment, place 0s in Register 1.

If the TCBPIE field is not equal to 0, this means an old SPIE environment exists, so place the OLDPICA address into Register 1 and make PIE points to new PICA.

Step 4 SPIE SVC routine gets the RBOPSW from PRB, takes the program mask (4 bits) from the RBOPSW, and saves in TCBP-MASK field in TCB. (In the formatted DUMP of TCB, this TCBPMASK is the last four bits of the first byte in TCBPIE

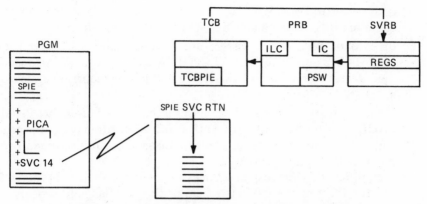

Figure 7.12 TCB-RB chain for SPIE macro processing.

field.) It takes the new program mask from the new PICA specified and places the mask in the RBOPSW field in PRB.

After this, control is given to EXIT PROLOGUE as in the case of any SVC routine. EXIT PROLOGUE, if determined to give control back to the program, issues LPSW instruction to load the current PSW from the RBOPSW. Now, with the new program mask, the interrupted program (which issued the SPIE SVC) gets control at the next sequential instruction after SVC 14. A SPIE environment now exists for the program.

7.3.5 Program Interrrupt Handler in a SPIE Environment

When a program check occurs, PCFLIH (Program Check First Level Interrupt Handler) gets control from the program check new PSW. PCFLIH does the following functions:

1. Saves Registers in LCCA (LCCAPGR1).
2. PI (Program Interrupt) OPSW is saved in LCCA.
3. Interrupt length code (ILC) and Interrupt Code is also saved in LCCA.
4. If the interrupt code is x'12' then it is a translation exception. A recursive indicator (LCCAPDAT) is set. If this is the first time this translation exception is marked as 0C4 and continue processing. For the first recursion loads control Register 1 with address of master segment table address and abend the address space. For the second recursion terminate the system and places the system in a wait state. Recursions in program check interrupt handler for address translation exception, segment translation exception, and translation exception indicate that the interruption handler may be unable to access critical data.

5. If the interrupt code is x'10', it is a segment translation exception. Same process explained in Step 4 above is repeated.

6. In case of recursion registers are moved from LCCAPGR1 to LCCAPGR2 and PSW from FLCPOPSW to LCCAPPSW. Also saves the interruption code in LCCAPINT and set the recursion indicator in the PSA.

7. If the interrupt code is x'11' then this interrupt is caused by a PAGE FAULT. If there is a SUPER SPIE routine specified to handle page faults, this routine is given control. Else, page fault suspend processor (PIX) is given control.

   For unlocked TCBs, suspend processing saves the register in the TCB and the PSW in the RBOPSW field of the RB. Suspend processing then sets the RB in a wait state by incrementing RBWCF field by 1 and by decrementing the count of ready tasks in the ASCBTCBS field of the ASCB by 1. Control is given back to the dispatcher. For locally locked tasks, suspend processing saves registers and PSW in the IHSA. Control is then given to a common suspend routine to complete suspension. For SRBs, suspend processing first obtains an SSRB and saves the register, PSW, and translation exception address in it. To complete the suspend processing a common suspend routine is evoked.

   According to the return code from the common suspend routine, control is given to the dispatcher (RC = 0, process suspended) or to the interrupted program (RC = 4 no I/O is necessary because the page can be reclaimed or it is the first reference after the GETMAIN); or continue the interrupt processing. (RC = 8, and mark this page fault as 0C4.)

8. For interrupts '0C1' through '0CF', PC FLIH has to determine where to give control, to a user written (SPIE routine) error handline routine or to RTM (Recovery Termination Manager) to terminate the task. PC FLIH asks the following questions and does the following process.

9. Was the PSW disabled for I/O and external interruptions? If the answer is "yes", give control to RTM by issuing CALLRTM TYPE=PROGMCK
   Else continue with next step.

10. Was this process in SRB mode? Check LCCADSF2/LCCASRBM field.
    If yes CALLRTM TYPE=PROGMCK
    Else continue with next step.

11. Any LOCKS held? Test this by issuing a SETLOCK TEST, TYPE=ALL macro.

If any locks held CALLRTM TYPE=PROGMCK.
Else continue with next step.

12. Take registers at the time of error which is in LCCA and places them in TCB. The way PCFLIH locate the TCB is from PSATOLD field. Also move the PSW to PRB (RBOPSW).

13. Next question to be asked is whether the process was in supervisor state. By checking the PSW this can be determined. If in supervisor control is given to RTM by issuing CALLRTM TYPE=PROGMCK. Else the process is in problem state, and SPIE routine can be given control if SPIE environment exist.

14. Is there a SPIE environment? Check TCBPIE field for 0s. If 0s, no SPIE environment exists, so call RTM to terminate the process; else continue process.

15. Get the address of SCA and initialize the SCA control block.
In the SPIE control area (SCA) there are pointers for the PIE and the RB. PSW at the time of error is placed into SCA and also the instruction length counter (ILC) and interrupt code (IC) is stored into SCA. Very adjacent to SCA is an SRB, and PCFLIH will fill these SRB fields. SRB will contain information such as ASCB address (from PSAAOLD), ASID (from ASCB), TCB address, and an entry point address of a service routine called *program interrupt service routine* for SPIE. This service routine will execute under control of the SRB that was just created. Parm field in this SRB will point to a 16-byte control area in SCA.

16. PC FLIH now sets the TCB as nondispatchable by setting TCB-FLAGS5 field. Decrement the number of ready TCBs in the address space by 1 (ASCBTCBS).

17. ISSUE SCHEDULE macro to place the SRB on the local SRB queue.

18. The last step performed by the PC FLIH is to give control to dispatcher.

7.3.6 *Program Interrupt Service Routine for SPIE*
When the SRB, that is scheduled by the PC FLIH for SPIE execution, is given control by dispatcher, the IEAVPSRB routine does the following:

1. Gets the SRB address from Register 0. It is a usual procedure for a service routine to release the SRB under which it is executing. But in this case the SRB is not released by IEAVPSRB routine.

2. Gets the TCB address from SRB. TCB address cannot be obtained from PSATOLD. Since an SRB is in control, this field will contain 0s.

3. Gets the address of SCA from TCBPIE field, and from SCA gets the address of PIE, and from PIE the address of PICA.

4. Check the first time logic switch in PIE. This field is called "PIE-BUSYBIT." This logic is necessary to accommodate the possibility of a page fault. PIE control block is in subpool 0 and PICA is imbedded within the program. These control blocks may or may not be in real storage. If any one of these control blocks is not in virtual storage when the IEAVPSRB routine gets control, a page fault occurs.

    This is the reason PCFLIH scheduled an SRB. Since PCFLIH executes disabled and cannot take an interrupt, it cannot take the possibility of a page fault for PIE or PICA; so it scheduled an SRB to handle this condition. Remember SRB execute enabled and page-faults are allowed. PIEBUSYBIT tells whether the program interrupt occurred again in a user-error-handling routine. If so, in order to avoid the recursive execution of PIE-error-handling routine, RTM is given control by issuing CALLRTM TYPE=ABTERM.

5. Next IEAVPSRB checks whether this current type of interrupt is specified in the SPIE environment by looking in PICA.

    To find what type of interrupt occurred, IEAVPSRB looks in SCA. SCA contains the ILC/IC fields at the time of error.

    If this interrupt is not specified in PICA then RTM is given control.

6. Registers 14, 15, 0, 1, and 2 are moved from TCB and placed in PIE.

7. PSW from SCA is placed into PIE.

8. Program MASK,IC,ILC and CC are placed into PIE.

9. Sets the first time logic switch in the PIE.

10. Take the address of the user SPIE exit routine from PICA and places this address in the address portion of the RBOPSW field.

11. Places the same address in Register 15 slot in the TCB.

12. Sets register 14 with an address of SVC 3 instruction. Actually PCFLIH code follows this SVC 3 instruction in nucleus.

13. Sets Register 1 with the address of PIE.

14. Sets TCB as DISPATCHABLE.

15. Increments the ready TCB count in ASCB.

16. Gives control to dispatcher.

NOTE: When this task becomes the highest-priority ready work in the system, the dispatcher will dispatch this task. Registers are loaded from the TCB, and the PSW is loaded from the PRB. This new PSW is pointing to the user SPIE exit routine. So this user routine will get control. The routine can correct the error by changing the register values or by changing the address portion of the PSW as described before. After the execution of this user routine a branch on Register 14 instruction is executed. We saw that Register 14 is loaded with an address of SVC 3 instruction. SVC 3 is called an EXITING SVC, and this SVC will do the 'cleaning' and give control back to the user program.

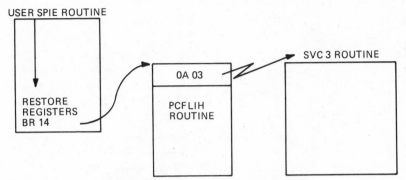

USER SPIE ROUTINE

RESTORE
REGISTERS
BR 14

0A 03

PCFLIH
ROUTINE

SVC 3 ROUTINE

Figure 7.13 Return from a SPIE routine.

7.3.7 Return From User SPIE Routine

Figure 7.13 depicts a routine sequence from a SPIE routine. When returning from the user SPIE exit routine, control is given to an address in Register 14. And this address points to SVC 3 instruction. This will cause an SVC interrupt and eventually SVC 3 routine gets control. This exit SVC routine is evoked from other routines such as TIMER routine, LINK routine, etc. Registers and PSW are stored in different places for different cases. To determine from where this exit SVC routine is given control, SVC 3 compares the address in SVCOPSW with the address of PCNPSW (Program Check New PSW). If equal, then the routine is given control through a user EXIT routine. (We saw that PCFLIH follows the SVC 3 instruction in nucleus.) If exit SVC evoked from a user exit, SVC 3 does the following for a SPIE environment.

1. Turn off the first time switch in the PIE.
2. Moves Register 14 through Register 2 from PIE into TCB. The rest of the registers were placed into TCB by the SVC interrupt status saving process.
3. Take the right half of the PSW from PIE and places it into RBOPSW.*
4. Branch on Register 14 instruction is executed to give control to EXIT PROLOGUE. Remember, all SVC routines exit through EXIT PROLOGUE. (Refer to SVC interrupt processing.)

   *NOTE: By performing steps 1-3, the exit routine is setting up the registers and PSW in the right places for the dispatcher to find.

Figure 7.14 gives an overview of SPIE processing.

7.4 OVERVIEW OF I/O INTERRUPT HANDLING

The input/output (I/O) interruption provides a means by which the CPU responds to conditions in I/O devices and channels. These conditions

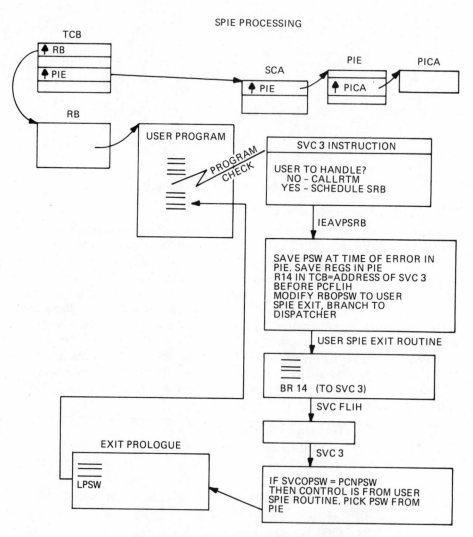

Figure 7.14 Overview of SPIE processing.

can be caused by the program or by an external event at the device.

A device attempts to initiate a request to the channel for an interruption whenever it detects Channel End, Control United End, Device End, or ATTENTION Condition. The channel may also, at command chaining, create an interruption at the device, which can be due to the following conditions:

- UNIT check
- UNIT exception
- Busy condition from device
- Program check
- Protection check

Mask bits in the PSW and the channel mask in control Register 2 determine whether the CPU is enabled for an I/O interruption, and the method of control depends on whether the current PSW specified the BC or EC mode. A request for I/O interruption may occur at any time and more than one request may occur at the same time. The requests are preserved and remain pending in channels or devices until accepted by the CPU. Priority is established among requests so that only one interruption request is processed at a time. Priority among requests is controlled by either a priority mechanism among interruption conditions associated with devices attached to the same channel, or by a priority mechanism established among requests from different channels.

Due to the interrupt, the swapping of PSW takes place automatically by hardware. The current PSWs from the CPU are stored at main storage, location 56, and a new PSW for I/O interruption handling is brought to CPU from storage location 120. Address portion of this PSW will give control to the I/O FLIH (first level interrupt handler) routine in nucleus.

The main functions of I/O FLIH routine are

- Save status (Register & PSW)
- Give control to the I/O supervisor and process the interrupt
- When finished processing, decide whether to return, either to the interrupted program or to the dispatcher.

8 Dispatcher

The functions of the dispatcher in MVS are to select and give control to the highest-priority dispatchable unit of work; save the status of the unit of work that is giving up control; and maintain the accounting information for the active task.

8.1 OVERVIEW

Dispatcher functions of older operating systems such as MVT were very simple. All the dispatcher has to do was search down the TCB queue for the highest-priority TCB. But in MVS a new unit of dispatchable work called "SRB" is introduced. Furthermore, a task is classified as GLOBAL and LOCAL. In this complex environment the dispatcher has to work with six different queues. In addition, the dispatcher must recognize requests for CPU affinity, redispatch of suspended SRB, and redispatch of interrupted or suspended LOCAL supervisor. The dispatcher also keeps track of tasks that are dispatched on each CPU to prevent the dispatching of the same process on two CPUs.

8.2 MEMORY SWITCH ROUTINE (MSR)

Before we look at the working of the dispatcher, let us look at a routine called *memory switch routine*. This routine provides the dispatcher with an indication that work is ready. The memory switch routine is called by supervisor functions such as ASCBCHAP, CMS LOCK RELEASE, STATUS, DEQ, etc., which will make work ready in the system. The dispatcher also calls this routine whenever an SRB is moved to a local service priority list (SPL) and makes work ready.

The memory switch routine using two fields per CPU gives indication to the dispatcher that work is ready in another address space. These two fields are PSAAOLD and PSAANEW. PSAAOLD indicates the current address space active on that CPU and PSAANEW indicates the highest-priority address space with ready work, except when a global SRB routine is dispatched. This is because GLOBAL SRBs are given priorities above that of any address space, regardless of the actual address space in which they are dispatched. In this case, PSAANEW field contains the highest ready address space, excluding the address space in which the SRB routine is running.

When MSR is called by other supervisor functions or by the dispatcher to indicate that work is ready, MSR compares the address space priority

155

of the newly ready work with the priority of the address space pointed by PSAANEW. If it is higher or equal to the address space pointed by PSAANEW, then the new ASCB address is stored into PSAANEW.

Dispatcher uses the PSAANEW field to determine whether an address space switch is necessary to dispatch the highest-priority work in the system. When searching for an address space to dispatch, the dispatcher starts at the address space pointed by PSAANEW. If PSAAOLD is equal to PSAANEW, then the dispatcher knows that there is no work ready in other address spaces and this will save the dispatcher a trip down the ASCB queue every time dispatcher is entered for dispatching.

When the dispatcher dispatches a unit of work in an address space, it stores the address of the ASCB into PSAAOLD field. It also stores the same address into PASANEW field. The only exception is when dispatching a GLOBAL SRB. In this case PSAANEW will not be updated.

In a multiprocessing system, MSR has to check the priority of address spaces that are active on both CPUs against the priority of the address space for which memory switch is requested. If MSR finds a low-priority ASCB address in one of PASANEW field of a CPU, then MSR will store the address of the new ASCB into PSAANEW field of that CPU. If MSR has to update PSAANEW field of a CPU, it generates an interrupt using single processor (SIGP) instructions and as the CPU takes this interrupt it causes an entry to the dispatcher. The reason the dispatcher entry is forced, rather than dependent on normal task switching activity, is to avoid the condition where the CPU is in wait state and there are no outstanding interrupts for the CPU. If the SIGP were not issued, the CPU would never come out of wait state. Another reason for the forced entry to the dispatcher is to provide better responsiveness to high-priority work.

8.3 DISPATCHER LOGIC

In MVS, dispatcher has to utilize various work queues to select and give control to the highest-priority dispatchable unit of work. These queues are

- The global service manager queue (GSMQ)
- The global service priority list (GSPL)
- The local service manager queue (LSMQ)
- The local service priority list (LSPL) (per address space)
- ASCB queue
- TCB queue (per address space)

As mentioned previously, a ready unit of work can be either a service request, represented by an SRB, or a task, represented by a TCB. The dispatcher searches for the work in a particular order, by first searching for ready SRBs and next searching for TCBs. By doing this, the dispatcher ensures that the most important work in the system receives control first.

8.3.1 Exit Processing

The first thing that the dispatcher looks for are any special exits to be taken. The exits possible are automatic CPU recovery, vary CPU, and time-of-day clock. The LCCA (LCCA + x '21C') will indicate what special exits are to be taken, and the dispatcher will give control to these exits. After processing, control is given back to the dispatcher.

8.3.2 GSMQ Processing

After special exits, the dispatcher processes SRBs. The first queue it looks at is the global service manager queue (GSMQ). CVT points to GSMQ header pointer which in turn points to SRBs. The process of dispatcher on GSMQ is removing the SRBs from the GSMQ and places them on GSPL. This is done via the SCHEDULE service. GSMQ can be considered as a staging queue of GLOBAL SRBs for the SCHEDULE macro. GSPL is also pointed by the CVT. Global service priority list consists of a HEAD that contains four fullwords. The first two fullwords point to the first and last of the non-quiesceable SRBs while the other two point to the first and last of the system SRBs. All SRBs on the GSMQ are distributed between the non quiesceable and system-SRB chains pointed by the GSPL field in the CVT.

8.3.3 GSPL Processing

Next, the dispatcher goes to the GSPL and does the following SRB dispatchability checks:

Step 1
- Pick up an SRB from the GSPL queue (non-quiesceable first).
- From SRB gets the address of ASCB.
- Check whether the system is non-dispatchable by checking the CSDSYSND bit in the CSDSCFL1 field of the CSD.
- If system is non-dispatchable, check whether this ASCB is exempt from system-wide nondispatchable state. (System could be nondispatchable, but some ASCBs have to be exempt from it; else system will never come up from wait states.) The exempt indicator from system-wide nondispatchability is in ASCBFLG2 (a bit called "ASCBXMPT"). If this ASCB is exempt, go to the next dispatchability check. If this SRB that the dispatcher is examining is nondispatchable, get the next SRB on the chain and start dispatchability check at STEP1.

If there is no SRB on GSPL, then the dispatcher will go to process the SRB on LSMQ.

Step 2 The next dispatchability check is for the address space. ASCB-DSP1 field will indicate whether this address space, associated with the SRB, is dispatchable or not. If dispatchable, go to the next step. Else move this SRB onto LSMQ.

Step 3 Check whether all SRBs STOP indicator is on (ASCBFLG2/ ASCBSNQS). If not all SRBs are stopped, go and check the next dispatchability indication. Else move this SRB onto LSMQ.

Step 4 If this SRB is a non-quiesceable SRB, then skip STEP5; else continue.

Step 5 Test ASCBSSRB field for a value greater than 0. If system-level SRBs are stopped, this SRB is moved to LSMQ. Else continue with STEP6.

Step 6 Once a GLOBAL SRB passes all the dispatchability tests, the dispatcher will dispatch it.

The dispatcher moves the ASCB address of this dispatchable SRB into PSAAOLD field; sets PSATNEW and PSATOLD to 0s indicating an SRB is in control; and establishes addressability to the address space by loading STOR value into control register 1. For the GLOBAL SRB, dispatcher sets SRB mode indicator in LCCA and increases the count of SRBs in the ASCBSRBS field; builds a PSW in low-core; and sets return address back to dispatcher in Register 14. After all these set-up procedures, dispatcher will issue a LPSW instruction to give control to the SRB. Note that PSAANEW field is not updated while dispatching GLOBAL SRBs.

8.3.4 LSMQ Processing

Finding no GLOBAL SRBs on GSPL, the dispatcher will dequeue any SRBs present on the local service manager queue (LSMQ) and move them to the local service priority list (LSPL) of the appropriate address space. The dispatcher does not attempt to dispatch any of the local SRBs at this time. It only places the SRBs on the appropriate SPL. The local SRB has the priority of the address space and will be dispatched with the same priority as the address space. Each time an SRB is moved to LSPL, memory switch routine is invoked. At the end of this process, PSAANEW has the highest-priority address space with ready work.

By comparing PSAANEW field to PSAAOLD field, dispatchers determine whether an address space switch is necessary. If so, addressability is made by loading the STORE value for that address space into control Register 1.

8.3.5 LSPL Processing

If there are no dispatchable GLOBAL SRBs, the dispatcher searches the ASCB queue, starting with the ASCB pointed by PSAANEW. The dispatcher will attempt to work with the same address space as long as possible. Only two things will cause the dispatcher to look for work in a new address:

1. PSAANEW is different from PSAAOLD.
2. The current address space has no dispatchable work.

If the current address space runs out of dispatchable work, the dispatcher will select the address space of the next lower priority. The dispatcher will look for work until it runs out of address spaces. At this point the dispatcher will dispatch the pseudo or WAIT task, and the CPU will then go into an enabled wait state waiting for work.

Once the dispatcher selects an address space, it will find what work has to be done within the address space and dispatch it. Work is selected within the address space in the following manner.

1. Local SRBs
2. Local supervisor (locally locked and interrupted work)
3. TCBs

The dispatcher looks at the SPL pointed by the ASCBSPL for the local SRBs. The top SRB is dequeued and dispatched after determining the dispatchability of this SRB as described in GSPL processing. If this SRB is not dispatchable, test the next SRB on this LSPL queue and continue testing.

If the SRB is dispatchable, indicate the SRB mode in LCCA. Check whether this SRB is a suspended SRB (SRBRMTR field). If it is, pick up the PSW and registers from the SSRB, free the SSRB and issue LPSW instructions to give control to the SRB. If this SRB is not a suspended SRB, the same procedure used to dispatch a global SRB is evoked.

8.3.6 Local Supervisor Dispatching

Next, the dispatcher looks to see if the local supervisor was interrupted. The local supervisor is the code in previous systems that ran disabled and is now running enabled in MVS. The dispatcher determines the mode of the address space by the contents of the lockword in ASCB. If the lock contains the interrupt ID of all 'Fs' or the lock contains the ID of the current CPU, then the address space is in local supervisor mode. In this case restore status from IHSA and issue LPSW instruction to give control to the local supervisor.

If the local lock contains a suspend ID of 7FFFFFFF, this means that this address space cannot be dispatched and the dispatcher will go to the next ASCB. If the local lock contains 0, the dispatcher will go to dispatch TCBs.

8.3.7 Task Dispatching

If the dispatcher gets past the checks for the local supervisor, it looks for and dispatches the highest-priority dispatchable TCB.

The first thing the dispatcher checks is whether all TCBs in this address space are marked nondispatchable (ASCBFLG1/ASCBSTND). If nondispatchable, the next address space is selected; else the dispatcher compares the ready TCBs in the address space (ASCBTCBS) to the total CPUs active in that address space (ASCBCPUS). If there are more ready TCBs waiting, dispatcher will select the highest-priority ready TCB. In order to check whether a TCB is nondispatchable, dispatcher checks TCBFLGS4/5 and also RBWCF for a value greater than 0. If this TCB is nondispatchable next TCB on this chain is selected. If a dispatchable, TCB is found, the dispatcher loads the register from TCB and PSW from RB (RBOPSW) and issues a LPSW to give control to the TASK.

8.3.8 WAIT Task

The WAIT task is dispatched when the dispatcher reaches the bottom of the ASCB ready queue. This bottom ASCB is a special ASCB that is hard coded into the nucleus and is called a "WAIT ASCB." It has an ASID of 0. WAIT task puts the system in an enabled wait state, waiting for work. Before dispatching the wait task, the dispatcher does a recursive search of the SRB queue and the ready queue to verify that no ready work exists. The CPU remains in wait state until an interrupt occurs either from the current CPU (because of previously started I/0 or timer requests) or from the other CPU when it has made work ready.

9 Virtual Storage Manager

Virtual storage manager (VSM) is responsible for maintaining the account of virtual storage. *Virtual storage* is the name given to the entire span of addresses available to the system through the dynamic address translations (DAT) feature. Using this feature, the size of virtual storage is limited only by the addressing capability of the system and not by the physical size of real storage. VSM has to keep track of what is allocated to each virtual storage address space by way of different sub-pools. Some of the functions VSM performs within an address space are

- Maintain the account of common system storage (CSA and SQA)
- Provide storage with different attributes
  - Key0 v/s non key 0
  - Fetch protect v/s non-fetch protect
  - Pageable v/s fixed
  - Common area v/s private area
- Monitor User Requests
  - Limit amount of storage (through IEALIMIT routine)
  - Require authorization for requests from SQA, CSA, LSQA, and SWA

In addition to the above functions, VSM also performs specialized functions at nucleus initialization, address space creation, step initialization, and task termination processings.

9.1 OVERVIEW

Virtual storage manager functions are not to be confused with paging. VSM functions are co-ordinated by real storage manager (RSM) and auxiliary storage manager (ASM). Some of the RSM responsibilities are the following:

- Maintain segment and page table.
- Maintain accounting of real storage usage.
  - Who uses what pages?
- Page fault processing.
- Keep only active pages in real storage.
- Assist in resolving a page fault.
- Assist in swapping.

161

As we can see, RSM administers the use of real storage and directs the movement of virtual pages between auxiliary storage and real storage.

Only virtual storage pages necessary for program execution are kept in real storage; the remainder reside on auxiliary storage, maintained by ASM. Some of the major responsibilities of ASM are

- Interface for paging I/O.
- Optimize usage of page data sets.
- Maintain accounting for address space pages.
- Main accounting for VIO pages.
- Find and retrieve page to resolve a page FAULT.

VSM routines service two macro instructions, namely GETMAIN and FREEMAIN. In this chapter we will concentrate on the working of these two macro instructions to find how VSM allocates virtual storage and releases the previously allocated virtual storage.

9.2 GETMAIN/FREEMAIN MACROS

Virtual storage can be explicitly requested for the use of the active task by issuing GETMAIN macro instructions and can be released by issuing FREEMAIN macro instructions.

There are two forms in expressing GETMAIN and FREEMAIN. One is storage type; the other, register type. These two classifications depend on how the parameters are supplied to the GETMAIN/FREEMAIN routines: through a parameter list or through a general register. In a storage type expression, the parameters are supplied in list form. The list will indicate the number of the sub-pool we wanted, its size and whether this request is conditional or unconditional.

Storage type parameters list also specifies whether the request is element type, variable type, or list type. Element type specifies a request for a single area of virtual storage of a specified length. Variable type specifies a request for a single area with a length between two specified values. List type specifies a request for one or more areas of virtual storage of specified lengths.

A GETMAIN/FREEMAIN macro instruction will expand into an SVC instruction. This instruction when executed will cause an SVC interrupt. As we saw in a previous chapter, SVC FLIH will get control. SVC FLIH, after examining the SVC number (in our case 4, 5, 10 and 120), gives control to GETMAIN/FREEMAIN service routines.

After finished processing by the service routines, control is given to EXIT PROLOGUE as in the case of other SVCs; from there control will be given to the program requesting GETMAIN/FREEMAIN.

SVC 10 and SVC 120 are used for both GETMAINS and FREEMAINS. Then, one may ask, how do the service routines distinguish whether these requests are for a GETMAIN or a FREEMAIN.

For SVC 10, if the high-order bit of Register 1 contains a 1, then the request is for a GETMAIN; else the request is for FREEMAIN. For SVC 120, the last byte of Register 15 contains an option byte. If the option byte is X'00', then the request is a conditional GETMAIN. If x'01', then the request is a conditional FREEMAIN. An x'02' indicates an unconditional GETMAIN, while an x'03' indicates an unconditional FREEMAIN. An X'04' indicates the request is for a page boundary.

9.3 MANAGING VIRTUAL STORAGES

As we saw before, an address space can be divided into common, private, and nucleus areas. Once the system is initialized, the nucleus area becomes fixed and no GETMAIN or FREEMAIN can be issued from this area. Since the nucleus area is fixed, VSM does not need to manage this area.

VSM manages the SQA, CSA, and private area of an address space. Sections within the private area to be managed by the VSM are:

1. LSQA/SWA and sub-pools 229/230.
2. Free area not assigned to a sub-pool.
3. Free area within sub-pools.

Virtual storage manager uses some of the pointers in the CVT to keep track of different areas of virtual storage common to all address spaces. For example CVT + x'80' points to the next byte after the nucleus, indicating the size of the nucleus. CVT+x'1A0' points to the beginning of CSA, and CVT+x'169' points to the PLPA. CVT=x'A4' points to the highest virtual storage address. (This is a carry over from MVT where this address represented the highest address of the region.)

9.4 MANAGING PRIVATE AREAS

Private area is allocated from the bottom and top of an address space and from the unallocated virtual storage between. Keeping track of virtual storage in the private area is more complicated than the SQA or CSA because virtual storage is allocated for these areas from one end only. The sub-pools managed in the private area are SP(sub-pool) 0 through 127, 229, 230, 233 through 237, 251, and 252. VSM keep track of the free area within each of the sub-pools allocated. Knowing how large the area is and where it begins, requests for GETMAIN in the private area are satisfied from the free area.

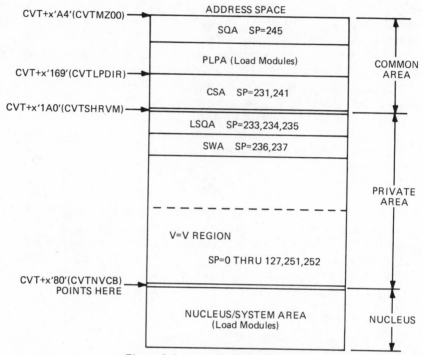

CVT+x'A4'(CVTMZOO) —

ADDRESS SPACE

SQA   SP=245

PLPA (Load Modules)

CVT+x'169'(CVTLPDIR)—

CSA   SP=231,241

CVT+x'1A0'(CVTSHRVM) —

COMMON
AREA

LSQA   SP=233,234,235

SWA   SP=236,237

V=V REGION

SP=0 THRU 127,251,252

PRIVATE
AREA

CVT+x'80'(CVTNVCB)
POINTS HERE

NUCLEUS/SYSTEM AREA
(Load Modules)

NUCLEUS

Figure 9.1 Virtual storage areas.

If we issue a GETMAIN for 72 bytes, VSM acquires 4K block of virtual storage from the total virtual storage allocated for our task. From this 4K block, VSM assigns 72 bytes to satisfy the request. If another request for 72 bytes from the same sub-pool is made, VSM now can allocate another 72 bytes from the 4K bytes of virtual storage already allocated.

Private area storage is associated with and is managed by the LOCAL SUPERVISOR. Management of the SQA and CSA is done by GLOBAL SUPERVISOR. One of the major control block used in managing the private area is called the *local data area* (LDA).

The LDA is created at address space initialization time and is located in LSQA. The LDA is pointed by the ASCBLDA field on the address space control block (ASCB) for the address space. Similarly, for global storage management there is also an anchor control block called *global data area* (GDA). The GDA is pointed by the CVTGDA field in the CVT. The GDA has pointers to other control blocks that describe system areas, such as the CSA, SQA, and nonpageable (V=R) region.

A pointer to the partitioned queue element for the address space is at offset X'8' into LDA. The PQE describes the private user area, such as the space assigned to subpools, the space not yet assigned, the size of the private user, and the starting location of the private area.

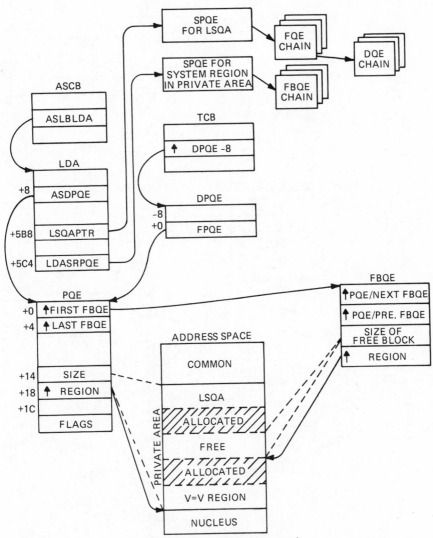

Figure 9.2 Local area control.

Offset '0' into the PQE is the pointer to the first FBQE (Free Block Queue Element) and is the pointer to the last FBQE at offset X'4'. The FBQE describes continuous free space. If free space is scattered, there will be one FBQE for each area of free space. FBQEs are chained together and anchored from the PQE. At offset X'8' into the FBQE is the size of the free area and at offset X'C' is the address of the first byte in the free area described by this FBQE. The first fullword of the FBQE points to the next FBQE or points back to the PQE if this FBQE is the last on the FBQE chain. The second fullword of the FBQE points to the previous

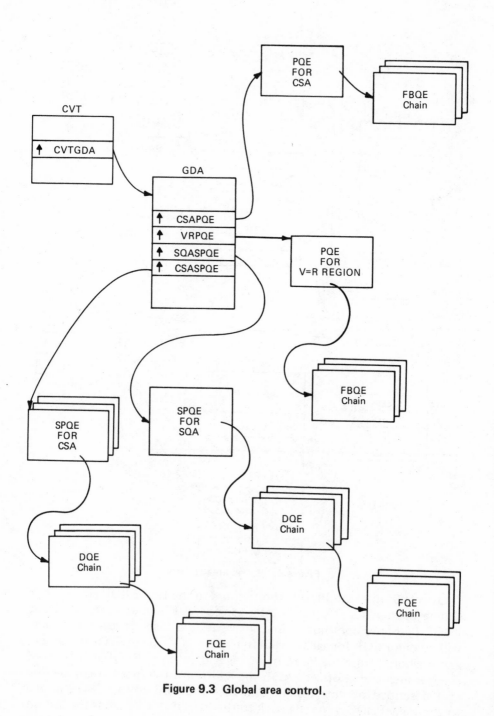

Figure 9.3 Global area control.

FBQE or points to the PQE if this FBQE is the first on the FBQE chain.

One way to get to the PQE is through the LDA that is pointed from the ASCB. Another way to get to the PQE is through the TCB. TCBDPQE pointer in the TCB points to an area 8 bytes ahead of the dummy partition queue element (DPQE). DPQE has pointers to the first and last PQE for the private area.

9.5 MANAGING SUBPOOLS

9.5.1 Characteristics

We were mentioning the name *subpool*, but we have not actually learned anything about subpools. So let us study subpools by examining their characteristics.

- SUBPOOL is all the 4K blocks of virtual storage allocated for a particular task under one label called the subpool number.
- Subpool numbers can range from 0 through 255. Subpool 0 through 127 are set aside for the user. Other subpools are for system usage and have special attributes such as fetch protection/nonfetch protect, fixed/pageable, special protect keys (0 thru 7) etc.
- Virtual storage make part of a subpool for any one request must be continuous.
- Virtual storage that makes up a complete subpool can be noncontinuous.

This last statement needs explanation. Let's say we requested 4K of subpool 0. VSM gives us 4K of continuous virtual storage. Next we may ask for 4K of virtual storage in subpool 1. VSM, after looking at the free block queue element, give us another 4K of storage labeled *subpool 1*. If we again request 8K of virtual storage in subpool 0, VSM will give us 8K of continuous virtual storage, if available.

We can see from this example that subpool consists of noncontinuous 4K and 8K areas of storage.

For a given address space there is only one subpool 251 and subpool 252. These subpools make up job pack area for an address space. This area of virtual storage contains load modules for the user. Subpool 251 contains load modules that are non-reusable, serially reusable, or re-entrant modules from nonauthorized libraries, while subpool 252 contains re-entrant modules from an authorized library. Tasks in an address space can share or have separate subpools 0 through 127.

9.5.2 Control Blocks Associated with Subpools

Subpool Queue Element (SPQE). It contains properties of a particular subpool. It has pointers to other control blocks which will further describe the subpool. SPQE is built each time a new subpool is created for a task.

The flag byte in the SPQE describes whether the particular subpool is shared or not shared and whether the subpool is owned or not owned by this task.

Description Queue Element (DQE). Each DQE represents one group of continuous blocks of storage assigned to a subpool by one request. DQE represents a minimum size of 4K block of virtual storage. A DQE is created for each GETMAIN issued by the task.

Free Queue Element (FQE). SPQE and DQE describe the properties and length of a particular subpool. But they have not described the length of the free area within a subpool. FQE describes the continuous free space within a subpool. It also gives the location and amount of virtual storage within a subpool that has not been assigned to a task.

9.5.3 *Relationship Between Control Blocks*

When initiator attaches a job step task, the first thing the initiator has to do is to GETMAIN out of subpool 0, 100 bytes for parameters from the EXEC card. Due to this GETMAIN, an SPQE is created for subpool 0. SPQE points to a DQE, which will tell us that a block of 4K of virtual storage is allocated for this task, of which 100 bytes are allocated for the parameter area. Besides having a DQE, there is a FQE that will describe the free area within subpool 0. Initiators TCB (TCBMSS) will point to SPQE for subpool 0. Since job step task is allowed to share subpool 0 owned by the initiator, the TCB for the job step task will point to a SPQE, that will in turn point to the owner SPQE. At this time the control blocks of VSM will look as in figure 9.4.

Before executing, load modules have to be brought into virtual storage and that GETMAIN is issued for subpool 251 or subpool 252. This will create SPQE, DQE, and FQE and will be chained from job step tasks TCB.

Suppose the program executing requested 6,000 bytes of storage from subpool 5. Since this is the first request for subpool 5, SPQE, DQE and FQE are created. This request is not a multiple of 4K. So the next higher multiple of 4K that satisfies the request (8K) is allocated, of which 6,000 bytes are assigned to the task. VSM chains these control blocks with appropriate values to the TCB and to the other SPQE chain. Again let us suppose the program issues a GETMAIN for 3,000 bytes from subpools. VSM checks whether the TCB already has a subpool 5 by searching through the SPQE chain. If it exists, VSM goes to DQE and FQE and checks whether there is enough continuous storage to satisfy the request. In our case there is not enough space, and VSM gets 4K of virtual storage. This time VSM does not create an SPQE, since an SPQE representing subpool 5 already exists. But this is a separate request, and hence a DQE and a related FQE is created. These control blocks are chained from the SPQE for subpool 5. If another request is made for 1,000 bytes of storage from subpool 5, VSM uses an algorithm known as BEST FIT to decide from

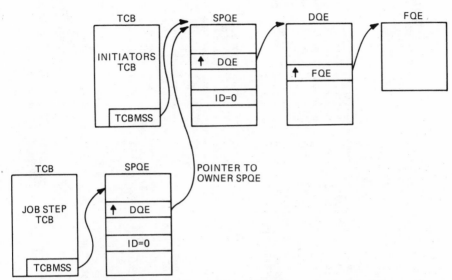

Figure 9.4 Control block structure at job step initiation time.

which of the available subpool 5 areas the request should be satisfied. VSM chooses the smallest area to fit the request, an approach known as the BEST FIT method.

If due to GETMAIN and FREEMAIN the subpool described by DQE is fragmented, free areas within the boundary of DQE are described by FQEs and are chained from the corresponding DQE. The first FQE points to the highest free area.

9.6 CONTROL BLOCKS FOR VIRTUAL STORAGE MANAGEMENT

9.6.1 Partition Queue Element (PQE)

The task control block (TCB) has a pointer (TCBPQE) to the PQE control block. In the formatted dump, the DPQE field points to DPQE minus 8 for the job step. In our example DPQE points to A3F548. This DPQE points to the first and the only PQE for the private area at A3F418 in figure 9.5. As we have already seen, PQE contains information about the beginning and the size of the private area and also pointers to the FBQEs which describe the free space within the private area. The first field in the PQE is the first free block (FFB), which contains the address of the first FBQE in the private area.

If there is no FBQEs or no free space within the private area then this field will contain the address of the PQE. The last free block (LFB) field points to the last FBQE for this private area; so, this field will also point to the PQE.

```
JOB CORTEST        STEP GO          TIME 140317   DATE 78032    ID = 000              PAGE 0001

COMPLETION CODE    SYSTEM = 0C1

PSW AT ENTRY TO ABEND  078D1000 000966C2         ILC 4   INTC 0001

ASCB 00FC5F18
  +0   ASCB C1E2C3C2  FWDP 00000000  BWDP 00FBAE28  CMSF 00000000  SVRB 00A3E7A8  SYNC 0000927A
  +18  IOSP 00000000  SPL  00000000  CPUS 00FC5FE8  IOSQ 00000001  IODP 00090011  STOR 0F281C00
  +30  LDA  00A3F548  RSM  00000000  CSCB 00FC32D8  TSB  00FC6028  EJST 00000000  XJST 18C70000
  +48  EWST 8C17C7AD  XWST E0BB0800  JSTL 00000685  ECB  00000685  URET P0A3E58   RESV 00000000
  +60  DUMP 00A3E3A0  FW1  FFFF0000  TMCH 00000000  ASXB 00A3F300  SWCT 8C12BD85  SSRB 00000000
  +78  VSC  00000018  TCBS 00000001  LOCK 00000000  LSQH 00000000  QECB 85110000  MECB 40000000
  +90  OUCB 00FC5E90  OUXB 00FBB480  FMCT 00230000  XMPQ 00000000  IQEA 00000000  RTWA 00000000
  +A8  MCC  00000000  JBNI 00FC8C70  JBNS 00FC603B  SRQ  00000000       00000000  PCTT 00000000
  +C0  SMCT 00000000  SWTL 0000DF4B  SRBT 00000000  ATME 01F36000  VGTT 00000000       00000000

TCB 9F62E8
  +0   RBP   00A3E6F0  PIE    00000000  DEB  00A1CF08  TIO  00A14020  CMP   900C1000  TRN  00000000
  +18  MSS   00A3C430  PK-FLG 80010000  FLG  000FFFFF  LLS  00A3C000  JLB   00000000  JPQ  00A3C770
  +70  FSA   0109 4FB0  TCB   00000000  TME  00000000  JST  009F62E8  NTC   00000000  OTC  00A3C920
  +88  LTC   00000000  IQE   00000000  ECB  00A3C234  TSF  20000000  D-PQE 00A3F548  AQE  009F6B88
  +A0  STAB  00A3D0A0  TCT   80A3C048  USER 00000000  SDF  00000000  MDID  00000000  JSCB 00A3CAAC
  +B8  RESV  00000000  IOBRC 00000000  XCPD 00000000  EXT  00000000  BITS  009F6C30  DAR  00000000
  +D0  EXT2  009F6410  AECB  00000000  TIRB 00000040  BAK  00A3C920  RTMWA 009F6C30  IOTM 00000000
  +E8  TMSAV 00000000  ABCR  00000000  XSCT 80000000  FOE  00000000  SWA   00A3C500  STAM 00000000
  +100 BID   E3C3C240  RTM1  80000000  ESTA 80000000  UKY  00A3FC60  CRVI  0000FFFF  BYT1 08040000
  +118 RPT   00000000  DBTB  00000000  SMAS 00A08F50  SCB  00000000  RESV  00000000  RESV 00000000
  EXT2 GTF   00000000  SVAB  00000000  EVNT 00000000  RES  00000000  RESV  00000000  RESV 00000000

ACTIVE RBS

PRB A3CA88  RESV 00000000  RESV 00000000  RTPSW1 078D1000  RESV 00000000  000956C2  RTPSW2 00040001  00A2E000
            FLG1 02000000  WC-L-IC 00040001
            RESV 00000000  APSW 00000000  SZ-STAB 00110082  FL-CDE 00A3C770  PSW 078D1000  000966C2
            Q/TTR 00000000  WT-LNK 009F62E8
  RG 0-7    00A3D0D8  00094FF8  00000040  00000000  00A3046C  00A30448  00A14018  FD000000
  RG 8-15   00A3C210  80A3C048  00000000  00000000  00A3E048  70DDE9C2  40DDECC0  00A3C240
```

```
SVRB A3E5F0   RESV 00000000   RESV 00000000      RTPSW1 00000000   00000000   RTPSW2 00000000   00D5ADC0
              FLG1 20000000    WC-L-IC 00020033
              RESV 00000000    APSW 00000000      SZ-STAB 001CD022  FL-CDE 00000000  PSW 070C1000   00D5A2B4
              Q/TTR 00000000   WT-LNK 00A3CA88
              RG 0-7  00000000   00096288   00A3046C   00096250   00096662   00095D40   000948F8
              RG 8-15 00095CB8   0009676E   00095CB8   00096558   0009669C   02000000
              EXTSA   00000000   00096288   00011BD8   009F62E8   00A3E5F0   00FC5F18   00029594   00000000
                                 FF0003CC   40000101   900C1000
              SCB 00A3D08C   00096C30   00000000   12A3E650   03A3E5F0   00000000
              FEPARM 00000000  80C1AAD0   00000000   6400DB00   00000000   00029594   00000000

SVRB A3E6E0   RESV 00000000   RESV 00000000      RTPSW1 00000000   00000000   RTPSW2 00000000   00D06000
              FLG1 02000000    WC-L-IC 0002000C

JOB COBTEST        STEP GO          TIME 140317   DATE 78032        ID = 000                     PAGE 0002
              RESV 00000000    APSW 00000000      SZ-STAB 001CD022  FL-CDE 00000000  PSW 070C0000   00DDE248
              Q/TTR 00000000   WT-LNK 00A3E5F0
              RG 0-7  000000F0   009F6D30   0080E600   00011BD8   00D5A723   50D59724   009F6C30
              RG 8-15 00A14034   00000000   00FE1F94   00A3C1D0   009F6DA4   009F6D30   00000000
              EXTSA   00000000   00A0FAB0   00A3E744   20FD0000   00000000   00000000   00000000
                                 00000000   00000000   00000000   00000000
              SCB 00A300A0   16A3E6E0   03A3E6E0   6400DB00   00000000
              FEPARM 00000000  80C1AAD0   00000884   00029594   00000000

LOAD LIST
              NE 00A3C010   RSP-CDE 00FE6A9R   CNT 00010001   NE 00A3CF28   RSP-CDE 00FBFA90   CNT 00010001
              NE 00000000   RSP-CDE 00FE7820   CNT 00010001

CDE
  A3C770   NCDE 00000000   RBP 00A3CA88   NM GO        EPA 00095CB8   XL/MJ 00A3D0C8   USE 00010000   ATTR 0820000
  FE6A98   NCDE 00FE6AC8   RBP 00000000   NM IGG019DK  EPA 00F86000   XL/MJ 00FE6A88   USE 00060000   ATTR B922000
  FBFA90   NCDE 00FC21A8   RBP 00000000   NM IGG019AQ  EPA 00BB4E00   XL/MJ 00FBFAB0   USE 00100000   ATTR B922000
  FE7B20   NCDE 00FE8ED0   RBP 00000000   NM IGG019DJ  EPA 0002F4C0   XL/MJ 00FE7840   USE 00260000   ATTR B922000
```

```
XL                                          LN       ADR       LN       ADR       LN       ADR

A3D0C8   SZ 00000010   NO 00000001          80002348 00095CB8
FE6AB8   SZ 00000010   NO 00000001          80000770 00F86000
FBFAB0   SZ 00000010   NO 00000001          80000200 00B84E00
FE7840   SZ 00000010   NO 00000001          800005A0 00D2F4C0

TIOT A14020      JOB COBTEST      STEP   GO
      OFFSET   LN-STA     DDNAME     TTR-ST     STB-UC
      + 0018   14010100   PGM=*.DD   A1F34000   80006BA0
      + 002C   14010102   SYSUDUMP   A1EB8000   80000000
      + 0040   14010102   CARDS      A1E7C000   80000000
      + 0054   14010102   PRINT      A1E64000   80000000
      + 0068   14010102   SYSDBOUT   A1E4C000   80000000

VSM
SPQE 00A3C430 NSPQE 00A3C370 DQE 009F6730 FL/RS 0000 SPID 251 KEY 8
DQE 009F6730 FQE A3C690 NDQE 000000 BLK 00095000 LN 0003000 FQE A3C690 FQE 80000000              LN 00000CB8 AREA 00095CB8
SPQE 00A3C370 NSPQE 00A3C410 DQE 00A3C410 FL/RS C000 SPID 000 KEY 8
SPQE 00A3C410 NSPQE 00000000 DQE 009F66E0 FL/RS 6000 SPID 000 KEY 8
DQE 9F66E0 FQE A3F0A0 NDQE A3C400 BLK 00094000 LN 00001000 FQE A3F0A0 FQE A3C6C0 FQE 80A3C6C0   LN 00000638 AREA 000948F0
                                                            FQE A3C6C0 FQE 80000000             LN 00000088 AREA 00094088
DQE A3C400 FQE 9F6600 NDQE 000000 BLK 0098000 LN 00001000 FQE 9F6600 FQE 80000000               LN 000009A0 AREA 009898A0

D-PQE A3F548      FIRST 00A3F418

PQE A3F418 FFB 009F6790 LFB 009F66D0 NPQ 00000000 PPQ 00000000
           TCB 00A3C920 RSI 009AC000 RAD 00094000 FLG 00000000
FBQE 9F6790 NFB 009F66D0 PFB 00A3F418 SZ 0095D000 AREA 00099000
FBQE 9F66D0 NFB 00A3F418 PFB 009F6790 SZ 0000F000 AREA 009F7000

***TCB SUMMARY***
```

Figure 9.5 Formatted dump of VSM control blocks.

9.6.2 Free Block Queue Element (FBQE)

The FBQE describes the free space within the private area not yet assigned to a sub-pool. The next free block (NFB) field points to the address of the next FBQE. If this is the only FBQE or the last FBQE, then NFB field will point to the PQE. The previous free block (PFB) field contains the address of the previous FBQE. If this is the lowest FBQE, then PFB field will point to the PQE. We can see that NFB and PFB fields produce a chained circle of FBQEs for the PQE.

9.6.3 Subpool Queue Element (SPQE)

Each SPQE describes a subpool and is used by VSM to keep track of subpools within the private area. SPQE field contains the address of this SPQE. In our example A3C430 is the address of the SPQE that is pointed by TCBMSS field. NSPQE field points to the next SPQE in the private area. If this is the last SPQE in the private area then this field will contain 0s. In our example NSPQE contains A3C370. Looking at the second SPQE in the dump we can verify this fact. The NSPQE field of the second SPQE contains 0s, indicating the last SPQE in the chain. Even though this SPQE should be the last one in the SPQE chains, we also see a third SPQE at location A3C410. Its NSPQE field also contains 0s, again indicating the last SPQE in the chain. This is because initiator-task acquired subpool 0 to pass parameters to the job step task, and job steps task is sharing subpool 0.

9.7 FREEMAIN

Requests to free virtual storage are serviced by FREEMAIN routines. These routines update control block queues to reflect the release of previously allocated virtual storage, thereby making the space available for reallocation.

FREEMAIN rounds the request up to an 8-byte multiple and searches for the requested subpool storage. If found the FQE is updated to reflect the new free space within the subpool. If more than a page of virtual storage is found, FREEMAIN notifies RSM to release the real pages. FREEMAIN also updates the FBQE to reflect the change in the region.

If FREEMAIN fails to do any of its operations, a nonzero return code is placed in register 15 for conditional requests. For unconditional requests, the requesting task is abnormally terminated if an error condition occurs.

10 Program Manager

Program management functions are divided into three categories: searching for and scheduling requested load modules, synchronizing exit routines to supervisor programs, and fetching modules into storage.

10.1 SEARCHING FOR AND SCHEDULING REQUESTED MODULES

Program management services find a load module by scanning control blocks from different queues. The order of search in the areas, queues, and directories for a module are as follows:

1. Job pack area queue (JPAQ)
2. STEPLIB or JOBLIB (task libraries)
3. Link pack area queue (LPAQ)
4. Pageable link pack area queue (PLPAQ)
5. LINKLIB

If the requested module is not found in any of the queues or associated areas, the requesting task is abnormally terminated. The program manager invokes the program fetch routine to load the requested module that is not in virtual or auxiliary storage. It is up to the program manager to identify what modules have been loaded into virtual storage, their names, starting addresses, entry points, and such attributes as their usability and re-enterability.

There are four macros that bring modules into an address space. They are LINK, LOAD, XCTL, and ATTACH. The DELETE macro, as the name implies, deletes a module. There are two additional service routines under program manager. They are IDENTIFY macro, which identifies alias names with modules, and SYNCH macro, which synchronizes exit routines.

The major control blocks associated with the program manager are

1. Request block (RB)
2. Content directory element (CDE)
3. Extent list (XL)
4. Load list element (LLE)
5. Link pack directory entry (LPDE)

175

10.2 CONTROL BLOCKS

This section summarizes the major control blocks associated with program management. These control blocks are conceptualized in figures 10.1 and 10.2.

10.2.1 Contents Directory Element (CDE)

We have seen that all modules that are brought into the private area of an address space are represented by CDEs in the job pack area queue.

The NCDE field in the CDE points to the beginning of the next CDE. If this is the last or the only CDE in the JPAQ, then this field will contain 0s. The RBP field contains a pointer to the request block (RB) for this CDE. If this CDE represents a module that is brought in by a LOAD macro, the RBP field will contain 0s.

The NM field gives the name of the module represented by this particular CDE. The EPA field contains the entry point address of the module in the address space. The XL/MCDE field points to another control block that will further describe this load module.

The USE field indicates the total number of successful requests for this module by ATTACH, LINK, LOAD, and XCTL macro instructions. The maximum use count is 32,757.

The FLAG or ATTR field provides the attributes of this module. If the first hex digit is 8 or more, it indicates either that the module is brought into link pack area during IPL by the nucleus initialization program or that this module is from fixed or modified link pack area.

10.2.2 Extent List (XL)

We have seen that for each module brought in by LINK, LOAD, XCTL and ATTACH macro, there is a CDE that represents its existence. For each CDE there is a corresponding extent list entry.

The LENGTH field in the XL provides the length of the module in hex bytes.

The ADR or BEG field contains the starting address of the first physical byte of the module defined by this XL entry.

10.2.3 Load List Element (LLE)

Each time the LOAD macro is executed, an LLE is created if one does not exist. The use count in the CDE is increased and the responsibility count in the LLE is also increased. The LLEs for each task in the job step are chained together to form the LOAD LIST. The NLLE field in the LLE points to the next LLE on the queue. The CDE field in the LLE points to the corresponding CDE for this module. The first 2 bytes of the CNT field contains the responsibility count for this module. This number represents the total number of LOAD macros executed against

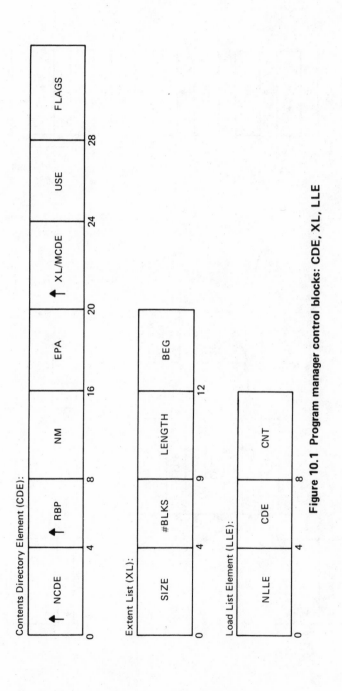

Figure 10.1 Program manager control blocks: CDE, XL, LLE

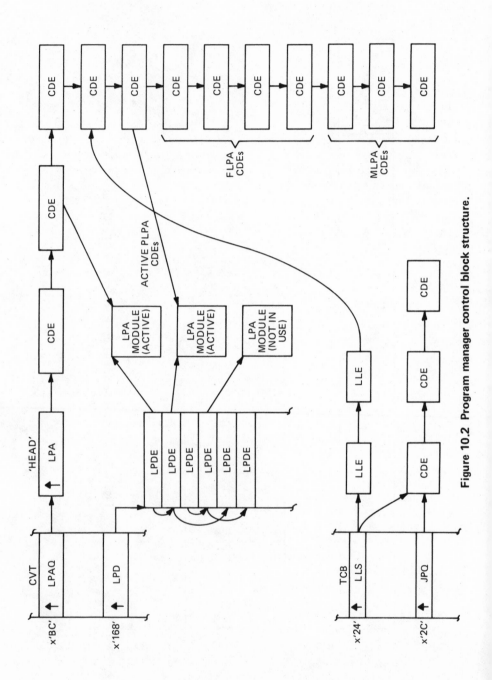

Figure 10.2 Program manager control block structure.

this module. The last 2 bytes of the CNT field contain the system responsibility count. This represents the total number of system requests for the module via the LOAD macro instructions.

10.3 METHOD OF SEARCH

10.3.1 Job Pack Areas (JPA)

The job pack area in virtual storage contains modules needed during the execution of tasks. The JPA resides in subpool 251 and subpool 252 of the region. Subpool 251 contains either non-reusable or serially reusable load modules or else re-entrant modules from nonauthorized libraries, while subpool 252 contains re-entrant modules from authorized libraries. Problem programs, including TSO tasks, execute in the JPA. Modules in the JPA may be executed only by the user in whose address space they are loaded.

Modules in the JPA are represented by contents directory elements that are chained together and collectively are anchored from TCBJPQ field in the job step task's TCB. This CDE chain is called the *job pack area queue* (JPAQ).

10.3.2 STEPLIB or JOBLIB Search

If the program manager cannot find the requested module in virtual storage by searching the JPAQ or LOADLIST, control is given to BLDL routine. This routine searches the auxiliary storage libraries specified in the STEPLIB or JOBLIB control card. The TCBJLB field in the TCB contains the address of the DCB for the library. If the module is found in any of these libraries, the BLDL routine reads the partition data set (PDS) directory entry for the modules into storage and a return code of 0 is passed to the requester. If the module is not found in these libraries, then BLDL routine passes a return code of 4 to its requester.

10.3.3 Link Pack Area (LPA)

The LPA is an area in virtual storage containing selected re-enterable and serially reusable routines that are loaded at IPL time and can be used concurrently by all tasks in the system. There are three link pack areas:

1. Pageable link pack area (PLPA)
2. Modified link pack area (MLPA)
3. Fixed link pack area (FLPA)

Let us see how the modules in each area are represented for program manager search. PLPA contains type-3 and -4 SVC routines, access method routines and other system or user read-only re-entrant modules. Every program in PLPA is represented by an entry in LPA directory. This directory is created during nucleus initialization and consists of LPA directory entries (LPDEs) for each entry point in the PLPA modules. The LPDEs for major entry points contain a CDE and a compressed XL; LPDEs for alias entry points contain the name of a related major entry instead of a compressed XL. Communication vector table (CVT) at off-set x'168' points to the link pack area directory.

Modified link pack area (MLPA) contains temporarily modified modules from SYS1.SVCLIB, SYS1.LPALIB, and SYS1.LINKLIB. The modules in MLPA want to be included in the bottom of LPAQ (link pack area queue). Fixed link pack area (FLPA) is used for system performance. Modules that are time dependent are placed in this area. This area is non-pageable and is above system nucleus. Modules are represented by CDEs and are chained above the CDEs for MLPA modules on the LPAQ. In effect makes the FLPA being searched for modules before searching the MLPA.

10.3.4 Link Pack Area Queue (LPAQ)

This is the active CDE chain that the system searches for modules in the link pack areas. This queue contains CDEs for MLPA modules which are chained from the bottom of FLPA CDEs. From this time onwards, any request for a module in the link pack area is done by searching the CDEs for FLPA and then CDEs for MLPA on the LPAQ. If not found on either queue, link pack area directory (LPAD) is searched. If a module is found in LPAD, then from the LPAD entry (LPADE), a CDE and an XL is created. The CDE is chained from the HEAD of LPAQ. Thus, currently active PLPA modules are first chained on the LPAQ. When a module in PLPA that is represented by the count = 0 in the CDE becomes inactive it is deleted and the CDE entry for the module is removed from the LPAQ.

10.3.5 LINKLIB

This library contains nonresident system routines, such as assembler language processor, linage editor, utility program, and service aids. Program manager searches this library by using BLDL routine. The DCB address for the linklib (SYS1.LINKLIB) is in the CVT. If the Program manager still cannot find the module requested, it will search all libraries specified in the LINKLIST. LINKLIST specification is in the SYS1.PARMLIB.

If, after searching for the modules in all the areas specified above, the program manager still cannot find the module, the requesting task is abnormally terminated with a completion code of S806.

In cases where the module is not found in virtual storage, program manager creates a CDE and places it on the JPAQ for the task. Program attributes from the program library directory are used to update the CDE flag field. Program FETCH is given control to bring the module into virtual storage.

If the module is found in virtual storage, there should be a CDE already existing. But in the case of an inactive PLPA module, a CDE and an XL are created from the LPDE and place the CDE on the LPAQ. Even though the module is found, program manager has to further check the attributes of the module to determine its usability. If the module is a re-entrant, then the module is immediately available and the program manager can start scheduling the execution of the module. PM does this by creating a PRB and chaining it to the TCB-RB chain. The only exception to this rule is when the module is marked "ONLY LOADABLE." In this case, only LOAD macro can be issued against the module.

If the module is serially reusable, program manager has to check whether anybody is using it by checking the CDERBP field in the CDE. If this field contains 0s, then no one is using this module and it is available immediately. But if this field is not 0, then, in the case of LINK, ATTACH and XCTL, the request is suspended and put on a queue of waiting requesters.

In the case of LOAD, since the control is not going to be given to the module immediately, the module is always available. PM makes sure that an LLE exists on the LOAD LIST, or the LLE is updated.

If the module is non-reusable, a new copy of the module is brought into virtual storage. In the case of LINK, ATTACH and XCTL, if a non-reusable module is found in virtual storage and the module is never used by any other task, the requested module becomes immediately available.

The program manager determines whether a module is ever used by a task by checking CDNFN bit in the CDE. If this bit is a 1, it means that some task has already used this module; hence, a new copy of the non-reusable module has to be brought into virtual storage. In the case of LOAD, a new copy of the non-reusable module is always brought into virtual storage. The search for a module always starts from JPAQ and ends up in LINKLIB or libraries in the link-list, as described in the previous steps.

10.4 PROGRAM MANAGEMENT OPERATIONS

10.4.1 Program Fetch

If the program manager cannot locate the requested module in virtual storage but has located it in auxiliary storage through BLDL, the program fetch routine is given control. This routine brings the module into virtual storage from auxiliary storage.

The program fetch routine checks the attributes of both the module and library to determine whether they are authorized. If both are authorized, a GETMAIN is issued for the module in subpool 252. Else, GETMAIN is issued in subpool 251.

The program fetch routine gives control to the channel programs that it creates in its work area. These channel programs transfer text records, RDL records, and the control records into virtual storage.

Using the RDL records, program fetch changes the values of the address constants in the loaded program according to the absolute virtual storage address.

An extent list (XL) is created. The physical beginning and the length of the module are placed in the XL. In order to acquire storage for the XL, program fetch issues a GETMAIN macro/instruction. GETMAIN returns the storage address from the XL, and the program fetch places this address in the CDE for the module. Also, the entry point of the module is placed in the CDE.

Abnormal conditions such as I/O errors while loading, invalid record type or insufficient storage space for program fetch are notified to program manager through conditions code setting in Register 15.

10.4.2 LINK

The LINK macro is issued when it is desired to bring in another module and pass control to it. After the execution of the module, it is expected that control will be returned to the calling module.

When the program execute a LINK, it causes an SVC interrupt. Since SVC6 is not a type 1 SVC, an SVRB is created by the SVC first level interrupt handle (SVC FLIH). SVC FLIH places the entry point of the LINK SVC routine in the SVRB. It also places the address of the EXIT PROLOG in register 14 and control is given to the LINK routine. The LINK routine will execute under the control of the new SVRB created. When the LINK routine gets control, it first checks the validity of the parameters passed to this routine through an address in register 15. The parameter list is 12 bytes long, and the first byte indicates the form of the module identification. If the first byte is x'80', it indicates the 'DE=' form of macro instructions and the next 3 bytes contains the address of directory entry list. If the first byte is x'00', it indicates the EP or EPLOC form of macro instructions and the next 3 bytes contains the address of entry point name.

Next, the link routine does the search for the module as described in section 10.3. The address of JPAQ is placed in register 8 before the search for the module. We have seen that if the search fails to find the module, then the task is abended with a system code of S806.

The LINK routine next determines whether the module can be used immediately. If the module cannot be used, then the search for the module is started and finally program FETCH is given control to bring a new copy of the module into virtual storage. If the module was link-edited with ONLY-LOADABLE attribute, then the task is abended with a system code of S406.

If the module found in virtual storage cannot be used immediately because it is being fetched into virtual storage or some other task is using it, the request for it is queued and the control is given to the dispatcher.

How does LINK routine defer the request and so place the requesting task in a wait state? From the CDE of the module that is in use, LINK gets the address of the RB that controls the module at that time. In the RB there is a field called RBPGMQ. This field is used to indicate that some other task wants to use the same serially reusable program. Link routine updates the RBPGMQ for the PRB with the address of the LINK's SVRB, and the use count in the CDE is incremented by one. The queue chained through the RBPGMQ is called an *SVRB suspend queue* (SSQ). By incrementing the wait count (WC) field in the SVRB, LINK routine places the requesting task in a wait state.

10.4.3 Schedule for Execution

If the module found in the virtual storage can be used immediately, then the use count in the CDE for the module is incremented by one. The LINK routine next creates a PRB for the requested module and chains the PRB behind the SVRB for the LINK SVC. The entry point address of the module is placed in the RBOPSW for the new PRB.

At this point, the link process is complete and control is returned to the EXIT PROLOG. (NOTE. Register 14 points to EXIT PROLOG at entry to LINK routine.) EXIT PROLOG routine removes the SVRB from the TCB-RB chain. It also moves the register from the SVRB to the TCB and control is given to the dispatcher. When this task becomes the highest priority task in the system, dispatcher gives control of the CPU to the task. Dispatcher does this by loading the current PSW in the CPU, from the RBOPSW in the RB pointed by the TCB. When this happens, the linked module gets control.

10.4.4 Exit From a Linked Program

When a problem program issues a RETURN macro, control is actually given to an EXIT SVC (SVC3). RETURN macro sets up register 14 with the address of SVC3 and does a branch register instruction (BR 14).

Since SVC3 is a Type 1 SVC, no SVRB is created for this EXIT routine. EXIT routine determines the type of exiting program. The program can be a user program, SPIE exit routine, an asynchronous exit routine or an SVC routine. EXIT performs some special processing for each type of the exiting program. We have already seen the process done by the EXIT routine for SPIE exits. Now let us look at the process done by the EXIT routine for user or system program.

EXIT routine first checks RBTCBNXT bit in the RB. This is to determine whether this RB is the last one on the chain that is pointing back to the TCB. In this case, EXIT routine invokes the end-of-task processing by issuing SVC 13. SVC 13 performs the normal termination of the task.

If the RBTCBNXT bit is not set, then EXIT decrements the use count in the CDE by 1. If the module represented by this CDE is serially reusable and if the RBPGMQ contains an address, then EXIT routine sets up an environment to enable a deferred requester for this module.

If the use count reaches 0 after the subtraction, this means *no outstanding request* for this module; the module is freed along with the CDE and the XL control blocks. EXIT routine removes the PRB from the TCB-RB chain and frees the area for the PRB.

After its processing, EXIT SVC routine gives up control to EXIT PROLOG. If the task can be redispatched, then current PSW in the CPU is loaded with the RBOPSW from the next level of RB. This in fact gives control back to the original program at the instruction next to the LINK SVC instruction. If for some reason the task cannot be redispatched, then EXIT PROLOG returns control to the dispatcher.

10.4.5 LOAD

The LOAD macro is used to bring a module into the virtual storage, but control is not given to the module. When a LOAD SVC instruction is issued, the LOAD SVC routine searches for the load module as discussed previously and brings a copy of it into virtual storage if no usable copies exist in storage. After the successful completion of the LOAD routine, register 0 contains the virtual storage address of the entry point specified for the requested module. Register 1 contains the length of the loaded module. The first byte of register 1 contains the authorization code. After the SVC interrupt, SVC FL1H gives control to the LOAD SVC routine. After validating the input parameters in register 1 and register 2, LOAD routine places the address of JPAQ in register 8. Then, LOAD routine sets the lower-order bit in RBCDFLGS (of the LOAD's SVRB) to 1 to indicate a load request. Using the TCB address in register 4, LOAD routine searches the LOADLIST pointed from the requester's TCB. If the module cannot be found in the load list, then the control is given to the search routines previously described. (These search routines are part of the LINK, and hence control is given to LINK.)

Once the module is found, LOAD routine considers three conditions to determine module usability. If the module cannot be used, control is given to LINK routine to search the libraries and bring in a new copy of the load module. If the module can be used later, then the requester is queued by a WAIT macro instruction. If the module is immediately available, LOAD routine increases the use count in the CDE for the module. If the use count exceeds 32,767, then the task is terminated with S906.

If none already exists, a load list element (LLE) is created for the loaded module and is chained to the caller's load list. LOAD routine also increases the responsibility count in the LLE by 1. If the count reached is more than 32,767, the task is terminated.

As in the case of LINK routine, LOAD routine also passes control to the EXIT PROLOG that will remove the SVRB for the LOAD routine. EXIT PROLOG gives control back to the interrupted task if dispatchable or to the dispatcher.

One important fact is that no PRB is created for the module in the case of a LOAD macro. This is because control is not given to the load module immediately, and hence no new level of control represented by a PRB is needed.

10.4.6 DELETE

The DELETE routine is used by the requester who previously issued a LOAD request to remove module that he brought into virtual storage. The DELETE SVC routine searches the requester's load list for the requested module. Register 4 will contain the requester's TCB address and TCBLLS field points to the load list for the task. LLE points to the CDE for the module.

If the module is not found by searching through the LLEs in the load list, a return code of 4 is passed in register 15.

If the module is found, then the responsibility count in the LLE is decremented by 1. If the responsibility count equals 0, then the LLE is freed. The DELETE routine also reduces the use count in the CDE for the module. If the CDE use count is 0, then the module is freed, along with the CDE and the XL. A return code of 0 is passed in register 15, indicating completion of DELETE.

As in the case of all other SVC routines, DELETE also passes control to EXIT PROLOG; from there control is returned to the dispatcher.

10.4.7 XCTL

The macro instruction XCTL, in addition to being used to pass control, is used to indicate that the program issuing the XCTL macro is completed. As in the case of the LINK routine, XCTL routine creates the linkage to a specified load module and ensures that the requester does not regain control after the specified load module has been executed. The load module that is given control executes with the same protection key and in the same state as the requester.

After validating the parameter list passed in Register 15, the XCTL routine passes control to the GETMAIN routine to obtain storage for a program request block (PRB). This PRB is initialized with information from the old PRB. Next the current RB pointer in the TCB is changed to point to the old RB, and the RB chain field in the old RB is changed to point to the SVRB for the XCTL routine. The RB chain field in the SVRB points to the new PRB that was just created.

The XCTL routine removes the old PRB by using SVC3 instruction. After this, TCB will point to the SVRB for XCTL routine; this SVRB in turn points to the new PRB. This PRB will point to the rest of the RB chain. By doing this switch, XCTL accomplishes the same level of RB control with the new module.

For the requested module, a search is done using LINK routines. A copy of the load module is loaded if necessary, and the entry point address is placed in register 15. The RBOPSW field of the new PRB is updated with the value in register 15.

The use count in the CDE is incremented for the load module to which control is to be passed. It is decremented for the module represented by the old PRB.

After its processing, the XCTL SVC routine gives control to EXIT PROLOG. EXIT PROLOG removes the SVRB for the XCTL SVC routine. If the task is dispatchable, control is given to the task. Since the RBOPSW field is used to load the current PSW in the CPU, the module specified by the XCTL macro will get control. If this task is not dispatchable, then control is given to the dispatcher.

11 Task Manager

Task manager provides services for problem and supervisor programs. The major functions provided by this manager's routines are the creation and control of the subtasks. Task manager routines can be activated through macro instructions such as ATTACH, DETACH, WAIT, POST, ENQ, DEQ, and CHAP. Such exit effections as STATUS, EVENTS, MODESET, and RESERVE are also classified under task management. Using these macros, control of the task execution can be done directly or indirectly.

11.1 OVERVIEW

The ATTACH macro is used to create a new subtask, and DETACH is used to terminate or delete a subtask. The WAIT and POST macros are used to synchronize the execution of tasks, while ENQ, DEQ, and RESERVE macros are used to serialize serially reusable resources between tasks. The CHAP, STATUS, and MODESET macros are used to alter the dispatchability of tasks.

EVENTS macro was added to the task manager to further enhance the synchronizations previously provided by WAIT and POST macros. The working of EXIT and EXIT PROLOG routines were covered in previous chapters. EXIT performs the exiting procedures for problem and system programs, while EXIT PROLOG performs the exiting procedures from SVC routines.

Task manager also provides informational services through two other macros, namely EXTRACT and TESTAUTH. EXTRACT enables the requester to extract information from control blocks such as TCB (task control block), JSCB (job step control block) and CSCB (command scheduling control block). TESTAUTH macro provides verification routines for authorization checks. This macro checks whether a task has the authorization to request a specific function.

11.2 ATTACH MACRO

A new task is created when the ATTACH macro is executed. The task that issued this macro is called the *originating task*, and the newly created task is called the *subtask* of the originating task. The idea behind creating subtask was to gain more frequent control of system resources by creating more competition for the resources within a job step. Thus, when a wait condition occurs within one of the tasks in a job step, it is not necessarily a task from another address space that obtains control, but it may be the one within the job step itself. If the execution of different functions within a task is overlapped, creating subtasks to do different functions will reduce the total run time required by a single job step task.

Let us assume that a program is executing under a TCB (TCB_A) and the level of control is represented by a PRB (PRB_A). The TCB-RB chain will look like figure 11.1. The PSW and the registers for the task are in the CPU.

Now, let us assume that the program A is issued an ATTACH to program B as follows:

ATTACH EP=B, PARM=(x,y,z), ETXR=ENDSUB1,ECB=MYECB.

As we know, ATTACH macro will generate a parameter list for the ATTACH-processing routine and finally generate a supervisor call (SVC 42) instruction. The end-of-task exit routine (ETXR) specifies the address of the exit routine to be executed when the subtask is terminated normally or abnormally. The event control block (ECB) indicates that the supervisor should notify the parent task about the completion of the child or subtask by posting the ECB·ETXR and ECB parameters used to communicate the status of the subtask to the originating (parent) task.

When the CPU executes the ATTACH SVC instruction, an SVC interrupt is generated and SVCFLIH obtains control. Since ATTACH is a Type 3 SVC, an SVRB is created and registers at the time the interrupt is saved in the SVRB. (For further details see chapter 7.) The PSW at the time of the interrupt was saved in the PRB, and the registers are saved in the SVRB.

Registers 13, 15, 0, and 1 in the CPU are then loaded with the values from the SVRB, but register 14 is loaded with the address of EXIT PROLOG. SVC FLIH will then give control to the ATTACH routines. At this time, TCB-RB chain will look like figure 11.2.

11.3 ATTACH LOGIC

At entry to ATTACH processing, register 15 will point to a parameter list. A validity check is performed on the input data and, if found invalid, terminates the task that issued ATTACH. ATTACH routines also make sure that the input data can be referenced with the callers protect key by changing the key using the MODESET macro. If invalid input is found, a program check occurs and diagnostic routines get control. After the check is done, protect key is changed back to 0 by using MODESET.

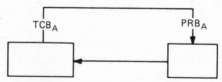

Figure 11.1 TCB-RB chain before the execution of ATTACH macro.

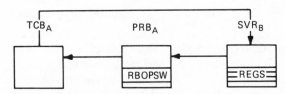

Figure 11.2 TCB-RB chain after an ATTACH SVC is executed.

Another validity check is performed to confirm that the ATTACH is not issued from a STAE exit. TCBNSTAE field in the TCB is checked for this; if set, a return code of x'04' is returned in register 15.

If the parameters passed are found to be valid, ATTACH routines acquire storage for a new SVRB in LSQA (SUBPOOL 255). Under this SVRB the LINK processing for the new program (Program B) will be scheduled.

Next, ATTACH routines get storage for the new TCB in subpool 253 (also in LSQA). If an ETXR parameter is specified in the ATTACH macro, then ATTACH obtains storage for an interruption queue element (IQE). ATTACH then searches through the current TCBs subtask queue for an interruption request block (IRB) that represents the same end-of-task exit routine. (IQEs are pointed by the TCBIQE field of the TCBs. And the IQEIRB field within the IQE points to the IRB. RBEP field in the IRB contains the address of the asynchronous routine.) If found, ATTACH increases (+1) the RBUSE count in the IRB and chains the IRB off of the new IQE. TCBIQE field in the new TCB is updated with the address of the new IQE.

But if the ETXR is not found in any of the subtasks IQE chains, then a new IRB is created by using SVC 43 (Create IRB) routine. SVC 43 is also called STAGE I EXIT effecter. This routine initializes the IRB and begins the scheduling of the asynchronous exit routine. IRBUSE Count is set to one at this time.

ATTACH then starts initializing the IQE. The LINK field in the IQE is initialized with 0 value. IQE PARAM field of the IQE is primed with the TCB address of the subtask. (This address will be passed to ETXR routine in register 1 when the subtask ends.) The IRB pointer in the IQE is initialized with the address of the IRB, and the IQETCBA field of the IQE is initialized with the address of the TCB for the mother task. This is necessary because the ETXR routine will be executed under the TCB of the mother task when the subtask terminates.

If STAI or ESTAI parameter is used in the ATTACH macro, then SVC 60 routine is invoked to build the SCBs and the SCBs are chained from the TCBSCB field of the new TCB (TCB_B).

In addition to updating the TCBIQE field of the new TCB, TCBFETXR field (BIT) is set to indicate that an ETXR to be scheduled at the end of this task. Next, certain invariant fields from TCB_A (such as TCBPQE, TCBTIO, TCBJLB, and TCBJSTCB) are propagated to the subtasks TCB (TCB_B).

If an ECB parameter is coded in the ATTACH macro, then the TCBECB field of the subtasks TCB is primed with the address of the ECB. According to the LPMOD and DPMOD parameter values, TCBLMP and TCBDSP fields in the TCB for the subtask are also updated.

The ATTACH routines build a queue of SPQEs off of the TCBMSS field according to the values specified in the SHSPL, SHSPV, GSPL, GSPV, and SZERO parameters in the ATTACH macro. If the "give subpool" parameter is specified, then the corresponding SPQE is de-queued from the originating (mother) TCB and is chained from the subtask (daughter) TCB. In the case of a "share subpool" parameter, a new SPQE is built chained from the subtask TCB. This new SPQE will point to the original (owning) SPQE for the subpool.

Possible errors in subpool transfer are

1. Subpool ID is greater than 127.
   In this case the parent task is terminated with an abend code of x'22A'.
2. An attempt is made to give up the control of a shared subpool.
   In this case the parent task is terminated with an abend code of x'12A'.

The ATTACH routine acquires an SVRB. This SVRB is chained from the subtask's TCB. Registers from the SVRB for the ATTACH routine are moved to the newly created SVRB. These registers contain values that obtain at the time of the SVC interruption for ATTACH. It is to be noted that Register 1 contains the problem program parameter list for program B.

The slot for Register 1 in the SVRB (for the ATTACH) is modified by the address of the TCB for the subtask (TCB_B). RBOPSW field of the $SVRB_B$ for the subtask is modified to point to a specialized routine in the ATTACH logic. Next, ATTACH routines will chain the subtask's TCB_B on the dispatching queue for the address space and also chain this TCB on the family queue of the mother TCB. Ready TCB count in the ASCB and the total TCB count in the ASXB are each incremented by 1. Now the ATTACH processing under the mother TCB_A is complete. Control is given to EXIT PROLOG routine. EXIT PROLOG frees the $SVRB_A$ from the TCB-RB chain for the mother task, and control is given to the dispatcher. When TCB_B gets control for the first time, according to the RBOPSW field in the $SVRB_B$ an ATTACH routine is activated. This routine obtains a problem program save area from subpool 0 (or subpool 250 if SVAREA=YES specified) and places the address of this save area into TCBFSA field on the TCB$_B$ and the slot for Register 13 in the SVRB$_B$.

Next, the ATTACH routine branches to an entry point in the program manager logic (LINK routine) to search the module for program B. LINK routine creates a PRB for program B and chains this PRB to the TCB$_B$. (See chapter 10, PROGRAM MANAGER LOGIC, for further details.) When the LINK routine finishes processing, control will be given to EXIT PROLOG. EXIT PROLOG will remove the SVRB$_B$, and control will be given to the dispatcher. When the TCB$_B$ becomes the highest-priority task, the dispatcher will give control to it. Now we have two tasks (TCB$_A$ and TCB$_B$) competing for the system resources.

11.4 EXIT PROCESSING

When the subtask finishes, it issues a RETURN macro. The last generated instruction from this macro is a BR 14 instruction. Register 14 will point to an SVC 3 instruction and then EXIT routine will get control.

We have already seen what the EXIT routine does when invoked through user SPIE routine. (See chapter 7, RETURN FROM USER SPIE ROUTINE, for more information.) EXIT routine also handles the exiting procedures for problem programs, asynchronous exit routines, and supervisor routines executing under an system interruption request block (SIRB). EXIT performs different functions for each type of exiting program. EXIT determines the type of the exiting program by examining the RBSTAB field associated with the RB.

The EXIT routine removes the RB under which the completed program was operating. Program-check routines which have no associated RBs are an exception to this rule.

In the case of a problem program RB, the EXIT before removing the PRB checks whether the RB is the last one. EXIT does this by checking RBTCBNXT field for the TCB address. If it contains the TCB address, it indicates the last PRB for the task and end-of-task processing is evoked. If the RB is not the last one, then the RB is marked as inactive and a program management subroutine (CDEXIT) is invoked to free the program. After the PRB is freed, control is given to the dispatcher.

11.5 NORMAL END-OF-TASK PROCESSING

The EOT routine checks the TCBEOT field in the TCB. If the task is going through the end-of-task processing for the first time, this field will contain 0 and the EOT routine does the following:

- Saves the return code which is in register 15 and it is moved into register 1. (Return code will become the condition code for the following job step.)

- Since the EXIT routine does not plan to go through the EXIT PROLOG at this pass, it clears the Type 1 switch in the ASCB. (Usually this switch is cleared by EXIT PROLOG.)
- EXIT routine also releases the LOCAL LOCK at this time. (Usually this function is done by EXIT PROLOG.)
- Next, this routine issues SVC 13 and control is given to RTM2. (Note: We are now executing out of the EXIT ROUTINE. By doing the above two steps, EXIT routine (an SVC) bypassed the normal procedure of exiting through the EXIT PROLOG.)

RTM2 recognizes it is a normal task termination by looking in Register 1. By looking at the first byte (high-order byte) RTM determines whether any abnormal conditions exist. If so recovery processing routine for the failing task is invoked. In our case RTM2 branches to task terminations processor.

Task termination processor checks whether the task is in a "must complete" state. TCBFJMC field is checked for this. If yes, then the task is terminated with an abend code of E03.

Next the TCBLTC field is checked for the existence of any subtasks for this task. If any subtask exists, then the task is terminated with an abend code of 'A03'. By following down the TCBLTC chain all subtasks are terminated by issuing DETACH.

Task termination processor then gives control sequentially to installation defined resource manager routines so that they can free task related resources. The module IEAVTRML contains the names of installation routines. After this, IBM-defined resource manager routines are given control to free task-related resources and control blocks. These routines are called in the following sequence:

1. Data Management*
2. TIMER
3. SPIE
4. ENQ/DEQ
5. WTOR
6. Region Control Task
7. VTAM/TCAM
8. Subsystem Interface
9. TIOC
10. POST
11. RSM
12. IQE
13. SRB Purge

*(To close data sets; if fails to close, abend with x'C03')

Next, the task termination processor places the address of SVC 3 in the RBOPSW field in the PRB, so that, when this RB gets control, the EXIT routine will be invoked again.

After setting the EOT flag in the TCB (TCBEOT) RTM2 will branch to EXIT PROLOG to get rid of the SVRB for SVC13. EXIT PROLOG after removing the SVRB gives control to the dispatcher.

When the dipatcher dispatches our PRB, according to the address set up in the RBOPSW, an SVC interrupt (SVC3) is generated. And, finally, EXIT routine will get control back again. But at this time TCBEOT flag will be on and final clean up for the task is started.

EXIT routine at this time frees all the programs loaded by this task. (LOADLIST entries represent all the programs loaded by this task. Note that no DELETES are issued for these programs.) After freeing the subpools for this task, EXIT ROUTINE reduces the ready TCB count in the ASCB by 1. Then control is given to the DETACH routine at a special entry point (IGC062R1) to handle the ETXR scheduling. This routine also posts the ECB specified in the ATTACH macro and releases the resources related to the TCB, such as the control block TCB and possibly the problem program save area.

DETACH checks for the existence of ETXR (TCBFETXR) and ECB (TCBECB). If TCBECB$_B$ is found to be waiting, the POST routine is given control to post the ECB. If there is no ETXR, then Stage II exit effecter is bypassed; else, after getting the IQE address from the TCB, control is given to the Stage II exit effecter.

We will examine the Stage II exit effecter later. But now let us continue with the process within DETACH.

DETACH removes the TCB from the dispatching queue and decrements the total TCB count in the ASXB by 1. If ECB or ETXR is specified, then the TCB is not freed and control is given to normal EOT processing, after setting the TCBFC field to 1. If neither ECB nor ETXR conditions exist, then the TCB and its problem program save area (if one exists) are freed. Control is then passed back to main line EXIT.

11.6 STAGE II EXIT EFFECTER

This routine is used by the supervisor and the data management routines to perform the second step in scheduling an asynchronous exit routine. This routine places the IQE on the IQE chain anchored at ASXB. ASXBFIQE field in the ASXB points to the first IQE, and ASXBLIQE points to the last IQE. If data management routine wants to schedule an asynchronous routine (represented by RQE), Stage II exit effecter places the RQE on the RQE chain beginning at ASXBFRQE and ending at ASXBLRQE. In the same way if an I/O supervisor wants to schedule an error recovery procedure (ERP), the SVRB representing the request is placed on a chain starting at ASXBFSRB and ending at ASXBLSRB. The address of the SRB is passed to the Stage II exit effecter through register 0, while the address of IQE or RQE is passed through register 1.

Next, the Stage II exit effecter sets the Stage III switch (ASCB3S) in the ASCB. This switch is checked by the dispatcher to determine whether there is work available in this address space. After this control is given to the caller, in our case—back to the DETACH code. DETACH will then give control back to the dispatcher.

When the dispatcher selects the above address space, it checks the ASCB3C switch. If found set, dispatcher go to the Stage III exit effecter to complete the scheduling of the asynchronous exit routine.

11.7 STAGE III EXIT EFFECTER

This routine searches the three asynchronous queue elements (IQE, RQE, and SRBs) chained off the ASXB for scheduling. The availability of an element depends on the availability of a corresponding IRB. EXIT effecter checks the RBFACTV for a value of 1. If found to be 1, then it indicates that the asynchronous routine represented by the IRB is in use and the next element is examined. Stage III EXIT effecter also checks whether the task that the asynchronous exit is to process is executing on another CPU. If found active, this element is deferred and the next element is examined.

Some other reasons why the exit effecter does not choose an asynchronous element for scheduling are the following:

- The IQE has been purged by DUMP (IQEPURGE=1).
- Asynchronous exits have been suppressed for this task (TCBFX=1).
- The asynchronous exit is being scheduled to the error task and an error recovery procedure is in process on that task.

Once an asynchronous element is found that is schedulable, then Stage III EXIT effecter does the following:

- The IRB is placed in the TCB-RB chain and then the IRB becomes the current RB for the task.
- The registers from the TCB (which was saved when the last interrupt happened) is moved to the IRB. This is necessary because the IRB is executing under the mother's TCB, and there should be a place to save the current registers for the program that was executing under the mother's TCB.
- The IRB is marked active (RBFACTV=1), so that any other requests for use of the same IRB will be deffered.

- The entry point of the asynchronous routine is placed in the RBO-PSW of the IRB.
- The RBIQE is set to point to the queue element that scheduled the asynchronous routine (IQE, RQE or SRB).
- If this task has been made ready and it previously was not, the count of ready TCBs (ACBTCBS) is incremented by 1.
- The registers in the TCB are initialized to set up for entry to the asynchronous exit. The registers are set with the following pointers:

  Register 0 points to IQE.

  Register 1 points to IQEPARM (TCB address of SUBTASK).

  Register 13 points to save area.

  Register 14 points to SVC 3 instruction.

  Register 15 points to EP of ETXR.
- Control is given to dispatcher.

11.8 RETURN FROM THE ETXR

When the end-of-the-task EXIT routine finishes processing, it issues a RETURN. This will cause an SVC interruption. (Remember Register 14 points to an SVC 3 instruction.) And control is given to EXIT routine.

We have already seen the processing that takes place in two different legs of the EXIT processing. The third leg is the exit processing from an IRB.

The exiting procedures for an IRB are the following:

- Registers that are saved in the IRB are moved back to the TCB to re-establish the environment for the PRB.
- The IRB is removed from the TCB-RB chain and now the PRB becomes the current RB.
- Decrement the IRB use count. If the use count is zero, then free the IRB.
- Go to the EXIT PROLOGUE and from there go to the dispatcher.

When the dispatcher redispatches this task, the original environment is established for the task and the program represented by the PRB resumes execution from the point of interruption.

11.9 DETACH PROCESSING

DETACH macro is used to remove a subtask from the TCB family queue and to free up all the resources used by the subtask. If the mother task issues an ATTACH macro with ECB or ETXR parameter in creating the subtask, it is the responsibility of the mother task to remove the subtask from the system using DETACH macro. Failure to remove subtask in this case will abnormally terminate the mother task and all of its subtask.

11.9.1 Detach Logic

When the DETACH logic gets control through the SVC interrupt handler, Register 1 supplies the address of a fullword containing the address of the subtask TCB to be detached. An initial validity check is done on the input parameter to determine any boundary violation (fullword boundary). Also, the validity of the TCB being passed is checked by searching the subtask queue of the caller.

If the input parameter is found invalid in any of the tests, an abend code of 23E is placed in Register 1 and control is passed to ABEND to terminate the Caller.

Next, the DETACH routine checks whether the subtask has already terminated by checking a bit of the TCBFLGS5 in the TCB called "TCBFC." The implication here is that a mother task can DETACH a subtask even before the subtask terminates. The TCBFC field is set by End-of-Task routine to indicate termination for the completed task and the TCB is not on the dispatching queue. If the TCBFC bit is on, then DETACH frees the task's problem program save area located in subpool 250, if one exists; unchains the TCB from the TCB family queue; and frees the subtask TCB. A return code of 0 is set and control is returned to the caller. The main line logic of DETACH finishes here for this particular condition.

If the subtask has not been terminated, then the DETACH terminates the subtask abnormally. In order to prepare the subtask for abnormal termination, DETACH routine first checks whether this TCB is active on the other CPU (in the case of MP). If active, DETACH routine issues a STATUS STOP to stop the active TCB.

DETACH routine then checks for an end-of-task exit routine for the TCB being detached. DETACH does this by examining both the TCBIQE field and the TCBFETXR bit being turned on for a nonzero value. If an ETXR exists, DETACH uses FREEMAIN to free the IQE and, using the IQEIRB field in the IQE, goes to the IRB for the exit routine. DETACH reduces the RBUSE count by 1. If the use count reaches 0, then DETACH routines uses FREEMAIN routine to free the IRB and its associated problem program save area. TCBIQE field and TCBFETXR bit are set to 0.

DETACH routine then sets an error code of 13E in Register 1 and invokes abnormal termination manager by issuing

```
CALLRTM   TYPE=ABTERM,COMPCODE=(1),
          TCB=(12), DUMP=NO
```

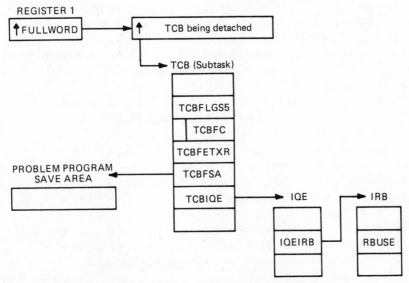

Figure 11.3 Control block structure at DETACH processing.

Register 12 contains address of TCB to be terminated and Register 1 contains the error code.

Since the DUMP=NO parameter is specified in this CALLRTM macro, no DUMP is produced. CALLRTM routine sets up the envronment for the subtask to be terminated when the subtask gets dispatched. It should be noted that the DETACH routine is executing under the mother task's TCB. The TCB-RB structure for both the mother task and the subtask are the following:

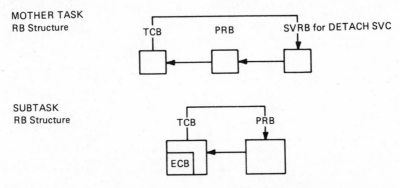

The SVRB on the mother task's RB chain represents the SVC routine for DETACH. DETACH routine saves the content of TCBECB field of the subtask's TCB. If the ECB parameter is coded in the ATTACH macro for this subtask, then Register 10 will contain the address of the ECB; else it will contain 0s. The TCBECB field in the TCB for the subtask is then changed with an address of an ECB that is located in the SVRB for DETACH SVC. Next, the DETACH routine will issue a WAIT on this ECB. This will put the mother task in a wait state.

When the subtask gets control next, ABEND routine gets control to terminate the subtask. ABEND finally posts the ECB when the subtask termination is completed.

Mother task now wakes up, due to the posting of its wait ECB; and detach processing resumed after the WAIT. The DETACH code next checks whether there was an original ECB by checking for a nonzero value in Register 10. If an ECB address exists, then DETACH gives control to the POST routine.

The subtask TCB is removed from the family queue, and through FREEMAIN routine the TCB is freed. After setting a return code of 0 or 4 (0 for normal completion, and 4 for an incomplete subtask detached with STAE=YES specified) in Register 15, control is given to EXIT PROLOG and from there to the dispatcher.

12 Wait and Post Logic

Task synchronization is achieved in the operating system through the WAIT, POST and EVENTS macro instructions. WAIT processing permits a problem program or system program to stop processing until a specified number of events have occurred, such as the completion of one or more I/O operations.

12.1 OVERVIEW

An event control block is associated with the above macro instructions and it is a fullword on a fullword boundary. A WAIT macro instruction can specify more than one event by specifying more than one event control block (ECB). If more than one event control block is specified, the WAIT macro can specify that all or only some of the events must occur before the task is taken out of the wait condition. When the specified events have occurred, the POST routine indicates the occurrence of the awaited event or events via the CS (compare and swap) instruction; and it makes the program ready (no longer waiting), so that its execution can continue.

12.2 WAIT ROUTINE LOGIC

The WAIT macro generates a Type 1 SVC and hence no SVRB is created for the execution of this routine. The registers and PSW at the time of the SVC interrupt are stored in the TCB and the PRB respectively.

The first thing the WAIT routine does is look at Register 0 for number of events or wait counts. If the value of Register 0 is 0, then control is given to EXIT PROLOGUE for exiting from the WAIT routine.

Sign bit of Register 0 will be on if an optional parameter LONG=YES has specified on the wait macro. This indicates that the task is entering a long rather than a regular wait. A long wait should never be considered for I/O activity, but can be specified for an operator response to a WTOR macro instruction.

Next the wait routine does validity checking on the ECB or list of ECBs whose address is passed in Register 1. If only one ECB is specified (ECB= ecb address), Register 1 will contain the true form of the address of the ECB. But if a list of ECBs is specified (ECBLIST = ecb list address), then Register 1 will contain the complemented form of the address of the ECB list. Each ECB address is checked for fullword boundary. If found invalid, the task is terminated with system code of 201. If the number of ECBs in the ECBLIST is less than the number of wait counts in Register 0, then the task is terminated with a system code of 101.

WAIT routine then examines the completion bit (POST bit) in the ECB. An ECB can be divided into two parts. The first part consists of only 1 byte and the second part consists of 3 bytes. Bit 0 of the first byte is called "the WAIT bit" and bit 1 of the first byte is called "the POST bit." If the POST bit is 1, this signifies that this event that we want to wait on has already completed. In this case an exit is made through EXIT PROLOG. In the case of an ECB list, the POST bit is searched on every one of the ECBs on the list, and, for each posted ECB, the wait count in Register 0 is decremented by 1.

If the POST bit is 0, then the wait routine checks the wait bit in the ECB. If the WAIT bit is on, it indicates that this ECB is already being waited on and a DOUBLE wait condition exists. The task is terminated with a system code of 301 in this situation. (Programming error of not initializing the ECB with binary 0s is the common cause of this situation.)

Next, wait logic sets the RBECBWT bit in the callers RB when the caller specifies a wait count less than the number of ECBs in the ECB list.

RBECBWT specifies that the caller awaits fewer events than the maximum number that can occur. We have seen that when the wait logic searches for POSTED ECBs in the ECB list, the wait count in Register 0 is decremented by 1 every time a posted ECB is encountered. When the wait count reaches 0, it means the task's WAIT request is fulfilled and the task can resume execution. In this case the WAIT routine clears all the WAIT bits in the unposted ECBs and, after clearing the search flag, (RBECBWT) control is given the EXIT PROLOG.

Each ECB in the ECB list is searched for the WAIT bit being turned on. If found, the task is terminated with system code of 301. If the WAIT bit is not on, then the WAIT routine turns on the WAIT bit and places the address of the PRB in the last 3 bytes of the ECB. This process is repeated on all the ECBs on the list.

Next the final adjusted wait count in Register 0 is placed into the RBWCF (RB wait count field) field in the PRB, and the explicit wait bit in the PRB (RBXWAIT) is turned on, indicating this task is waiting due to the issuence of a WAIT macro.

The number of ready TCB count in the ASCB (ASCBTCBS) is decremented by 1. If the ASCBTCBS count reaches 0 then the short wait count field in the ASCB (ASCB SWCT) is incremented by 1.

If the user issued a long wait request, then the long wait bit on the RB (RBLONGWT) is turned on.

If all the TCBs in the address space are either in a wait condition or non-dispatchable, then system resource manager (SRM) is notified through

SYSEVENT macro. SRM will decide whether this address space should be swapped out or not. In either case, exit from the WAIT SVC routine is done through EXIT PROLOG.

12.3 POST ROUTINE LOGIC

The POST processing routine signals to a waiting program of the occurrence of an unexpected event. The POST routine does this by changing the indicator in the ECB that is shared by the program issuing the POST and the program that is waiting.

The first thing the POST routine does is the validity check on the ECB address passed in Register 1. If the ECB is not on a fullword boundary, the task is terminated with a system code of 102. Next the RB address in the ECB is checked for validity. In order to do this, the POST routine has to scan through each of the TCB-RB chains for an address match for the RB address found in the ECB. If no match is found, the task is terminated with a system code of 102. If the ECB is not being waited on and is not posted, then the POST bit in the ECB is turned on and the POST code is placed in the last 3 bytes of the ECB. Control is then given to EXIT PROLOG to exit from the SVC. If the ECB POST bit is on, then no processing is necessary and the post routine exists using EXIT PROLOG. If the POST routine finds the WAIT bit on in the ECB and the explicit WAIT bit on (RBXWAIT), it will turn off the WAIT bit and turn on the POST bit. It also moves the POST code into the ECB. RBWCF is decremented by 1. If the RBWCF is still nonzero, exit the POST logic through EXIT PROLOG. If RBWCF goes to 0, POST increases the number of ready TCBs (ASCBTCBS) in the ASCB for use by the dispatcher. It also resets the explicit WAIT bit (RBXWAIT) in the PRB. POST next checks the search flag (RBECBWT) for a list of unposted ECBs. If this bit is on, and the RBWCF reached 0, then POST gets the address of the ECB list and goes down the chain of ECB addresses. Outstanding WAIT bits in any of the ECBs are cleared. POST also resets the RBECBWT, RBLONGWT, and RBXWAIT bits to make the RB ready. After this, WAIT SVC routine gives up control to EXIT PROLOG.

13 ENQ/DEQ/Reserve Processing

In a multiprogramming system, almost any sequence of instructions can be interrupted, to be resumed later. If that set of instructions manipulates or modifies a serially reusable resource (for example, a control block or a record in a data set), the control program must prevent any other programs from using the resource until the interrupted program has completed its processing of the resource.

13.1 OVERVIEW

In MVS, the supervisor program provides two techniques for serializing the use of resources: one by enqueueing and the other by locking. We have already discussed the use of LOCKS in a tightly coupled multiprocessing environment for serializing resources by processors. In this chapter, the mechanisms by which MVS supervisor provides serialization for a resource in a multiprogramming environment are discussed.

The ENQ routine, working with the DEQ routine, permits program issuing a ENQ macro instruction to gain control of a resource or set of resources. The requested resource may be one or more data sets, records within a data set , program control blocks, or any work areas within main storage. ENQ uses the symbolic name of the resource to control access to the resource.

The requester of a resource uses the ENQ macro to reserve the resource. and also by a *scope* indicator. These names may or may not have any relation to the actual name of the resource. Supervisor program does not associate the name with the actual resource; it merely processes requests having the same qname, rname, and scope on a first-in–first-out basis. It is up to the users of the resource to use the same qname, rname, and scope to represent the same resource.

13.2 ENQ MACRO

The format of the ENQ macro is as follows:

```
         ┌                                    STEP    ┐        CHNG
  ENQ   (  qname    rname   E  ,  rname     SYSTEM  )    ,RET = HAVE
         │  address ⸴ address ⸴  S  Length ⸴ SYSTEMS │        NONE
         └                                            ┘        TEST
                                                              USE
```

Qname address specifies the address of an 8 byte long character string. *Rname address* specifies the address of the name used in conjunction with qname to represent a single resource. *E* specifies the request is for exclusive control and *S* specifies the shared control of the resource. Exclusive control is required while the resource is being modified to keep the integrity of the resource. If the requester does not modify the resource, then the request should be for shared control. *Rname length* specifies the length of the rname used. Length can range from 0-255. If 0 is specified, the length of the rname must be contained in the first bytes at the rname address specification.

Qname and rname are used to increase the availability of the whole resource while only a part of it is being updated by a task. For example, rather than holding up the entire master file for the duration of a single record update that uses the qname for the entire master file (probably the file name) and the rname for the specific record (probably the record identifier or key), only the specific record is locked out from the other tasks that want to access the master file. Table 13.1 lists the qnames and rnames used in the ENQ/DEQ macros used by the MVS system and the resources they represent.

The scope of the resource usage is identified by specifying STEP, SYSTEM or SYSTEMS. If STEP is specified, a request for the same qname and rname from a program in another address space addresses a different resource. In other words, the scope of serialization is within an address space only when STEP is specified, MVS prefixing the rname specified with the ASID of the address space. Thus, each request from different address spaces specifying the same qname and rname, with the scope of STEP, are treated as different resources. If SYSTEM is specified, serialization is maintained for all the address spaces within the operating system. If SYSTEMS is specified, requests for the same qname and rname from programs of other address spaces in the various systems denote the same resource.

RET parameter specifies the type of request for the resource.

RET=CHNG specifies that the status of the resource specified is to be changed from shared to exclusive control.

TABLE 13.1 Qnames, Rnames and Associated References

Qname	Rname	Resources
SYS DSN	Data set name	System data sets
SYS IAT	CKPT	JES check point dataset
SYSIEA01	IEA	Dump datasets
SYSIEFSD	CHNGDEVS	UCB (Unit Control Block)
	DDRTPUR	SWAP UNIT (Tape Unit)
	DDRDA	SWAP DASD Device
	Q4	UCB
	Q6	Protect key resource
	Q10	CSCB (Command Scheduling Control Block)
	RPLL	Job Journal Data set
	STCQUE	Started task control
	TSOQUE	TSO data sets
SYSIGGV1	MCATOPEN	Master Catalog
SYSIGGV2	Catalog name	User catalog
SYSIKJBC	RBA	TSO Broadcast data set
SYSIKJUA	OPENUADS	User attribute data set
SYSIKJUA	Userid	TSO user
SYSIEWLP	dsname	SYSLMOD data set for linkage editor
SYSSMF01	data set	SYS1.MAN data set (SMF data set)
SYSZUSRL	ucbaddr	User label tracks
SYSVSAM	ccccnnnx	VSAM data set (cccc=ACB address, nnn=Control Interval number, x = status)
SYSVTOC	VOLSER	VTOC
SYSZCSD	CSDCPUJS	CSD (Common System Data area) field
SYSZEC16	PURGE	Purge data set
SYSZIGG1	ASID	TSB (terminal Status Block for TSO)
SYSZOPEN	dsname	System data set
SYSZPCCB	PCCB	Private Catalog Control Block
SYSZPGAD	PAGEADD	Serialize PAGEADD Command
SYSZPSWD	dsname	Password data set
SYSZSIPS	IRARMSET	SYSEVENT
SYSZSMF1	BUF	SMF buffer
SYSZTIOT	ASID+DSAB	Queue Descriptor Block for TIOT (Task I/O Table)
SYSZVARY	CPU	Reconfiguration Commands
	VALIDATE	Storage Validation Process
SYSZVMV	ucbaddr	Virtual Volume
SYSZVOLS	volserno	System Volume

RET=HAVE specifies that the control of the resource is requested only if a request has not been made previously for the same task.

RET=TEST specifies that the availability of the resource is to be tested, but control of the resource is not requested.

RET=USE specifies that the control of the resource is to be assigned to the requester only if the resource is immediately available. If any of the resources are not available, the requester is allowed to continue processing without the resource.

RET=NONE specifies that the control of all resources is unconditionally requested.

13.3 RESOURCE QUEUES

The control program constructs a list for each qname, rname, and scope combination and chains them from a pointer in CVT. This pointer (CVTFQCB) points to the first major QCB on the control block queue that represents an ENQed resource.

A major QCB entry contains the pointers given in figure 13.1. The first 4 bytes point to the next major QCB and the next 4 bytes point back to the previous major QCB. These two fields form forward and backward chains of major QCBs. Associated with each major QCB, there can be one or more minor QCBs. The next two fields within the major QCB form a chain of minor QCBs for this major one. The last 8 bytes of the major QCB contain the major name or the qname for the resource specified in the ENQ macro. The minor QCB contains the fields shown in figure 13.2. The first 4 bytes point to the next minor QCB and the next 4 bytes point to the previous minor QCB. These pointers form a link in the minor QCB chain.

Associated with each minor QCB are one or more control blocks called *Queue Elements* (QEL). At offset +8 into the minor QCB is a pointer to the first QEL, and the next 4 bytes point to the last QEL associated with this minor one. The next bytes contain the length of the rname on the minor name. The flag field identifies the scope of this ENQ. An x'80' indi-

Figure 13.1 Major QCB entry.

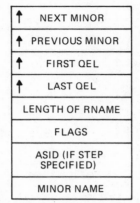

Figure 13.2 Minor QCB entry.

cate a scope of SYSTEM and an x'20' indicate a scope of STEP. An x'40' represents a scope of SYSTEMS. If the scope is STEP, then the next 2 bytes contain the address space ID of the requester. Finally, the minor QCB contains the variable length rname specified in the ENQ macro.

Queue element (QEL) represents a request for the serialization of a resource represented by the corresponding major and minor QCBs. The fields in the QEL are shown in figure 13.3.

The QEL contains pointers to the next QEL and to the previous QEL. The QEL also contains a pointer to the TCB for which ENQ is issued. The flag field identifies the type of ENQ requested, such as EXCLUSIVE (x'00') or SHARED (x'80'). Finally, the QEL contains counts for the number of active requests and for the number of requests waiting.

13.4 RESERVE MACRO

In an environment where multiple processors share the devices, RESERVE macro is used to reserve a device for use by a particular system. Once reserved, the device cannot be accessed from any other system sharing the device. The task issued the RESERVE should release the device by issuing a DEQ macro instruction.

The format of the RESERVE macro is similar to that of ENQ, except for some additional parameters such as UCB and ECB.

The unit control block (UCB) keyword specifies an address of a full-word that contains the address of the UCB for the device to be reserved.

The event control block (ECB) keyword specifies the address of an ECB and conditionally requests the resource named in the macro instruction. RESERVE is basically an ENQ with UCB specification. Both of these macros generate the same SVC instruction (0A38) and invoke the same SVC routine.

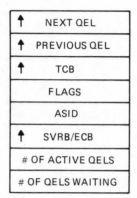

Figure 13.3 Queue element (QEL).

13.5 ENQ/RESERVE LOGIC

The ENQ/RESERVE routine gets control when the program executes an SVC 56 instruction. This routine first checks for valid input parameters passed to it in Register 1. (Register 1 contains the address of a parameter list.) If an invalid minor name length is found, control is passed to the abend routine with an abend code of S238. Or if the caller is not authorized for specified function, the task is abended with a code of S338. (Required authorization is verified by invoking the TESTAUTH macro.) For any other discrepency recognized in the parameter list, the requesting task is abnormally terminated with a code of S438.

Next the ENQ/RESERVE routine searches the major QCB chain for a major QCB that contains the specified qname. At this time, if the ENQ resource queue is not referable, control is passed to ABEND and the task is abended with a code of S838.

If ENQ routine finds the qname in the major QCB, it means that at least one resource in the set of resources is in use. Then it searches the associated minor QCB for the specified rname.

If the rname is found in the minor QCB, it means the requested resource is in use. ENQ then compares the ASID and the TCB address in the QEL against the requesters ASID and TCB. If found equal, the task already has or is waiting for the resource. In this case, depending on the type of request, the task is abend with a code of S138 or a condition code is returned to the requester.

When the ENQ/RESERVE routine finds a qname-rname combination in QCBs (which means the resource is in use), then depending on the type of request the following processing is done.

In the RET=TEST Option, the requester only wants to test the availability of a resource but does not want the control of the resource.

If the resource is immediately available the task would have been given immediate control of the resource; a return code of 0 is returned to the requester.

A return code of 4 means that the resource is not immediately available and the task would have been placed in a WAIT state if request was unconditional. A return code of 8 means the task previously requested the same resource and has control over the resource. If the task has requested the resource previously and does not have control over the resource, then a return code of 20 is returned to the requester.

The RET=USE Option indicates to the ENQ/RESERVE routine that the requester wants to control the resource only if it is available for immediate use. Else the requester wants to continue processing without the use of the resource.

If the resource is available, then a QCB-QEL combination is created and placed on the major QCB chain. Control of the resource is given to the requester with a return code of 0.

Return codes of 4, 8, and 20 have the same meaning as in the case of RET=TEST.

The RET=CHNG option indicates that the requester wishes to change the control of a resource from SHARED to EXCLUSIVE. A return code of 0 indicates that the resource is already under exclusive control of the requester or exclusive control is just given to the requester. Flags in the QEL are changed from SHARED to EXCLUSIVE if the requester already has control of the resource and no one else is sharing it.

A return code of 4 is passed to the requester if the request cannot be honored because the requester is currently sharing the resource with other users.

A return code of 8 indicates that that requester has not queued previously for the resource and hence no change can be made. Even though this is an error condition, control is returned to the requester.

A return code of 20 means that a previous request for the resource has been made but the task does not have the control of the resource.

The RET=HAVE option specifies a conditional request for a resource. The requester in specifying that the control of the resource is needed only if a request has not been made previously. A return code of 0 means that the resource is given to the requester after creating a QCB-QEL pair and after chaining from the major QCB. A return code of 8 implies that the requester has control of the resource already.

A return code of 20 indicates that the requester already has a request for the resource in the QCB chain but does not have control of the resource.

Note that there is no condition code of 4 for this type of request.

The RET=NONE option is an unconditional request for the resource. The omission of the RET operand in the ENQ macro has the same meaning as a RET=NONE specification. This implies that the requester is willing to wait for the resource until it becomes available. No return code is set for this type of request. If the resource is available, control is given to the requester immediately after chaining the major and minor QCBs along with the QEL. If the resource is not available, then the newly created QCBs and the QEL are chained off the major QCB chain, and the requesting task is placed in a WAIT state.

If there is already a request in the QCB chain, then the requesting task is abnormally terminated with a code of S138.

13.6 RETURN FROM THE ENQ/RESERVE ROUTINE

In the case of conditional requests, control is given to the requester through the EXIT PROLOG.

In the case of unconditional requests, the task is placed in a WAIT state by incrementing the RBWCF in the TCB. The resume PSW in the SVRB (for the ENQ SVC routine) will point to a special routine in ENQ/RESERVE logic. The control in this case is given to the dispatcher.

Any abnormal conditions will be handled by the ABEND processing.

13.7 DEQ LOGIC

Using the DEQ macro, a task informs the control program that the use of a resource is complete.

DEQ routine gets control from the SVC interrupt handler which was invoked when the program executed an SVC instruction (0A30) for DEQ.

DEQ routine first examines the content of the parameter list passed to it. If any invalid parameter is found, control is given to ABEND and the requesting task is abnormally terminated. If invalid minor name length is found, the task is terminated with a code of S230. If the request is not authorized for a function, the requesting task is terminated with S330 code. For any other discrepencies in the input parameters, the task is terminated with a code of S430.

Next, DEQ routine determines whether the specified resource is in ENQ resource queue. This is done by searching the major and minor QCBs for the qname and rname specified in the DEQ macro. It then verifies that the callers TCB address matches the TCB address in the QEL associated with the QCBs containing the qname and rname. If a match is found, it means that the requester of DEQ has in fact issued an ENQ for that resource. By scanning the position of the QEL on the QCB chain, DEQ determines whether the caller owns or shares the resource. If the caller owns the resource, then the QEL should be on top of the queue. DEQ removes the QEL and the storage is saved for future use. If there are no more QELs left on the minor QCB, then the minor

QCB can also be freed. It then examines the minor QCB chain to decide whether a major QCB is needed. If there are no minor QCBs left, then the major QCB is released and saves the storage for later use.

When the caller of the resource does not own or share the resource, the task is abended if it is an unconditional request (RET=NONE) or an appropriate return code is returned to the requester if it is a conditional DEQ.

Depending on the characteristics (shared vs. exclusive) of the DEQed QEL and the next top QEL on the chain, DEQ routine determine whether the next waiting requester should be ready.

Three possibilities exist:

1. The DEQed QEL is shared and the next top QEL is also shared. In this case DEQ routine does nothing for the dispatchability of the task that owns the QEL.

2. The DEQed QEL is either exclusive or shared and the new top QEL is exclusive. In this case DEQ routine invokes the POST routine which will decrement the RBWCF field in the RB of the task that owns the new top QEL. The task is taken out of the WAIT state when the RBWCF field reaches 0.

3. The DEQed QEL is exclusive and the next top QEL is shared. In this case DEQ routine decreases the RBWCF fields of each shared QELs invoking the POST routine.

RESERVED QELs being dequeued from an owning group will cause the UCBSQC count to be decreased. When the count reaches 0, the DEQ routine issues a STARTIO instruction. This causes the I/O supervisor to release the shared direct access device.

During the search for specified resource in the ENQ resource Queue, if no QEL is found, this indicates that it is not being ENQed. The caller who requests an unconditional (RET=NONE) DEQ, is terminated with a code of S130. When a conditional DEQ was requested, the appropriate return code is returned to the requester.

At the end of the processing, DEQ passes control to the EXIT PROLOG and then to the dispatcher.

14 MVS Summary

14.1 MVS ENVIRONMENT

14.1.1 Overview

The environment of modern operating systems has evolved from serial job processing on computers with limited resources to complex multi-job processing on high speed comprehensive computing facilities. A modern computing system, for example, could have a main storage size of 64 megabytes, a processing unit cycle time of 26 nanoseconds, and up to 24 data channels. Moreover, the transfer rate of a block multiplexer channel could be as high as 3 million bytes/second. Even printing rates of 17,000 lines per minute are readily obtainable.

Clearly, sophisticated and powerful software is needed to fully utilize hardware resources such as these. In addition to providing for the concurrent processing of several jobs, the dynamic allocation of the totality of system resources, including CPU time, main storage, and I/O devices, is required. The MVS operating system satisfies a set of needs, such as these, for a complex operational environment, characterized as follows:

- A large computer system
- A large number of concurrent users
- Teleprocessing applications
- Data base facilities
- Time sharing service
- Batch processing facilities

Thus, MVS is a multipurpose operating system designed to enhance the functional capabilities of the underlying computer system.

14.1.2 Software Structure of MVS

It is convenient to view the software structure of MVS as being divided into three major functional areas: job management, supervisor management, and data management. *Job management* activities include command processing and job processing. *Supervisor management* activities are concerned with resource management, and *data management* activities involve file and input/output operations.

Command processing consists of receiving a command from a program or console and scheduling it for execution. *Job processing* involves reading the JCL jobstream, converting it to internal text for processing, job

213

initiation, creation of control blocks, allocation of data sets, and attaching the job step for execution. After execution, the system output is handled and the job is terminated.

Supervisor management is the class of MVS routines that essentially "run" the system by handling all system-related functions, such as interruption handling and scheduling, task management, program management, virtual storage management, real storage management, auxiliary storage management, timer supervision, system resource management, and recovery and termination management.

Data management routines handle the system catalog, provide I/O support (such as open, close, and end-of-volume processing), and supply the access methods for the user.

14.1.3 Hardware Structure of MVS

The five main hardware resources in an MVS system are devices, control units, data channels, main storage, and one or more central processing units. Clearly, the various components are interrelated and the key objective of the MVS is to utilize the precise nature of the interrelationship to achieve maximum performance of the total system.

A *multiprocessing system* (MP) allows more than one CPU to share the same computing workload, thereby increasing both performance and availability. In the former case, the throughput of the system is increased. In the latter case, the system can continue processing in the event of a single CPU failure, even though the total system runs in a somewhat degraded state. In a *tightly coupled multiprocessing system*, the CPUs share main storage and the operating system code. In an *attached processor multiprocessing system*, one CPU is used only to increase computing throughput and does not support any channels. In a *loosely-coupled multiprocessing system*, tandemly operating CPUs communicate via a channel-to-channel adapter but operate independently.

The MVS system is uniquely designed to fully utilize the channel programming and interrupt structure of the host computing systems.

14.2 VIRTUAL STORAGE

14.2.1 Overview

An important function of an operating system is storage management, which has historically evolved through the following technical phases:

- Serially operated single-user facilities
- Multiple user systems with fixed-size partitions
- Multiple user systems with variable sized partitions
- Multiple user systems with dynamic relocation of programs and data

Through dynamic address translation facilities, the MVS system supports a virtual storage concept that provides each user with an address space of 16 million bytes, or 2 billion bytes with extended addressing.

14.2.2 Virtual Storage Concepts in MVS

The basic concept underlying virtual storage is the relaxation of a physical constraint on program address space. Thus, a program is no longer bounded by the physical amount of real storage, and a virtual address space is mapped into a combination of real storage and direct-access storage.

Each address space—both in real and virtual storage—is divided into fixed-size units called *pages*. In MVS, the page size is 4096 bytes, known as 4K. Thus, a complete program need not be in real storage in order for it to execute. Only the pages required to sustain execution are required to be in real storage. Other pages are brought in when needed. The process of retrieving pages on a demand basis is know as *paging*.

14.2.3 Virtual Storage Management and Addressing

In MVS, each user and most system components have a unique address space that is 16 million bytes long. This address space is organized into 256 segments, each containing sixteen 4K pages.

Page and segment tables correspond to an address space and are used to manage virtual storage. To keep track of pages within a segment, the MVS system maintains a page table for each segment. A page table entry is associated with each page to help determine whether it is active, in real storage, or on direct-access storage. Moreover, a segment table is used to keep track of the page tables.

14.2.4 Virtual Storage Hardware

The tables used to manage virtual storage are software entities. Three hardware entities are used to support virtual storage operation:

- Control registers
- Dynamic address translation hardware
- A translation lookaside buffer

Since each address has its own segment and page tables, a control register is used to locate the segment table. This register, known as the *segment table origin register* (STOR), is loaded by MVS when an address space is given control of the CPU. The STOR register is control register number 1.

Dynamic address translation (DAT) is the process of translating virtual addresses to real addresses through the segment and page tables. The translation of addresses is performed dynamically during program execution by a special hardware unit known as the DAT box.

The *translation lookaside buffer* (TLB) is a relatively small associative memory used to hold the most recently used pairs of virtual and corresponding real addresses. Through the use of the TLB, also known as the associative array registers, normal dynamic address translation, which is reasonably fast but still time consuming, can be speeded up.

14.2.5 MVS Storage Organization

A virtual storage address space is divided into three major areas: the common area, the private area, and the system area. The *system area* contains the basic routines of the operating system and consists of the nucleus load module and the nucleus extension. The *nucleus load module* contains hardware dependent operational code and some system-wide tables. The *nucleus extension* primarily contains system-wide information. The nucleus is fixed in real storage.

The *private area* starts on the first 64K boundary after the nucleus and contains user programs and operational information about the user. The private area can only be addressed by programs running in the user's address space. This is readily obvious since each user has a unique set of segment and page tables.

The *common area* is shared among all address spaces in the system and is divided into three parts: the system queue area, the pageable link pack area, and the common system area. The *system queue area* (SQA) contains tables and queues relating to the entire system. The *pageable link pack area* (PLPA) contains SVC routines, access method routines, and other system programs. The *common system area* (CSA) is a pageable data area and is used to communicate between address spaces.

There can be two types of regions in the private area for a user. In a V=R region, virtual storage is mapped one-to-one into real storage and is fixed in real storage. V=R regions are used for time dependent functions. In a V=V region, pages are subject to page faults, which means that they can be paged out when their space is needed.

14.2.6 Program Loading

Prior to execution, a program is loaded into main storage in the conventional manner and the segment and page tables are built. However, only a working set of pages are kept in real storage and the other pages are written to a direct-access device, known as *external page storage* (EPS). Pages can then be retrieved from EPS on a demand basis.

14.3 CONTROL BLOCKS

14.3.1 Overview

Control blocks are used in MVS to manage the work and the resources of the system. Because MVS manages work within an address space and also for the system as a whole, the supervisor is divided into two parts called the local and global supervisors.

The *local supervisor* performs operational functions for a specific address space, such as to add a control block to an existing chain of control blocks. Routines in this class are coded reentrantly so that a single copy of the routines exists in the system and is used for all address spaces.

The *global supervisor* performs operational functions for the system as a whole, such as to schedule a task for execution. Accordingly, there are two types of control blocks in MVS: those needed for the overall operation of MVS and those needed for the management of an individual address space.

14.3.2 System Control Blocks

System control blocks contain information that concerns the operation of the total hardware and software system. Within system control blocks, there is no orientation to a specific unit of work, even though these control blocks do contain user information. The major system control blocks in MVS are summarized in the following list:

- *Common System Data Area* (CSD)—contains information about the CPUs in the system
- *Communications Vector Table* (CVT)—contains the addresses of the other control blocks and tables used by the supervisors. This is the major control block in the system.
- *Physical Configuration Communications Area* (PCCA)—contains information about the physical facilities associated with each CPU. There is a PCCA for each CPU.
- *Physical Configuration Communication Area Vector Table* (PCCAVT)—contains an array that has a slot for each of 16 possible CPUs.
- *Logical Configuration-Communication Area* (LCCA)—contains information needed by the software about an operating CPU, such as the contents of machine registers.
- *Logical Configuration-Communication-Area Vector Table* (LCCAVT)—contains the LCCA addresses for the 16 CPUs.
- *Prefixed Save Area* (PSA)—resides in the nucleus and refers to the unique 4K (i.e., addresses 0–4095) for each CPU.

The system control blocks are related and chained together in an operational sense. The key element is the CVT, which is used to locate other control blocks.

14.3.3 Address Space Control Blocks

Address space control blocks are needed to manage resources within an address space. While the local supervisor code is shared among address spaces, each set of control blocks is unique. The three major control blocks associated with an address space are:

- *Address Space Control Block* (ASCB)—contains information needed for address space control, such as whether the address space is swapped out, dispatching, priority, assigned real storage, number of ready task control blocks (TCBs) in the address spaces, and the number of CPUs active in this address space. The ASCB is not swappable and is used primarily by the global supervisor.

- *Address Space Extension Block* (ASXB)—contains address space information that is not of interest to most system components and other address spaces. The ASXB can be swapped out and is used primarily by the local supervisor.

- *Address Space Vector Table* (ASVT)—contains control information about the various address spaces in the system. There is only one ASVT for the entire system.

The ASVT is located through the CVT and can be used to locate an ASCB directly. The ASCBs are chained together and anchored in the CVT.

14.3.4 Task Control Blocks

A task is a unit of work to the system and is represented through a *task control block* (TCB), which contains operational data about a task. The CVT is anchored in the PSA and points to the ASVT, which in turn points to the ASCB. The ASCB points to the ASXB which points to the TCB. The TCB points to several address space control blocks and save areas.

14.4 TASK MANAGEMENT

14.4.1 Overview

One of the most powerful features of MVS is the high degree of generality inherent in task management. Most modern operating systems, except perhaps in the microcomputer area, permit several jobs to co-reside in the system at varying stages of their execution. This facility is commonly known as *multiprogramming* and it permits CPU delays, possibly for input or output, in one job to be used to process other work. This feature has been taken one step further in MVS.

There can be several load modules associated with a task. When one task spawns another task that essentially competes for CPU time, the process is known as *multitasking*. When the new task does not compete with its originator for CPU time, it is known as *subtasking*. In any session, both multitasking and subtasking can occur at differing levels of execution.

In a multiprocessing (MP) environment, it is possible that two tasks from the same address space can be in execution on both CPUs at the same time.

14.4.2 Task Representation

When a job step is initiated, the initiator gives control to the associated task with the ATTACH macro that loads the module and gives control to it. At this time, the load module is represented in the system by a control block called a *request block* (RB), that is pointed to by the TCB for the task. The TCB is also created by the program manager that handles the ATTACH macro. The reason that both a TCB and a RB are needed is based on the multitasking and subtasking facilities. The TCB always points to the current RB, which in turn may point to the previously active RB.

The manner in which request blocks (RBs) are used is inherent in the methods for passing control from one load module to another. When an executing program issues a LINK macro to another program, that program is loaded for execution and a RB is created for it. There are now two levels of control. The TCB points to the new RB, which points to the old RB. When an executing program issues a LOAD macro, the referenced program is loaded but not executed directly. No new RB is created, in this case, and there is no new level of control. A program that has been loaded, as in the latter case, must be referenced with a CALL macro, as in the case of a subroutine within a load module. Control always returns to the issuing program after the execution of "linked" or "loaded" programs has been completed.

When an executing program issues a XCTL macro, the referenced program is executed as in the case of the LINK macro, covered above. The only difference between XCTL and LINK is that the request block (RB) of the issuing program is removed from the chain in the XCTL case so that control can return to a calling program.

The request block (RB) concept is a control mechanism and it does not refer to actual code blocks. Clearly, a load module is only loaded if a copy is not available in virtual storage.

14.4.3 Task Queues

There are always two TCB queues associated with an address space: the TCB dispatching queue and the TCB subtask queue. The TCB dispatching queue is pointed to by the ASXB control block and the various TCBs in the queue are chained by priority. The TCB subtask queue is implemented through pointers within the address space TCBs that represent a family history of address space activity.

14.4.4 Task States and Priority

A task can be in any of three states: active, ready, or waiting. An *active task* is executing in a CPU. A *ready task* is one that can be dispatched when its turn comes up. A *waiting task* cannot be dispatched because it is either waiting for an event completion or its no-dispatch ability bit is set. Task status is reflected in the TCB.

Task priority is actually based on three priorities: address space, task, and subtask. These priorities are based on job control and control program parameters.

14.5 SERVICE MANAGEMENT

14.5.1 Overview

At various times during normal operations, the MVS system requires functional support from tasks running in the system. The subtask concept could satisfy these needs but requires an inordinate amount of overhead for most system-related functions that are relatively short in duration and perform a small number of heavily used tasks. Functions that are placed into this category are called service requests and are represented by service request blocks (SRBs).

A service request usually operates on behalf of an address space and is dispatched before any TCBs. Some service requests have an effect on the system as a whole and are known as *global SRBs*. They reside on a global SRB queue and are dispatched before any address space SRBs. A SRB associated with an address space is called a *local SRB*.

14.5.2 Utilization

A typical application in which a local SRB is used is in the handling of input and output interruptions. As a result of normal I/O delay, a task commonly loses the CPU during I/O processing, such that the I/O completion interrupt may be received by the CPU when another address space has CPU control. The I/O interruption handler simply creates a local SRB for the condition to be handled the next time the relevant address space is dispatched.

A case in which a global SRB is needed involves paging operations for which it is necessary to release main storage page frames in one address space for use in another address space.

14.5.3 Processing

Service request blocks are created and placed on appropriate queues using in-line code from within the MVS nucleus. In a single CPU environment, the inherent serialization of processing essentially eliminates any problems with queue management. In a multiple CPU environment, however, implicit serialization is not available and a "compare and swap" instruction is used to provide interlocking between CPUs.

14.6 LOCK MANAGEMENT

14.6.1 Overview

In the MVS system, serialization of resources is achieved with an operational technique known as *lock management*. Lock management is implemented through the use of a designated storage location, called a *lock word*, set by a CPU before it uses any serially reusable resource. Clearly, a lock is released after the use of the associated resources has been completed. A CPU that is waiting for a lock to become free is said to be *spinning on the lock word*.

14.6.2 Philosophy of Locking

MVS is a very large and complex operating system requiring hundreds of serially reusable resources. Therefore, a single lock for the entire operating system or for each resource is neither practical nor efficient. A compromise solution was to analyze the MVS system for components having a minimum of interaction between them and assign a lock for each class. The basis for lock management is the set of local supervisor and global supervisor functions.

14.6.2 Classes of Locks

A *local lock* provides serialization within an address space. Only one lock exists for each address space and it is used by the local supervisor to serialize with other local supervisor functions in the same address space. Local supervisor functions acquire the local lock before they use resources associated with the local supervisor. These functions do not physically disable the CPU by setting bits in the PSW. Local supervisor functions are logically disabled by the local lock but in a hardware-enabled state.

Global supervisor functions that have a minimum of interaction between them can be divided into four classes:

- The dispatcher
- The storage manager
- The input/output supervisor
- Other miscellaneous functions

Each of these functions is assigned a *global lock*. The dispatcher lock is used to serialize the functions involved with changing queues and modifying control blocks used for dispatching. The storage management lock is used by the virtual, real, and auxiliary storage managers to handle their resources. The input/output control blocks and queues are referenced by the I/O supervisor while holding the input/output supervisor lock. The remainder of functions in the global supervisor are executed while holding the miscellaneous lock.

14.7 INTERRUPT HANDLING

14.7.1 Overview

An interrupt mechanism is used to switch the CPU status from the problem state to the supervisor state. When an interrupt occurs, the following machine action takes place: the current PSW is stored in the "old PSW" location and a "new PSW" is invoked as the current PSW. At this instant in time, the new PSW controls the execution of the CPU. Moreover, the address portion of the new PSW points to an interrput-handling routine for the type of interrput that occured.

The primary function of the interrupt handler is to save the environment of the system at the time of the interrupt. The machine registers are saved in the main storage save area and control is then passed to a specific routine for the interrupt.

14.7.2 SVC Interruptions

An SVC instruction is used to change the state of the CPU from an executing program. There are 256 possible SVC interruptions in the system and they are grouped into 6 mutually exclusive classes, numbered 1 through 6. SVC types 1 and 2 are link edited in the nucleus and execute with the lock mechanism. SVC types 3 and 4 execute in a link pack area and have limited locking capability. SVC types 5 and 6 are used for special cases.

SVC interrupt processing is accomplished through a first level interrupt handler (FLIH). A variety of control blocks, including the TCB, PRB, SRB, and SVRB, are used during SVC interrupt processing.

14.7.3 Program Check Interruptions

Program check interruptions handle three types of conditions: monitor call, program event recording, and programs checks. As with SVC processing, a FLIH is used to handle program check interruptions and control blocks are employed to store machine conditions. Program masks govern the extent of conditional interruption processing.

14.7.4 Input and Output Interruptions

The input and output interruption mechanism provides a means by which the CPU can respond to the state of the input/output system. Interruptions in this class are caused by external events or are initiated by an executing program.

14.8 DISPATCHER

14.8.1 Overview

The functions of the dispatcher in MVS are to select and give control to the highest-priority dispatchable unit of work in the system. In the process, the status of the unit of work giving up control is saved and the accounting information is maintained.

14.8.2 Logic

The dispatcher uses six queues to manage the MVS workload and keeps track of the tasks that are dispatched on each CPU to prevent operational duplication on differing CPUs. The queues are:

- The global service manager queue
- The global service priority list
- The local service manager queue
- The local service priority list
- The ASCB queue
- The TCB queue

A ready unit of work can be either a service request, represented by a service request block (SRB) or a task, represented by a task control block (TCB). The dispatcher first searches for ready SRBs and then for ready TCBs.

14.9 VIRTUAL STORAGE MANAGER

14.9.1 Overview

The *virtual storage manager* (VSM) keeps track of the state of a virtual address space by performing the following functions:

- Common system area (CSA) and system queue area (SQA) allocation
- Attribute management
- User request processing for private storage allocation

The VSM uses a real storage manager (RSM) and an auxiliary storage manager (ASM) to create and maintain the tables used by the paging process.

14.9.2 Real and Auxiliary Storage Managers

The real storage manager (RSM) maintains an accounting of real storage usage, maintains segment and page tables, and handles paging and swapping conditions. The RSM effectively administers the use of real storage and directs the movement of virtual pages between auxiliary storage and real storage.

The auxiliary storage manager (ASM) maintains the interface for paging input and output, optimizes the use of paging data sets, and performs various page accounting functions.

14.9.3 Virtual Storage Services

Virtual storage space can be explicitly requested with the GETMAIN macro and released with the FREEMAIN macro. Both functions involve the virtual storage manager that uses the RSM facilities to adjust segment and page table entries.

Virtual storage macros invoke the manager through SVC instructions that are processed as described previously by the GETMAIN and FREEMAIN service routines. The virtual storage manager handles the following areas of private storage:

- LSQA/SWA and subpools 229/230
- Free area not assigned to a subpool
- Free area within subpools

as well as the SQA and CSA, mentioned previously.

14.10 PROGRAM MANAGER

14.10.1 Overview

The program manager searches for and schedules load modules, synchronizes exit rountines to the supervisor, and fetches modules into storage. A load module is located by scanning control blocks on different queues and if a load module is not found therein, the task is abnormally terminated.

The program manager invokes the program fetch routine to load a module that is not in virtual storage. In so doing, the program manager keeps track of modules that have been loaded into virtual storage, along with their names, starting addresses, entry points, and various attributes.

14.10.2 Methodology

The program manager uses a variety of control blocks to perform its primary functions. The major control blocks in this category are the request (RB), the content directory element (CDE), the extent list (XL), the load list element (LLE), and the link pack directory element (LPDE).

14.10.3 Search

The program fetch routine searches the following areas, queues, and directories, in the given order, for a load module:

- Job pack area queue (JPAQ)
- Task libraries (STEPLIB or JOBLIB)

- Link pack area queue (LPAQ)
- Pageable link pack area queue (PLPAQ)
- System library (LINKLIB)

When a requested load module is not found in virtual storage, a CDE is created by the program manager and placed on the JPAQ for the task. Program attributes from the program library directory are used to update the CDE and the program fetch routine is given control to bring the module into virtual storage.

14.10.4 Operations

The operations performed by the program manager are summarized as follows:

- Program fetch
- Link (load a module and pass control to it)
- Schedule for execution (for an already loaded module)
- Exit from a linked program
- Load a module into virtual storage
- Delete a module from virtual storage
- Load and transfer control through a module (XCTL)

Program manager functions are initiated through macros, such as LINK and LOAD, that issue SVC instructions to invoke the supervisor.

14.11 AUXILIARY FUNCTIONS

14.11.1 Task Manager

The *task manager* functions provide services for problem and supervisor programs, such as the creation and control of subtasks. Task manager routines are activated in the following ways:

- Macro instructions, such as ATTACH, DETACH, WAIT, POST, ENQ, DEQ, and CHAP
- Exit effections, such as STATUS, EVENTS, MODESET, and RESERVE

The philosophy underlying task manager functions is to use the subtask concept to gain more comprehensive control over system resources by creating tasks within a job step to compete for these resources. Thus, when a wait condition occurs in one subtask, it is not necessary for CPU control to pass to another address space. Control may be passed to another subtask within the same job step.

The task manager additionally handles asynchronous exit conditions from supervisor and data management routines.

14.11.2 Wait and Post Logic

Task synchronization is achieved in MVS through the WAIT, POST, and EVENTS macro instructions. WAIT processing permits a problem program or a system program to suspend execution until a specified event or condition has occured, such as the completion of an input or output operation.

An event control block (ECB) is associated with each condition that is observed. A WAIT macro instruction, as outlined above, can specify one or more ECBs. When the events have occurred, the POST routine is used to indicate that condition.

A WAIT macro may specify that all or only some of a set of events must occur for processing to continue. The wait and post conditions are implemented through SVC interruptions.

14.11.3 ENQ/DEQ/Reserve Processing

The MVS supervisor supplies two methods for serializing the use of resources: locking and enqueueing. The use of locks, which emphasize a tightly-coupled multiprocessing environment has been covered previously. Enqueueing supports a multiprogramming environment.

In order to maintain operational control over a system with multiprogramming facilities, the supervisor must prevent any routine from using a resource until the interrupted routine has completed its working. This control is achieved by queueing requests for a resource, so that scheduling can be provided in an orderly manner.

The ENQ routine, working with the DEQ routine, permits a program issuing an ENQ macro instruction to gain control of a resource or set of resources. The supervisor maintains a queue for each resource and relevant information on the requestor is stored in a queue control block (QCB). Accordingly, resources are allocated to the first entry on each queue.

The RESERVE macro is used to reserve a device for use by a program element.

Glossary

ABEND Abnormal END. ABEND Is the term used to indicate an abnormal termination of a program, routine or task.

ACR Alternate CPU Recovery. In a multiprocessor environment, if one CPU fails, the other CPUs will take charge of the resources of the failing processor. This process is called alternate CPU recovery.

ALGOL A programming language used to express computer programs by algorithms.

ALU Arithmetic and Logic Unit. This is the component of a central processing unit that does the arithmetic and logic operations.

AM Access Method. Programming support to move data between main storage and input/output devices. Access Methods build channel programs and manage data in buffers. Some on-line access methods such as TCAM (Telecommunication Access Method) and VTAM (Virtual Telecommunication Access Method) have their own address spaces.

AP Attached Processor. In order to increase the processing power of a uniprocessor, a second central processor is connected to it and it's memory. Usually this add-on CPU will not have any data channels.

APL A Programming Language. This language is primarly used in mathematical applications.

ASCB Address Space Control Blocks. This control block represents the existence of an address space in an MVS system.

ASID Address Space Identification. This is a numeric value assigned to each address space in our MVS system.

ASM Auxiliary Storage Manager. This is a component of MVS which manages the virtual storage resides on the external page storage. ASM with the help of IOS (I/O superior) do both the paging and swapping operation.

ASMVT Auxiliary Storage Manager Vector Table. Auxiliary storage manager uses this control block to store relevant information to do its function.

ASVT Address Space Vector Table. This table contains a list of all possible address spaces and their IDS within the MVS system.

ASVTENTY   Address Space Vector Table ENTrY. Each entry for an address space in the ASVT is called ASVTENTY.

ASXB   Address Space Extension Block. This control block, along with ASCB, contains information and pointers needed to control an address space.

BASIC   Beginners All-purpose Symbolic Instruction Code. This is a programming language used for numerical applications.

BC   Basic Control Mode. This is a mode in which System/370 emulates system/360 features.

BDAM   Basic Direct Access Method. An access method used to directly retrieve or update particular blocks of data on a Direct Access Storage Device (DASD).

BISAM   Basic Indexed Sequential Access Method. This is an access method that uses index structures to access and update data on a Direct Access Storage Device (DASD).

BPAM   Basic Partitioned Access Method. This is an access method that can be used to create program libraries and to retrieve or update individual programs in the library. The program library should be on a Direct Access Storage Device (DASD).

BSAM   Basic Sequential Access Method. This access method is used to read and write sequential files.

BTAM   Basic Telecommunications Access Method. BTAM is an access method that will provide low-level services for reading and writing data from remote devices.

CAW   Channel Address Word. This is a fixed location in main memory where the address of the channel program is stored before initiating an I/O operation on a channel.

CCW   Channel Command Word. This is the instruction for a channel to do its I/O operations. A set of channel command words makes a channel program.

CD   Chain Data. This is a flag in a CCW indicating that the transfer of data from/to main storage locations are non-consecutive.

CDE   Contents Directory Entry. This is a control block that describes the characteristics of a load module.

CMS (MVS)   Cross Memory Services. This is a facility in MVS to communicate between address spaces in the system using the Dual Address Space (DAS) facility.

CSA   Common Service Area. This is part of the common area of an address space which contains system and user data areas.

CSCB   Command Scheduling Control Block. This control block contains run time job description data that are passed to command execution routines.

CTC   Channel-To-Channel adaptor. This is a device that transfers data between two channels of two different CPUs at channel speeds.

CVOL   Catalog VOLume. This is an older version of the catalog.

CVT   Communication Vector Table. This is the primary MVS control block from which any other control block can be reached. CVT resides in the nucleus and its address is always in a fixed location in memory.

DAS   Dual Address Space.

DASD   Direct Access Storage Devices.

DAT   Dynamic Address Translation. The process at which virtual addresses are translated into real storage addresses. This is done by a combination of both the hardware feature in the System/370 and the MVS system software.

EC MODE   A mode in which all the features of a System/370 computing system, including dynamic address translation, are operational.

ECB   Event Control Block. This control block is the subject of wait, post and events macro instructions. It is used for communications among various components of the control programs as well as between problem programs and the control programs.

ENQ/DEQ   These macros provide a programming mechanism by which MVS allows a user exclusive access to a resource and, at the end of the use, deallocates the resource.

EOT   End Of Transmission.

EOV   End Of Volume.

EP   Entry Point. This is the address of the first instruction executed upon entering a computer program.

EPS   External Page Storage.

ETXR   End of Task eXit Routine. This routine is executed when a subtask terminates.

EXCP   Execute Channel Program. This macro instruction is used to request that a channel program which the user has built be executed on a specified device.

EXCPVR   EXecute Channel Program Virtual Real. It is the name of the OS/MVS macro instruction used to request the start of an I/O operation. No address translation is done when this macro is used to start an I/O operation.

FBQE   Free Block Queue Element. Describes the 4K of contiguous free space within an address space.

FLIH   First Level Interrupt Handler. When an interrupt happens, these routines get control depending on the type of interruptions.

FLPA   Fixed Link Pack Area. Modules loaded into this area are kept in real memory. For performance reasons, users specify certain modules to be stored in FLPA.

FRR   Functional Recovery Routines.

GDA   Global Data Area. This control block contains system related virtual storage manager, control blocks and pointers.

GSMQ   Global Service Manager Queue.

GSPL   Global Service Priority List.

GTF   Generalized Trace Facility.

HASP   Houston Automatic Spooling Program. This provides control of job flow and output spooling. This program is the predecessor of Job Entry Subsystem (JES).

IAR   Instruction Address Register. This register contains the address of the next instruction to be executed.

IC   Interrupt Code

ICU   Instruction Control Unit. This unit controls the execution of an instruction.

IHSA   Interrupt Handler Save Area.

ILC   Instruction Length Code.

I/O   Input/Output. It is the process of transferring data between the main memory and the auxiliary storage devices.

IOS   Input Output Supervisor. This MVS component sets up and monitors the execution of channel programs supplied by the drivers and issues start I/O instruction to begin the execution.

IQE   Interruption Queue Element. This control block represents a request to be scheduled asynchronously for an exit routine.

IR   Instruction Register.

IRB   Interruption Request Block. Contains information needed by the supervisor concerning programs and routines.

JES   Job Entry Subsystem. This component of MVS reads the jobs into the system, schedules their execution and spools the output for later printing, either locally or remotely.

JPA   Job Pack Area. An area in virtual storage where the program modules are loaded for the execution of a job.

JPAQ   Job Pack Area Queue. This queue contains entries for all program modules loaded into Job Pack Area.

JSCB   Job Step Control Block. This control block contains job or step related information.

JST   Job Step TCB.

LCCA   Logical Configuration Communication Area. This control block contains information about processors in the complex.

LDA   Local Data Area. This control block contains address space, related virtual storage manager control block printers and working storage for the use of VSM reentrant routines.

LIT   Lock Interface Table. This table is used by the lock manager to indicate the type of setlock macro that was issued.

LLE   Load List Element. This control block contains information for loading and deleting a particular load module into or from an address space.

LPA   Link Pack Area. This area in virtual storage contains selected reenterable and serially reusable routines that are loaded at IPL (Initial Program Load) time.

LPAD   Link Pack Area Directory. Every program in PLPA (Pagable Link Pack Area) is represented by an entry in LPAD.

LPAQ   Link Pack Area Queue. This queue contains entries for all modules in the Link Pack Areas.

LPDE   Link Pack Directory Entry. Each LPDE represents a particular load module which is loaded into the Pagable Link Pack Area.

LPSW   Load PSW. A machine instruction which loads the program status word into the CPU.

LRU   Least Recently Used.

LSMQ   Local Service Manager Queue. This queue contains local SRBs (Service Request Blocks) for an address space.

LSPL Local Service Priority List. This list contains SRBs that are to be dispatched locally.

MAR Memory Address Register.

MCU Memory Control Unit.

MDR Memory Data Register.

MFA MalFunction Alert.

MFT Multiprogramming with a Fixed number of Tasks.

MLPA Modifiable Link Pack Area. Since the MVS supervisor searches this area before the PLPA, changed modules may be loaded into MLPA for testing. Therefore the main use of MLPA is for maintenance convenience.

MP MultiProcessing. A processing environment where more than one processor shares the same memory and is under the control of a single operating system.

NFB Next Free Block.

NSPQE Next SubPool Queue Element.

OLTEP OnLine Test Executive Program. A diagnostic aid that tests I/O devices, control units and channels concurrently with the execution of programs.

OS Operating System.

OS-MFT Operating System - Multiprocessing with Fixed number of Tasks.

OS-MVT Operating System - Multiprocessing with Variable number of Tasks.

OS-PCP Operating System - Primary Control Program.

PCFLIH Program Check First Level Interrupt Handler. This routine will get control when there is a program check interrupt.

PDS Partitioned Data Set. This type of data set composed of a 'directory' and associated 'members'. This data set can only reside on Direct Access Storage Devices.

PFT Page Frame Table. This table contains entries for each 4K of real storage in the system.

PGM. ProGraM.

PICA Program Interrupt Control Area. This control clock contains information on interruptions which the user SPIE exit routine will service. It also contains a program mask to be used in the PSW along with the address of a user SPIE exit routine.

PIE Program Interrupt Element. This control block is used to pass necessary data to the user specified exit routine for program check interruptions.

PLPA Pagable Link Pack Area. An area of virtual storage which holds programs used by more than one address space at a time. It also holds programs whose function requires that they execute in commonly addressable storage. PLPA is created at IPL time when CLPA option is specified.

PQE Partitioned Queue Element. This control block describes the space held by the region.

PRB Program Request Block. This control block contains information needed by supervisors concerning programs and routines. It also contains save areas for registers.

PSA Prefixed Storage Area. Each CPU in an IBM multiprocessing system has its own PSA.

PSW Program Status Word. An 8 byte control register whose contents are jointly managed by the MVS operating system and hardware. PSW contains information about the program the CPU is currently executing.

PVR Prefix Value Register.

QCB Queue Control Block. This is used to describe a global resource that needs to be serialized.

QEL Queue ELement. This represents a request for serialization of a resource represented by the corresponding major and minor QCBs.

QSAM Queued Sequential Access Method. This is an OS/VS access method used to read and write sequential files. QSAM manages buffers for the user and blocks and deblocks records.

RB Request Block. This control block contains information needed by the MVS supervisor concerning programs and routines.

RCT Resource Control Table. This table contains constants and statistics used by the system resources manager routines.

RQE Request Queue Element. This control block is used by the EXCP processor to describe an I/O request and its status.

RSM   Real Storage Manager. This MVS component controls the allocation of memory frames.

RTM   Recovery Termination Manager. This MVS component is responsible for system recovery from failures. If it cannot recover from an error, it terminates the process (task) and does the "clean up" to free up the resources held by the task.

SCA   Spie Control Area. This control block provides information to program check FLIH in its processing of program interruptions covered by a SPIE exit.

SCB   STAE Control Block. The SCB is used to make STA/ESTA recovery known to the system.

SGT   Segment Table. This table contains entries for each segment allocated to the address space. Each entry contains a real address of page table origin.

SIGP   SIGnal Processor. A System/370 machine instruction which allows a CPU to force another (or itself) to perform a specified operation.

SIO   Start I/O.

SMF   System Management Facility. This facility of MVS captures system wide data for management reporting and control.

SPIE   Specify Program Interrupt Exit.

SPL   System Parameter List.

SPQE   SubPool Queue Element. This control block describes the space in a subpool.

SQA   System Queue Area. This is a portion of the MVS common area used for MVS control blocks which must be both fixed and globally addressable.

SRB   Supervisory Request Block. (see PRB and RB)

SRM   System Resources Manager. SRM monitors the critical resource usage (such as CPU usage, page fault rate, etc.) and attempts to keep the performance of the total system within the installation specifications. SRM does this by swapping ready users, in or out, and thus adjusts the multiprogramming level.

STAE   Specify Task Asynchronous Exit. This macro instruction specifies a routine that will receive control in the event of the issuing tasks abnormal termination.

STC   Started Task. STCs are tasks started from the operator consoles.

STOR   Segment Table Origin Register.

SVC   SuperVisor Call. This is a System/370 machine instruction which causes a machine interruption. The main use of SVC is to allow a problem state program to invoke a function which runs in supervisor state.

SVS   Single Virtual Storage System.

SWA   Scheduler Work Area. This area is located at the high end of the private area and is used to store control blocks created as a result of JCL interpretation.

TCAM   TeleCommunications Access Method.

TCB   Task Control Block. This control block serves as a repository for information and pointers associated with a task.

TIC   Transfer In Channel. This is a channel command.

TIOT   Task Input/Output Table. This table provides the I/O support routines with pointers to JFCBs and to allocated devices.

TLB   Translation Lookaside Buffer. A hardware facility that speeds up the dynamic address translation in virtual storage systems.

TP   TeleProcessing.

TSO   Time Sharing Option.

UCB   Unit Control Block. UCB describes the characteristics of a device to the I/O supervisor. There is a UCB for each device attached to the system.

UIC   Unreferenced Interval Count.

VIO   Virtual Input/Output. A programming support in MVS for simulating DASD I/O devices by using virtual storage.

VSM   Virtual Storage Manager. This MVS component is responsible for maintaining the virtual storage.

VTAM   Virtual Telecommunications Access Method. An IBM subsystem which manages the flow of data between terminal and application programs.

VTOC   Volume Table Of Contents. This table on each DASD volume contains the names of all datasets and their location on the volume.

Selected References

Auslander, M.A., Larkin, D.C., and Scherr, A.L., "The Evolution of the MVS Operating System," *IBM Journal of Research and Development,* Volume 25, Number 5 (1981), pp. 471-482

Katzan, H., *Operating Systems: A Pragmatic Approach*, New York: Van Nostrand Reinhold Company, 1973

Scherr, A.L., "Functional Structure of IBM Virtual Storage Operating Systems, Part II—OS/VS2-2 Concepts and Philosophies," *IBM Systems Journal*, Volume 12, Number 4 (1973), pp. 382-400

IBM Reference Documents:

- OS/VS2 MVS Overview, Form GC28-0984
- OS/VS2 Systems Logic Library, Volumes 1-7, Forms SY28-0713 TO SY28-0720
- OS/VS2 Systems Programming Library: Supervisor, Form GC28-0628
- IBM System/370 Principles of Operation, Form GA22-7000

Index